DOCTRINE IN THE CHURCH
OF ENGLAND
(1938)

DOCTRINE IN THE CHURCH OF ENGLAND

(1938)

Church of England

The Report of the Commission on Christian Doctrine
appointed by the Archbishops of Canterbury and York

With a new Introduction by

G. W. H. LAMPE

London
SPCK

First published 1938
Reprinted with a new Introduction 1982
SPCK
Holy Trinity Church
Marylebone Road
London NW1 4DU

Reproduced from copy supplied,
printed and bound in Great Britain
by Billing and Sons Limited and Kemp Hall Bindery,
Guildford, London, Oxford, Worcester.

ISBN 0 281 03847 3

CONTENTS

viii CONTENTS

viii CONTENTS

PAGE

APPENDICES:

I. On the Psychological Aspects of Sin — 221

II. On Finitude and Original Sin — 223

III. On the Meaning of the Terms "Body" and "Blood" in Eucharistic Theology — 224

IV. On the Relation of the Sacraments to Grace — 230

THE 1938 REPORT IN RETROSPECT

by

G. W. H. LAMPE

THE rather tattered cover of my copy of *Doctrine in the Church of England* still bears intact on its front page a roundel framing a curiously grim silhouette of what looks like a Victorian prison but is in fact the gatehouse of Lambeth Palace. This was presumably meant to remind the reader that here was the report of a commission officially appointed by archiepiscopal authority. It might also be taken as a symbol of the somewhat disproportionate amount of space given by the Commission to the doctrine of the ministry and to episcopacy in particular.

In the circumstances in which the report was called for this lack of balance was almost unavoidable, but it was criticized in a review-article by the Bishop of Gloucester (A. C. Headlam), contrasting the 143 pages (out of 242) devoted to the Church, the ministry and the sacraments with the Report's treatment of the Holy Spirit in about three pages and the Trinity in about a page, and quoting a comment of Dean Hastings Rashdall that "if you believed in episcopacy it did not matter what else you disbelieved in the Church of England."[1]

Inside, the book is defaced with the marginal comments, underlinings, queries and exclamation marks with which, as a brash and rather opinionated assistant curate, I annotated it in the spring of 1938 for the purpose of reading papers about the Report to my ruridecanal chapter and other meetings of clergy in the diocese of Exeter and reviewing it in local papers and church

1. *Church Quarterly Review* (April–June 1938), pp. 83-94.

magazines. For *Doctrine in the Church of England* was for a short time front-page news, at any rate in the ecclesiastical press, and a main subject for discussion in clerical gatherings until as a news item it was extruded by the crisis over Czechoslovakia later in the same year. As a theological document it came, very mistakenly and undeservedly, to be ignored and forgotten as neo-orthodoxy swept over the churches of Europe, answering the strident assertions of Nazi irrationalism with its almost equally strident and unfounded assertion of " the revealed Word of God," while the Church of England clergy often took advantage of the stress of national emergency, and the comforting belief that orthodoxy was being vindicated, to get on with the job and leave the intractable problems raised by the Report to the theological experts whose business or hobby these things were.

It was especially unfortunate that much of the wide publicity received by the Report during those few months was both misguided and misleading. It had recorded a quite remarkable measure of agreement among Anglican theologians and church leaders over very wide areas of Christian doctrine, though, admittedly, it remains a matter for discussion to what extent this agreement was superficial and only apparent. Where they differed from one another they were for the most part content to agree to differ without disrupting their common fellowship within the boundaries of the Church of England. The spirit of the entire Report was strikingly tolerant and eirenic. The tone of the whole discussion was set by the memorable dictum of the chairman, William Temple, in his Introduction: " To admit acrimony in theological discussion is in itself more fundamentally heretical than any erroneous opinions upheld or condemned in the course of the discussion." Yet some of the first reactions to its publication came from partisans of traditional orthodoxy to whom the concessions made in the Report to liberal theology, especially in its tolerance of divergent beliefs

concerning the historicity of the virginal conception and
bodily resurrection of Christ, seemed a betrayal of the
faith. It was therefore almost inevitable that the press
should focus public attention on the relatively few
controversial passages in the Report to the exclusion of
what was really at least the equally newsworthy achievement of agreement and reconciliation which it embodied,
and that the document should have been presented as
though it were merely the trigger which had set off yet
another major row in the Church—one more in the long
series reaching back to the appearance of *Essays and
Reviews*.

The Dean of St. Paul's (W. R. Matthews) was fully
justified in his complaint[2] that attention had been
concentrated on the few points where the Commission
agreed to differ, rather than on the far more numerous and
weighty matters on which they agreed to agree. " When
we ought to have been thanking God," he said, " for the
revelation of a deep unity of the Spirit, many of us were
calling Heaven to witness the intolerable dissensions in the
Church." " One sometimes wonders," he went on,
" whether the great sin of the Church of England is not its
distrust of its own particular genius and mission to combine unity with freedom." Indeed, the Report had
received comparatively little objective and informed ap-
praisal before it was overtaken in the public mind by
more pressing concerns. Many churchpeople, especially
(as I can testify from personal experience) the clergy, were
glad to see this bone of contention safely buried out of
sight, to be dug up again, if at all, only by those whom
Canon E. T. Kerby in the debate on the Report described
as " the theological intellectuals."[3] Canon Kerby, in fact,
represented a very common attitude on the part of the

2. " The Demand for Restatement," in *The Gospel to this
Generation*, Report of the Proceedings of the 66th Church Congress
at Bristol (Hodder & Stoughton 1938), pp. 123-31.

3. Lower House of the Convocation of York, 3 June 1938.

parochial clergy: " Sometimes we are tempted almost to despair in our endeavours to forward the work we have been commissioned to perform, and while naturally I am prepared to value all that the theological intellectuals contribute to the Church by their thought and by their minds, at the same time I do wish they would give the Church for ten years, at any rate, a rest, so that we can get on with our proper work of saving souls."

Against the attitude of those who now, as forty years ago, want only to be left in peace to get on with the work of saving souls, regardless of the bearing upon that task of questions concerning the truth or falsity of the Church's teaching, *Doctrine in the Church of England* stands as a symbol of seriousness, sincerity, and paramount concern for truth in the furtherance of the Church's mission. After the upheaval of the Second World War theology moved into a changed climate. As William Temple and his colleagues had realized, and as he recognized in his Chairman's Introduction, the world of 1938 was already very different from that of September 1923 when the Commission held its first session at Oxford. " If we began our work again today," he wrote, " its perspectives would be different. But it is not our function to pioneer. We may call the thinkers and teachers of the Church of England to renewed devotion of their labour to the themes of Redemption, Justification and Conversion. It is there that, in my own judgment at least, our need lies now and will lie in the future. To put the matter in another way: theology in the half-century that ended with the war was such as is prompted by and promotes a ministry mainly pastoral; we need and must work out for our own time a theology such as is prompted by and promotes a ministry at least as much evangelistic as pastoral."

Even before the beginning of a second " post-war " era the new developments which the Archbishop had foreseen had actually begun to take place, though the basic change lay primarily in the area of the Christian understanding of divine revelation. " As the world closed in," writes Dr. F. W. Dillistone,[4] " the Church also closed in to become the Church of the authoritative Word or the Church of the authoritative Order. The times were becoming too serious, it seemed, for every man to do what was right in his own eyes. The call was for a new obedience to God's Word, a new discipline within God's Order—a closing of the ranks, a rediscovery of the distinctiveness of the Christian Gospel, a determination to stand for the faith against all assaults of the enemy in whatever guise he might come." To a generation preoccupied with the theology of crisis and of divine irruption into the temporal order, as it were from outside it, with dialectical theology and with the working out of a doctrine of revelation in terms of biblical theology, the traditional Anglican approach to theological problems, which had been followed by the Commission, made comparatively little appeal. It was now no longer true that the subjects to which Anglican theology paid most attention were " not the same as those which cause most concern to Continental theologians." It was much less appropriate, therefore, in the era of the Second World War and its aftermath to assign as the principal causes of the " difference of habit in theological thought " between England and the Continent our characteristic Platonism, the greater indebtedness of the English Reformers to the Greek Fathers (and not to Augustine alone), and the strengthening of this link with Eastern theology through the influence of Westcott and the *Lux Mundi* school. At the same time the renewed interest predicted by Temple in Redemption, Justification and Conversion found expression in the post-war revival of Anglican Evangelical theology and in the attention given to these very themes in the series of three reports called for by Archbishop Fisher: *The Fulness of Christ*, in

4. *Charles Raven* (Hodder & Stoughton 1975), p. 278.

which they were explored positively, and *The Catholicity of Protestantism* which corrected the misunderstandings of the Reformers' teaching, especially about Justification, which had been shown by the authors of *Catholicity* who had, significantly, thought it necessary to deal at some length with this same area of theology.[5]

It is not surprising, then, that the Commission's work had largely been forgotten by the time that the pressures towards a greater degree of ecumenism began again to create the need which the Commission itself had been set up to try to meet: to explain where the Church of England stood, so far as doctrine was concerned, and to promote agreement and fuller understanding between its divergent and opposed theological schools of thought. In the year 1947 I remember hearing a teacher of theology say that he had been asked by a Continental student whether he would recommend *Doctrine in the Church of England* as a guide to the current state of Anglican theology. His reply had been that the Report was now so dated that it would be wise to ignore it altogether; the live issues of contemporary theology found little or no place in it, and no one could seriously claim that it reflected the mind of the post-war Church of England.

Yet, although most of the clergy and laity of the Church

5. *Catholicity* was produced first, by a distinguished group of Anglo-Catholics. *The Fulness of Christ* was the work of an Evangelical group, of which I was a member, most of whom would nowadays be regarded as "liberal." The group responsible for *The Catholicity of Protestantism* consisted of Free Church theologians. The task of these three bodies closely resembled that which was entrusted to the Commission on Christian Doctrine in 1922: to examine the possibility of closer agreement between the main traditions in English theology and, where this seemed unattainable, to consider how far the chief differences of theological outlook could coexist within the framework of a single Church. These reports should be read as a kind of supplement to *Doctrine in the Church of England*, illustrating the extent to which the primary concerns of theologians had shifted in the course of a decade to a decade and a half in this country.

soon lost sight of this document, it has always been highly valued by the more discerning students of Anglican theology. They have recognized its lasting importance, not only as a fair and objective report of the actual state of agreement and diversity within the Church of England during the inter-war years, but also as a careful and scholarly exposition of doctrine, particularly in the field of the Church, the ministry and the sacraments. We have not, I think, been told whether the Anglican–Roman Catholic International Commission used the Report's presentation of the doctrine of the Eucharist in the discussions which led to the Agreed Statement on that subject.[6] It was certainly a pity that the brevity of their Statement made it impossible for them to publish a detailed discussion of the Report's admirably thorough examination of such topics as Eucharistic Sacrifice and Presence, and its even more important attempt to resolve the difficult question of the meaning, within the context of the Eucharist, of " the Body and Blood of Christ." Had the International Commission been able to record general agreement after working through the Report's discussion of these issues, the extent of its achievement would have been impressively demonstrated; if it had had to report agreement to differ on some of them, its Statement would at least have been proof against any charge of superficiality.

Now that the theological climate has again changed, and the reign of " biblical theology " has ended, it is high time for *Doctrine in the Church of England* to be rediscovered by a wider public. The fundamental questions raised by the theologians of the first thirty years of this century still remain unanswered and have lost none of their importance. The conviction of the Bishop of Derby (A. E. J. Rawlinson)[7] was justified: " The . . . document,

6. SPCK 1972.
7. *Church Assembly News*, April 1938.

whatever its formal status (whether at the present time or hereafter) is one which it would be quite impossible for either the Church of England or the Anglican Communion to repudiate in practice; and it must be expected to bear its chief fruit in the next generation. The Report constitutes, upon any theory of it, an historic landmark in the story of Anglicanism. It must inevitably come to be used as a text-book in theological teaching; and its method of approach, undercutting all the traditional lines of partisan cleavage, must be expected to operate powerfully in the direction of unity. It is a document which can hardly fail to promote not only mutual understanding, but actual synthesis, as between the various traditional ' schools of theological thought in the Anglican Church '."

The *Church Times*[8] attacked the Bishop in a leader: " His article would possibly have been better unwritten. It certainly ought not to have been published in the guileless official organ of the Church Assembly." But it was he, and not his critics, who judged the situation correctly. His " next generation " has taken longer to emerge than he expected, and now that basic questions concerning the grounds of belief, the relation of Christian claims to have received divine revelation to the similar claims of other religions, and the historical relativity and cultural conditioning of Scripture, creeds, and all other theological formulations are being raised again with renewed urgency, such consideration as the Report gave to these fundamental issues seems far too slight and superficial. In some of its aspects it was not nearly radical enough; some major problems it ignored, others it did not explore in depth. It would seem complacent now to echo Rawlinson's conclusion: " Taking the Report as a whole, I cannot personally understand how any intelligent reader can fail to regard its main outcome as constituting an impressive reaffirmation, upon the basis of complete

8. April 1938.

intellectual freedom, of the substance of Christian orthodoxy." It does, nevertheless, constitute " an historic landmark in the story of Anglicanism " and it does deserve " to be used as a text-book in theological teaching." If its method does not strike us as out of the ordinary, that is only because it anticipated the way in which theological discussion is now usually carried on by theologians of different traditions, whether within a single communion or across the boundaries of different churches.

The defects of the Report are partly, at least, an inevitable consequence of the circumstances which led to the appointment of the Commission and the terms of reference given to it. The background of the long process which ended in the publication of the Report was, first, the sharp and long-standing conflict between Anglican Catholics and Evangelicals, reflected in divergent ritual and ceremonial practices and therefore directly affecting the worship of ordinary congregations, and, secondly, the series of bitter controversies between liberal theologians and traditionalists which, following the unhappy example of the wrangles about *Essays and Reviews*, Bishop Colenso, and *Lux Mundi*, had resulted in a succession of protests and *gravamina* in Convocation, answered by emphatic but futile affirmations and reaffirmations of the Church of England's unshaken adherence to the orthodoxy embodied in the Creeds, including the " historical facts " of the virgin birth and the bodily resurrection of Christ which they assert.

In the new post-war situation it seemed to thoughtful churchpeople that what was needed was an effort, actually sponsored by the leadership, to break away from this pattern of sterile and frustrating party strife. The constitution of the Church of England had been radically altered by the passing of the Enabling Act of 1919, and the champions of the " Life and Liberty " Movement had fought for this change in the belief that it would clear the way for a profound revitalization of the whole Church for mission and service in a world which was being deeply and rapidly transformed socially and politically. The Lambeth Appeal of 1920 opened up a new prospect of reunion as a practical possibility and at the same time challenged Anglicans to clarify the ambiguities inherent in their public statements about the Church and the ministry and to define their position. The dangers of double-talk on this subject and on doctrine generally became apparent in 1922 with the publication of an agreed statement by a Joint Conference of Anglican and Free Church representatives at Lambeth and, at almost the same moment, a Declaration of Faith, drawn up by a committee of the English Church Union and addressed to the Patriarch of Constantinople. Meanwhile, the first Anglo-Catholic Congress of 1920 with its strongly militant line, particularly on the cultus of the reserved sacrament in a paper by G. A. Michell, demonstrated the need for some official action to promote inter-party dialogue with a view to greater mutual understanding within the Church.

The first move[9] was an approach to the Bishop of Oxford (H. M. Burge) by a lay Anglo-Catholic theologian, Will Spens (later Master of Corpus Christi College, Cambridge), with a group of younger theologians, as a result of which a series of meetings took place and after about a year of discussion a draft letter proposing a Commission was sent to Archbishop Davidson for his reactions. They expressed the view that, in a situation where party disputes were becoming wearisome, it was likely that a thorough investigation of fundamental principles could lead to agreement among all but a comparatively small minority of extremists upon a positive statement of the faith of the Church of England. It was hoped that a statement of this kind could serve as a

9. The story is narrated in detail by G. K. A. Bell, *Randall Davidson* (3rd edn, OUP, 1952), pp. 1136-50.

general norm of Anglican teaching and thus as a guide and standard for the clergy. " No one would be silenced or made liable to heresy hunts, but no one would be able to claim the authority of the Church of England for what was opposed and contradictory to this statement of doctrine thus generally agreed and approved." The letter asked that a Doctrinal Commission should be appointed and solemnly commended by authority to the prayers of the Church, that it should be allowed ten or twenty years for its labours, and that it should be largely composed of younger men of wide sympathies, trusted by their respective parties and representing all parties in the Church of England, however extreme in whatever direction, which were willing to seek a common basis of agreement.[10]

The Archbishop at first disagreed with them on the ground that a formally established commission could not possess the degree of authority required to set up an officially approved statement and norm of the doctrine of the Church—a task more appropriate to a Council. He was evidently alarmed at the prospect that a commission would lead to the establishment of new and rigid canons of orthodoxy and, in the long run, produce fresh divisions rather than unity. In his view it would be better for an independent group to proceed privately, on the lines of the Tractarians and the collaborators in *Lux Mundi* or *Foundations*. The Bishop of Oxford, replying in a letter dated 24 September 1921, pointed out that " the method of approach which this Committee desire is something different: it is not a question with them of a group of 'like-minded ' men, interested in investigating the subject of the supposed comprehensiveness of the Church of England, and giving the Church and others the benefit of their investigations: they want to see the Church, through its authorities, deliberately setting itself to decide, in the light of the controversies and criticisms which distract

10. Bell, p. 1137.

and dishearten so many of its members, and in the light of its own development, where it now stands—and I think the Committee would say that in this way and this way alone would you be able to make the position and the policy of those in authority, what at present it is not, intelligible and consistent and convincing."[11]

The letter proposing a commission was formally sent to the Archbishop in January 1922, signed by Burge and eight other diocesan bishops with eighteen other signatories, including such well-known theologians as O. C. Quick and C. E. Raven (later Regius Professors of Divinity at Oxford and Cambridge respectively), W. L. Knox, E. G. Selwyn, Will Spens and L. S. Thornton. Davidson's reply, dated 15 February, still expressed reservations arising from his fear that an official statement of doctrine might become a rigidly applied test of orthodoxy. By adopting the method of conference instead of controversy, endeavours might usefully be made to obtain a basis of doctrinal agreement. If, however, one object was to be the drawing up of " an unambiguous statement . . . to be regarded as an expression of the Church's official teaching," he did not know to what body of picked younger men he could assign the task, or " what character or authority would belong to such ' expression of the Church's official teaching ' when ultimately produced." He asked for a clearer indication of the sort of questions to which such a commission might address itself, and in what sort of shape its answer should be formulated, and he enquired about the number of members that might be envisaged, and the relation of the proposed body to the constitutional structures of the Church.[12]

To this the Bishop of Oxford replied that they had no desire " to frame a statement which would be binding on the Church or the clergy, or even a statement of doctrine

11. Bell, p. 1139.
12. Bell, pp. 1147-8.

which would *ipso facto* be held to be the official teaching of the Church." They maintained that " both an enforced uniformity, and acquiescence . . . in grave doctrinal differences which closely affect the religious life of every member of the Church, seem to us to be serious dangers to the well-being of the Church." They repeated their conviction that a laborious and systematic effort ought to be made " to reconcile different points of view in a clearer apprehension of those truths of which the different points of view give a partial presentation," and that, although informal conferences were valuable, an initiative from the bishops was required to persuade the Church of the importance of " finding and appreciating the real agreement that lies behind divergencies and of diminishing as far as possible these divergencies." Official action was needed in order both to create the right atmosphere for the enquiry and also to give sufficient authority to the issuing of a call to participate in what would be a most onerous as well as important task.[13]

At last, on 28 December 1922, the Archbishop wrote to the Bishop of Oxford in his own name and that of the Archbishop of York (Cosmo Lang), appointing the Commission. Bell's suggestion[14] is probably right, that the case for a commission had been strengthened for Davidson by the latest example of fierce and destructive controversy: the theological battle which followed the Modern Churchmen's Conference at Girton in the summer of 1921 and which occupied the Convocations in February and May 1922, coinciding with the correspondence between the Archbishop and the Bishop of Oxford and his committee.

The theme of the Girton Conference was " Christ and the Creeds." Of the Christological papers the most notable were Hastings Rashdall's " Christ as Logos and

13. Bell, p. 1149.
14. Bell, p. 1143.

Son of God," J. F. Bethune-Baker's " Jesus as both
Human and Divine," and H. D. A. Major's " Jesus the
Son of God." In some respects, especially in the area of
New Testament criticism, some of the Girton papers are
now dated, but they deserve to be reprinted, for, taken as
a whole, they are astonishingly relevant to the present-
day debate about the person of Christ. Most of the issues
raised by *The Myth of God Incarnate*,[15] by the controversy
which followed its publication, and by my own Bampton
Lectures for 1976[16] (among a number of writings of the
1970s), were anticipated by these short but seminal essays.

Rashdall, for instance, tried to say " in twenty five
minutes " what liberal theologians mean when they use
the traditional language about the " divinity of Christ."
Jesus, he pointed out, did not claim divinity for himself.
He was a man, as much so as any other human being,
having not only a human body, but a human soul,
intellect, will. It is entirely unorthodox to suppose that
the human soul of Jesus pre-existed. His divinity does not
necessarily imply the virgin birth or any other miracle.
If it could be historically proved, the virgin birth would be
no demonstration of Christ's divinity, nor would the
disproof of it throw any doubt upon that doctrine.
Christ's divinity does not imply omniscience. There is no
reason to suppose that he knew more than his contemporaries about the true explanation of the mental
diseases which current belief attributed to diabolic
possession; and it is difficult to deny that he entertained
eschatological expectations which history has not verified.
" Divine " and " human " are not to be regarded as
mutually exclusive terms; there is a certain community
of nature between God and man. Yet although it is
impossible to maintain that God is fully incarnate in
Christ and not incarnate at all in anyone else, it is possible

15. Edited by John Hick. SCM Press 1977.
16. *God as Spirit*. OUP 1977.

to believe that in one Man the self-revelation of God has been " signal, supreme, unique." " That we are justified in thinking of God as like Christ, that the character and teaching of Christ contains the fullest disclosure both of the character of God himself and of his will for man—that is . . . the true meaning for us of the doctrine of Christ's divinity. The ancient doctrine of the Logos expressed in the language of a bygone philosophy the truth that in Jesus the world has received its highest revelation of God; and it must be remembered that in the teaching of Augustine and the Schoolmen the Logos is not a separate mind or Person in the sense of a centre of consciousness, but a distinguishable activity of the one and only divine Mind."[17]

This brief summary of one of the principal contributions to the Girton Conference may serve as a reminder that part of the background of the Commission's work was a major controversy about precisely the same fundamental problems of Christology which are a chief concern of theologians at the present time. Other Girton papers discussed the nature and use of creeds—the subject of the report of Archbishop Ramsey's Doctrine Commission in 1976, entitled *Christian Believing*.[18] There could be no doubt that this was a damaging and disruptive quarrel. A *gravamen* on behalf of the English Church Union was presented to the Lower House of the Convocation of Canterbury on 15 February 1922: " Inasmuch as certain erroneous opinions concerning the Godhead of our Lord and Saviour Jesus Christ and His Holy Incarnation, and concerning the doctrine of the Holy, blessed and glorious Trinity as set forth in Holy Scripture and the Catholic Creed have been advanced by certain clergymen of the Church of England . . . and inasmuch as these opinions have been published far and wide in the Daily Press and

17. *The Modern Churchman* 11 (1921-2), pp. 278-86.
18. SPCK 1976.

the minds of many have been deeply distressed thereby, the enemies of the Faith encouraged and the honesty of the clergy as a body seriously called in question: *Reformandum*, That this House humbly desires his Grace the President and their lordships of the Upper House to declare that such opinions are contrary to the teaching of the Bible and the Church."

In the Upper House the Bishop of Gloucester (E. C. S. Gibson) presented a Petition from the Council of the English Church Union, humbly showing " that the said book[19] contains teaching that is contradictory of the Faith—to wit: (1) The doctrine of the unique and distinctive character of the Being of God is denied; (2) The doctrine of the Incarnation as taught in the Creeds and in Holy Scripture is repudiated; (3) The idea that a divine character was infused into a human person is substituted for the scriptural doctrine that ' The Word was made Flesh '; (4) The authority of the Creed of the whole Catholic Church is repudiated; (5) A desire is expressed either to abolish Creeds or to formulate new in place of the existing Creeds. Your Petitioners submit that such teaching is entirely subversive of the Christian Faith and the Christian Religion and therefore calls for authoritative condemnation. Your Petitioners therefore most humbly and most earnestly pray your Venerable House to take the doctrinal teaching contained in the said book into consideration and to pass judgment upon it."

The fundamental theological issues in the controversy evidently interested the Archbishop much less than the diplomatic problem of preventing the Church of England from blowing itself apart—his constant preoccupation throughout his primacy—and he was therefore concerned above all else to lower the ecclesiastical temperature and damp down the explosive material which was being eagerly collected and piled up by both sides. " I am very

---

19. *I.e., The Modern Churchman*, 11, nos. 5 and 6, Sept. 1921.

anxious," he said in his reply, " that on this matter we should not drift into a condition of exaggerated apprehension or exaggerated feeling. To judge from some of the things which have been said and written it might be supposed that there was a great phalanx of heresiarchs set in battle against the doctrine of the Church Catholic, and that we were called upon to rally the Church in defence of the Christian Faith . . . In my belief the whole of that is grossly exaggerated. It would be a very real danger if we were supposed to be face to face with any such array of battle forces on both sides as some people have suggested. I do not think the danger anticipated is what is supposed, or that the means for meeting it are of the kind that many outsiders have suggested. . . When the matter comes up next time my earnest hope is that it may be possible to expediate such action as is desired. There will be time between now and then to think out what it ought to be." It was this unexcited, civilized, detachment which provoked Bishop Gore's letter to the Archbishop, dated 17 February,[20] describing the latter's speech in Convocation as " a grievous affliction." " I venture to say that this sort of chaff, or apparently light-hearted disparagement of the gravity of the situation, tends to drive us wild. . . It appears to me that if under these circumstances the Bishops do not at the least rebuke them by a solemn reaffirmation of the basis on which the Church of England stands . . . it will have assented to the idea that Major and Rashdall's teaching is legitimate—a ' school of thought ' within the Church of England. They *are* heresiarchs, and very fundamentally so, and very formidable. . . I never felt ' official optimism ' so sickening."

The " next time " mentioned by the Archbishop was a debate in the Upper House on 2 May 1922. The Bishop of Oxford clarified the issues raised by the English Church

20. Bell, p. 1140.

Union's Petition and *Gravamen* under the following heads:

1. Whether the views impugned are formally heretical.
2. Whether they are essentially true or false.
3. What ought to be the attitude of the authorities of the Church towards those who reverently try to develop new aspects of truth?

The resolution which the House adopted, however, merely followed the familiar pattern of reaffirmation of traditional doctrine, combined with gestures of encouragement towards critical scholars and theologians, with a warning, nevertheless, that they should take care not to disturb the peace of the Church.

The Bishop of Gloucester (Gibson), proposing the resolution, began by attacking the Modernists. " One of those present at the Conference . . . actually admitted that ' one or two seemed to doubt whether the Jesus of history was the unique Person in whom St. Paul and St. John saw the only begotten Son.' One of those who spoke absolutely identified the living Christ and the Holy Spirit, and claimed the authority of St. Paul for that as if it were an ascertained truth, relying of course on a single passage of doubtful interpretation,[21] and ignoring altogether the number of passages in which St. Paul mentioned together the Eternal Son and the Holy Spirit. . . Again, one . . . seemed to deny the pre-existence of Christ in any true sense, and His claim to eternal Godhead. Several . . . were apparently anxious to get rid of the Nicene Creed, and to substitute something else for it, and some raised claims for a creed confined to the actual words of Scripture . . . I do say it is a very serious tning when teachers holding responsible positions made some of the utterances that had been made." The Bishop contended, however, that the synodical condemnation demanded by the petitioners was not the proper

21. The allusion is to 2 Cor. 3. 17 as all too commonly misunderstood.

method of procedure. The episode of *Essays and Reviews* had demonstrated this. Argument must be met by argument.

He accordingly proposed the motion: " This House declares its conviction that adhesion to the teaching of the Catholic Church as set forth in the ' Nicene ' Creed—and in particular concerning the eternal pre-existence of the Son of God, His true Godhead, and His Incarnation—is essential to the life of the Church, and calls attention to the fact that the Church commissions as its Ministers those only who have solemnly expressed such adhesion. Further, this House recognizes the gain which arises from enquiry, at once fearless and reverent, into the meaning and expression of the Faith, and welcomes every aid which the thoughtful student finds in the results of sound historical and literary criticism, and of modern scientific investigation of the problems of human psychology; and it deprecates the mere blunt denunciation of contributions made by earnest men in their endeavours to bring new light upon these difficult and anxious problems. At the same time it sees a grave and obvious danger in the publication of debatable suggestions as if they were ascertained truths, and emphasizes the need of caution in this whole matter, especially on the part of responsible teachers in the Church.''

In retrospect it seems that the resolution proposed that the Church of England should have several different cakes and eat them at the same time. As had so often happened during the past sixty years, adhesion to the Nicene formulation of belief about the person of Christ was affirmed as " essential to the life of the Church." To this there was attached the warning that only those who were ready to commit themselves to that formulation could expect to be accepted for ordination. Nevertheless, the results of " fearless and reverent enquiry " and " sound historical and literary criticism " (no attempt being made to offer any criteria of " reverence " and " soundness ") are welcomed, and " blunt denunciation " (which, it might be supposed, the mover of the resolution had himself directed at the Modern Churchmen's Conference in the opening part of his speech) is deprecated. On the other hand, the results of fearless and reverent enquiry and sound criticism, being (like all theological and philosophical propositions, including those enunciated by the Council of Nicaea) " debatable," ought not to be published as if they were ascertained truths, and clergymen as responsible teachers in the Church ought to be especially cautious in " this whole matter."

The controversy thus fizzled out into verbiage, and the Archbishop's aim of defusing it had been achieved. It is reasonable, however, to suppose that the whole episode made him more ready to agree to the demand for some less futile method of dealing with the conflicts of opinion in the Church. The paramount need, as he saw it, of avoiding a renewal of head-on confrontation between the parties led him, nevertheless, to define the Commission's terms of reference rather narrowly. As the Introduction to the Report tells us, the Archbishop's letter to the Bishop of Oxford of 28 December 1922, laid down its task as follows: " To consider the nature and grounds of Christian doctrine with a view to demonstrating the extent of existing agreement within the Church of England and with a view to investigating how far it is possible to remove or diminish existing differences." The Commission's Report was not to be an authoritative statement, but, when prepared, it was to be laid before the Bishops for them to consider what further action (if any) should be taken. Thus the work of the Commission was to be investigative only, and not normative. Davidson refused the original suggestion of Burge and his committee that the Church should deliberately set itself to *decide* where it now stood. Instead, it was to *ascertain* where it, or rather where the divergent opinions of its members, were actually standing. If the terms of reference were interpreted strictly there could be no statement to serve as a general guide and standard for the clergy as the Church's accredited teachers. The Commission would have the important and valuable task of surveying the extent of existing agreement within the Church, underlying and persisting through its many controversies, and of exploring the possibility that objective, non-partisan, discussion of major theological issues might broaden the area of agreement, but there could be no attempt to define the limits of permissible variety. In fact, the terms of reference were not strictly observed. At a number of points in the Report the Commission went beyond their allotted task and expressed an opinion as to the permissibility or otherwise of some theological position. There is thus an inherent confusion in the professed aims of the Commission and this gives rise to some ambiguities in the Report.

The Introduction informs us that the members of the Commission were chosen as representing different traditions or points of view. " But there have been no clear lines of division. It has often happened that the chief champion of some part of a tradition has been one not reckoned as belonging to the school chiefly attached to it. This has been due in part to the fact that all members adopt in varying ways the critical method and outlook." What this means in effect is that the very distinguished group of twenty-five younger theologians under the chairmanship, for a short time, of the Bishop of Oxford, then, after his death, of William Temple (then Bishop of Manchester)—it would be hard today to pick so impressive a team—almost all shared a common educational background and a similar outlook. Twenty-one of the original members were clergymen; fourteen of these had been educated at Oxford, six at Cambridge, one at London (W. R. Matthews, then Professor of the Philosophy of Religion and Dean of King's College, London). Almost all the Oxford men had read Greats, most of them after

Classical Honour Moderations, one after Mathematical Moderations (L. W. Grensted, then Principal of Egerton Hall, Manchester, later Nolloth Professor of the Philosophy of the Christian Religion at Oxford). Some had followed Greats with the Honour School of Theology. Three of the Cambridge clergy had read Part 1 of the Classical Tripos followed by Part 2 of the Theological Tripos, one had confined himself to the Classical Tripos and two to the Theological Tripos. The four laymen, Professor W. H. (later Sir Walter) Moberly, Mr. (later Sir) Will Spens, Professor A. E. Taylor and Professor C. C. J. Webb, were all highly distinguished scholars from the same academic background. As any international conference soon reveals even today, when English theologians are much less insular than they were in the nineteen-twenties (when it took them an extraordinarily long time to pay serious attention either to Barth's theology or to the work of the Form critics), the traditional approach to theological study by way of an English-style classical education tends to produce a distinctively English (rather than specifically Anglican) method of doing theology: historically orientated, rooted in the study of the biblical and patristic texts, accepting the principles of critical scholarship but applying them cautiously and conservatively, uncomfortable with dogmatics or systematic theology which have never formed a real element in the syllabus of either the Honour School of Theology or the Theological Tripos.

As Anglicans of the Oxbridge stamp the members shared not only a common method of approaching theological questions but also a common liturgical inheritance and, to some extent, a shared spirituality grounded in the Prayer Book. Amidst the clamour of controversy in the church press and up and down the dioceses, these mainly academic theologians spoke a common language and understood one another's cast of thought. It was much easier for them to join in discovering areas of agreement and to move towards fuller unity of outlook among themselves than to commend their agreements to the different parties in the Church at large. It is a striking sign of the temporary eclipse of what would now be called conservative Evangelicalism that, as Dr. C. Sydney Carter pointed out in a review of the Report,[22] the Commission included " no real representative of definite Evangelicals." His complaint was well founded. The Evangelical tradition was represented by Canon J. R. Darbyshire, formerly Vice-Principal of Ridley Hall and in 1922 Vicar of Sheffield Cathedral Church (later Bishop of Glasgow and Galloway), by the Principal of Wycliffe Hall, H. B. Gooding, who almost immediately resigned on going overseas, and by C. J. Shebbeare, Rector of Stanhope, Canon V. F. Storr of Westminster and Canon H. A. Wilson, Rector of Cheltenham (later Bishop of Chelmsford). Of this small minority, theological light-weights in comparison with most of the members, none was representative of the hard core of conservative biblicism or of the dogmatically self-conscious Evangelicalism which held rigidly to the theology of the Reformers and its formulated expression in the Thirty Nine Articles. Some of them, such as Wilson and especially Storr, belonged to a liberal Evangelical tradition in which there was little to differentiate them from the more " non-party " members like Professor Grensted or Canon F. R. Barry. Such a virtual exclusion of what has since become a strong, articulate and theologically sophisticated wing of the Church of England would nowadays be inconceivable. It was regrettable in 1922, in view of the nature of the Commission's task.

The subject for investigation included, first, the areas of longstanding controversy between Anglican Evangelicals and Catholics. Here divergencies of sacramental teaching issued in differences of ritual and ceremonial which directly and unavoidably affected every parishioner.

22. *The Churchman*, NS 3 (1938), pp. 219-22.

In the years preceding the appointment of the Commission the focal point of controversy in this field had come to be the question of the permissibility of reservation. A draft rubric had been adopted by the Upper House of Convocation in 1911, allowing reservation at a celebration of Holy Communion of some of the consecrated bread and wine for the communion of the sick " on the same day and with as little delay as may be." " If," the rubric continued, " the consecrated bread and wine be from any urgent cause not taken immediately to the sick person, they shall be kept in such place and after such manner as the Ordinary shall direct, so that they be not used for any other purpose whatsoever." A memorandum accepted by a special meeting of the bishops in July 1917 reaffirmed this policy, adding that " if a bishop believes that owing to special conditions it is desirable that a parish priest . . . should be allowed by him to go beyond what would, if the Rubrics became law, be set forth as the permissible rule or custom in the Church, his action in giving such sanction will be individual and exceptional, and will lie outside what the episcopate has assented to."[23] By the time of the Commission's first meeting in September 1923, the controversy on this issue had been sharpened, not only by the continuing growth of the extra-liturgical cultus of the reserved sacrament, especially in Winnington Ingram's diocese of London, but, more specifically, by the appeal made on 13 July 1923, by the Bishop of Zanzibar (Frank Weston) to the Anglo-Catholic Congress to " insist on their right to worship Christ in the Tabernacle."[24]

The Commission certainly did their best to break through the surface of the Catholic-Evangelical controversies about the sacraments and bring to light deeply buried strata of theological agreement. They devoted about a third (and much of this the best) of the Report to

23. Bell, pp. 813-4.
24. Bell, p. 1154.

sacramental doctrine. In the extended Note on Reservation and Devotions, however, they found it difficult to avoid going beyond their sphere of responsibility and expressing an opinion on questions of pastoral administration. It was not easy to draw a line on this issue between the problem of the truth or falsity of the theology underlying these practices and the question whether the practices themselves were desirable or legitimate. In fact, they reached an impasse at this point. They focused their attention on the practical pastoral and administrative question which was the actual centre of controversy, and tried in vain to work back to the theological principles which it involved. It would have been more in keeping with their general terms of reference, and might have led to a less inept conclusion, if they had started from their previous exposition of the principles of eucharistic theology and related these deductively to the concrete issue of extra-liturgical devotions. They might then perhaps have avoided committing themselves to the curious opinion that " Even if it be judged that the practice of Devotions does not itself logically involve any wrong theological doctrine, it is still possible that in given circumstances a permission of the practice might on the whole be harmful. And, on the other hand, even if it be judged that the practice does logically involve a doctrine which in principle is erroneous, it might still be inexpedient to attempt to put an end to it by any direct or absolute prohibition."

This departure of the Commission from their proper theological sphere and their excursion into the realm of pastoral expediency earned from me, I notice, two marginal queries and an exclamation mark forty-one years ago. The passage is followed by a distinctly loaded question: " If then devout Christians find (as multitudes have found) that, when the consecrated elements are reserved, they are helped to adore their Lord by offering their adoration in the presence of those outward things by means of which He offers Himself to be the food of the faithful, is there any theological principle involved which renders the encouragement or even the permission of such a practice inadmissible?." " To that question," they had to admit, " we are unable to give a decisive answer, because we are not agreed upon the application of the determining consideration. That consideration is that the special sacramental Presence of our Lord is to be sought only within the context of those sacramental acts with which the original promise of it was associated." One might suppose that the question would then be whether, if this is in fact agreed to be the determining consideration, there is still any reason to doubt that it excludes the propriety of extra-liturgical devotions. Surprisingly, however, the Commission " are not agreed whether or not its application provides a sufficient theological *justifica-tion*[25] for the practice of ' Devotions '."

This was one of the weaker parts of the Report. It shows the confusion which persisted about its aim : was it meant to examine the existing situation, discover agreement, and explore the possibilities of further agreement, or was it also to lay down norms and limits of acceptable Anglican teaching and even, in this instance, devotional practices? It also suggests that the contribution of a good systematic theologian in the old tradition of Evangelical dogmatics could have been useful and salutary, although Carter's review[26] suggests that the Evangelicals of that time might have been too content to take refuge in legalism. He complains that the Report treats reservation as a normal and legitimate practice despite the " Archbishops' Opinion " of 1900 which condemned it, and that " they consider Adoration capable of an inoffensive use and interpretation, yet it was condemned and forbidden even by the 1928 Prayer Book."

25. My italics.
26. See above.

A more weighty opinion on this aspect of the Commission's work came from one of its own members, J. M. Creed, Ely Professor of Divinity at Cambridge, in an address to the annual meeting of the Modern Churchmen's Union on 18 May 1938. While agreeing that his colleague the Bishop of Derby (Rawlinson) had been right to call attention in his Convocation speech welcoming the Report to the " remarkable measure of consent on fundamental points," he was wrong in his claim that the divergencies were only on points of quite minor importance. Among the two which were of great importance one was " teaching and practice with regard to the Holy Communion."[27] On this there were unresolved differences, " and the agreements do not cover those issues which were responsible for the rejection of the Deposited Book. Hence there is not the slightest chance that Reservation of the Sacrament could be given the status of a fully-recognized practice of the Church of England as a whole."

It came as a surprise to me when I joined the Doctrine Commission set up by Archbishop Ramsey that one of the tasks requested of us was to take up this same topic of the theology of reservation and report on it. We, too, failed to reach a common mind, though there was general agreement on the propriety of the reservation of the sacrament for the sick; but we discussed the question with little enthusiasm and no heat on either side. Much had changed since the nineteen-twenties. Instead of being confined to comparatively few " extreme " churches, perpetual reservation had become common in cathedrals and parish churches throughout the country, but the theological and devotional impact of the Liturgical Movement both in Anglicanism and in Roman Catholicism, and, in particular, the changed climate of thought brought about by the Second Vatican Council, meant that

27. The other was " the kind of authority which the Creeds possess and the measure of freedom which may legitimately be claimed in their interpretation."

the attraction of Counter-Reformation teaching and practice had lost its power, extra-liturgical cultus had not spread widely, and " the tide of . . . longing to get as near as possible to the Sacramental Presence of our Lord " which Winnington-Ingram had found " too urgent "[28] had rapidly ebbed. None of us, I think, believed that this was still a really live issue, and nothing effective came of our work.

If eucharistic controversy was, so to speak, the first item on the Commission's agenda, the second might be said to be the doctrine of the Church and the ministry, on which the practical politics of inter-church relations made it so important to determine the position of the Church of England, especially in view of the dangerous tendency of its representatives at that time to speak with one voice to the Free Churches and with another to the Orthodox and the Old Catholics. The section of the Report on this subject includes what can be seen in retrospect to have been some notable statements. It is also of continuing value as a concise scholarly exposition of the historical development of church order itself and of its theological rationale. For instance, it explicitly teaches the doctrine of " internal schism," of which much was to be heard in inter-church theological conversations in the years following the Second World War.[29] The Christian Body " is not

28. Convocation of Canterbury, Upper House, 9 February 1917.
29. In the Anglican–Free Churches conversations (in which I took part) which produced the report *Church Relations in England* (SPCK 1950) an interpretation of schism on these lines was implied (see especially pp. 23f), though not explicitly affirmed. A Joint Committee of the Convocations, reporting in 1955 on the implications of *Church Relations in England*, gave consideration to a prior condition for conversations with the Church of England on intercommunion, stipulated by the Faith and Order Committee of the Methodist Church in England: that it must be acknowledged that " our divisions are within the Christian Body which is throughout in a state of schism." The Joint Committee refused to commit themselves to one particular interpretation of the word " schism," but agreed that it would " regard all discussions

to be thought of as consisting of a single true Church, or group of Churches, with a number of ' schismatic ' bodies gathered about it, but as a whole which is in a state of division or ' schism '. The various ' denominations ' may and do differ in respect of the degree in which they approximate either to orthodoxy of doctrine or to fulness of organised life; but just in so far as their very existence as separate organisations constitutes a real division within Christendom, it becomes true to affirm that if any are in schism, all are in schism, so long as the breaches remain unhealed . . . and this irrespective of the question on which side rests the major responsibility for the schism." It is hard for churches to persuade themselves to pay more than lip-service to this principle, but, to the extent to which they become willing to acknowledge that all Christian bodies, not excepting themselves, are " separated brethren," it has the radical effect of opening up the real possibility of moving into union as a new dimension of church life, as opposed to mere " reunion," a reversion to a previous state of affairs.

On the other hand, this section, like that on the sacraments, to which it leads up, could have presented a truer, if less rosy, picture of the extent of agreement among Anglicans if more attention had been paid to the attitude of those who do not share the Tractarian presuppositions concerning the " apostolic ministry." It is surprising, in view of that outstanding New Testament scholar, B. H. Streeter's, active membership of the Commission until his death shortly before the work was completed, that some strangely uncritical assumptions

---

between the Methodist Church and the Church of England as taking place within the Body of Christ." See also W. Nicholls, *Ecumenism and Catholicity* (SCM Press 1952), S. L. Greenslade, *Schism in the Early Church* (SCM Press 1953), Kenneth M. Carey, ed., *The Historic Episcopate* (Dacre Press 1954), A. E. J. Rawlinson, *Current Problems of the Church* (SPCK 1956).

are made about the historical validity of the concept of apostolic succession. It baldly asserts that the Church is called " apostolic " because it preserves the essential tradition of the apostolic preaching and teaching, and maintains, as a safeguard of that tradition, a duly appointed order of ministers, who derive their commission in historical succession from the original apostolate. This last is a highly dubious claim. Further, while rightly maintaining that " the New Testament bears witness to the principle of a distinctive Ministry, as an original element, but not the sole constitutive element, in the life of the Church," it assumes a greater historical reliability in the early chapters of Acts than most scholars would now accept. Incidentally, the election of Matthias is cited as evidence of a concern for " the Apostolate as an element within the Church," yet nothing is said about the equally significant fact that Luke does not believe that there was any need to maintain the " Apostolic number " when James was martyred. More curious is the assertion that " a distinction corresponding to that drawn later between clergy and laity—*cleros* and *laos*—is there from the outset." It is usually thought that, according to the evidence of the Pauline Epistles, this distinction was strikingly absent from the primitive Church; much ink was, in fact, expended during the decades following the appearance of the Report to make the point, so important for the " declericalization " of the Church, that in the New Testament the *laos* is not the " laity " as contrasted with the clergy, but the whole people of God collectively and corporately.

There are signs that the Commission themselves were uneasy with their sometimes almost pre-critical approach to Christian origins. They admit that " in a historical process of growth the appearance of formality is often increased in retrospect," and their previous statement about the Church's ministers receiving their commission in succession from the original apostolate is somewhat modified, at the cost of greater obscurity: " Whether or not the succession of the Ministry as known from (at latest) the end of the second century can be traced through all its stages to the Apostles, yet the Ministry exists in succession to the original Apostolate."

Anglican apologetic often tends, by a kind of sleight-of-hand, to substitute *the ministry* for *a ministry*: to demonstrate that ministerial order is essential to the Church's life, and then to create the illusion that what has been shown is the necessity of the particular, historic episcopal, form of ministry. The Report is no exception. Yet the Commission agree that neither Scripture nor tradition can establish any one form of church order as being of binding necessity for all ages; they make the important point that " we no longer regard precedents, as such, as decisive for all time;" and they reject the idea either that ministerial succession alone constitutes the essence of the Church, or, on the other hand, that the ministry is merely representative of the congregation or of the whole body of the laity. Their defence of the claims of episcopacy thus turns out in the end to be largely pragmatic. The ministry should be an expression of the Church's unity and historical continuity. To be such a sign it needs to be constituted by an " agreed, universal and traditional " rite of ordination. The historic episcopate alone can, *de facto*, provide this. The episcopate symbolizes apostolic mission and authority; it fulfils (in some manner which the Report understandably leaves vague) its ancient function of safeguarding the true tradition of apostolic teaching; and by representing the whole Church to each diocese, and *vice versa*, it symbolizes the unity and universality of the whole body. *Episcope* or oversight there must be. This need not necessarily be always exercised in the traditional fashion. Conceivably there could be a collegiate episcopate; but then *episcope* would no longer be embodied in a single paternal overseer: " An assemblage of persons cannot be a ' father in God '."

The whole section on the episcopate is a characteristic example of sensible and moderate Anglican apologetic. Time was to show that the transition from vindicating the indispensability of *episcope* in general to demonstrating the necessity of bishops in particular involves a similar conjuring trick to the change-over from *a ministry* to *the ministry*. In the post-war decades the merits of *episcope* were proclaimed with increasing enthusiasm by Anglican spokesmen, but the connection between *episcope* and the (historic) episcopate was never successfully made, and churches which lacked the latter but believed that their systems made ample provision for the former remained unimpressed. It is rather ironical that one of the stronger points in the Report's exposition of the pragmatic value of episcopacy, the advantages to a diocese of having a single " father in God," and not a committee of overseers, is now being undermined to some extent by the growing practice of joint administration by the bishop in " collegiality " with a team of suffragans or " area bishops."

What does not emerge from the Commission's treatment of this subject is any theological justification for making episcopal ordination an exclusive criterion of a valid ministry of the sacraments. The general official policy of the Church of England did this, at any rate in practice, by refusing to countenance reciprocal intercommunion with non-episcopal bodies; intercommunion was to be regarded as the goal of the movement towards unity and not as a means to its achievement. The question to which the situation following the Lambeth Appeal of 1920 required an answer was whether Anglican teaching on the ministry did or did not allow that non-episcopal ministries were real ministries of Christ's sacrament, the Church's Eucharist; and intercommunion (never discussed in the Report) was the touchstone. The moderate claims made by the Commission for the historic episcopate might appear not to support a rigidly negative attitude, but to leave room for flexibility—for divergencies of practice as well as of doctrine. This important issue, however, was not faced by the Commission. They only recorded, with unusual terseness, that " on the larger question concerning the validity . . . of sacraments performed by ministers who have not received their commission in the historical succession of the episcopate, there is divergence of opinion amongst us."

A major controversial issue was thus left concealed among the Commission's unfinished business. An attempt to bring it into the open was made in the Open Letter of thirty-two theologians which, on the initiative of Canon Max Warren and myself, was addressed to the Archbishops in 1961.[30] In the spirit of the Report we affirmed that " the historic episcopate constitutes an important expression of the continuity of the Church in time and the unity of its fellowship across space. We therefore hold that acceptance of this traditional Ministry is the best means by which a reunited Church may be given a fitting outward form in which its inward unity in Christ may be manifested." " Nevertheless," we continued, " we believe that our Lord conveys through these " (*i.e.*, non-episcopal) " ministries the same grace of the Word and the Sacraments as He bestows through the historic ministry . . . and that He does this, not as an act of uncovenanted mercy, but because they are real and efficacious ministries within the Body of His Church. . . We have no doubt that every faithful minister of the non-episcopal communions who has been duly called and commissioned to act as such exercises the one priestly ministry of Christ no less than do his Anglican brethren."

This unambiguous statement of one possible reply to the question which the Commission left unanswered evoked much controversy in 1961. The subsequent history of the scheme for Anglican-Methodist union and the recent hesitations of the Church of England over the

30. Chansitor Publications, London, 1961.

" Ten Propositions " show that doctrinal agreement on this issue is still remote. On the other hand, the practice of intercommunion has broken down much of the former rigidity. A combination of the rapid growth of ecumenicity at all levels in all the churches, including especially Rome, with the very widespread Anglican acceptance of the Eucharist as the main, or only, congregational Sunday service, the establishment of areas of ecumenical experiment, and the extent of theological sanction allowed by the Report of the Archbishops' Commission on Intercommunion in 1968[31] and other documents have changed the atmosphere. Today it is the Church of England through the Archbishop of Canterbury which asks Rome to give official approval in practice to the view of our Open Letter that " the Holy Communion is not only the goal of unity but also an efficacious means of the grace of unity, as of all grace."

This same section of the Report contains what is perhaps its most interestingly " dated " passage: Note B: The Papacy. About 250 words are enough for the Commission to declare themselves united in holding that the Church of England is still bound to resist the claims of the contemporary papacy. " The account which we have already given of the nature of spiritual and doctrinal authority supplies in large measure the ground of our conviction on this point." " With regard to the Church of the future," this Note ends, " some of us look forward to a reunion of Christendom having its centre in a Primacy such as might be found in a Papacy which had renounced certain of its present claims; some, on the other hand, look forward to union by a more federal type of constitution which would have no need for such a Primacy." In the light of even the rather inadequate Agreed Statement on Authority of the Anglican–Roman Catholic International Commission,[32] my marginal comment against

31. *Intercommunion Today*. Church Information Office 1968.
32. SPCK and CTS 1977.

the former alternative, " What a hope! " is happily beginning to look as " dated " as anything in the Report itself.

More important in the actual context of 1938 is the Commission's method of expounding the doctrine of the Church. They recognize that some schools of thought prefer to start from the freshness of the new covenant, without denying the continuity of the Church with Israel, while others lay the primary emphasis on the latter without denying the former. It is, on the whole, the second approach which they follow, and they define the Church historically, with a survey of the history of the people of God from the call of Israel onwards, and institutionally. It is the line usually followed by Anglican and much Roman Catholic theology, and it is congenial to all who share that historical, as opposed to systematic, method of theology so characteristic of English thought. The Commission show little sign of realizing that this method cannot expect to win uncritical acceptance in ecumenical circles. That this is the case was shown when a double report (European and North American) on " Christ and the Church " was presented to the Fourth World Conference on Faith and Order at Montreal in 1963.[33] The European Section, of which Bishop Anders Nygren was chairman with myself as vice-chairman, presented what was in fact a basically British study, treating the history of the institutional Church from " The People of God under the Old Covenant " to " The Church and the Consummation." The North American Section, led by Professors Calhoun and Pittenger, proceeded deductively from Christology to " The Church in the World." Here were two different theological models; another, pressed upon us from the side of German theology, was the idea of the creation of the Church, almost *de novo*, wherever the word is proclaimed and evokes the response of faith from the hearers. In the wider ecumenical debate

33. Faith and Order Paper No. 38. Geneva 1963.

to which Lambeth had helped to open the way in 1920, a much fuller enquiry into the theology of the Church than the Commission could undertake has turned out to be among its unfinished business.

If the Church and ministry formed the second main item on the agenda of the Commission, the third and ultimately the most important could be said to be that " thorough investigation of fundamental principles " which Burge and his committee had originally hoped might lead to a wide measure of agreement. Fundamental principles had now been brought into the open by the Girton controversy. They included the basic principles of authority in doctrine; the question of the sources and norms of truth in the sphere of Christian belief was now urgent. The reaction of the English Church Union to the Girton papers had proceeded on the assumption that the answers to all questions concerning the content of Christian doctrine can be read off, in the last resort, from Scripture interpreted in the light of the Creeds and the Church's tradition. The same assumption underlay the long series of attempts to stave off criticism of traditional doctrine by dogged reaffirmations of loyalty to Scripture and the Creeds, to which some, like Carter in his review of the Report, would add the Articles as the norm of " official Anglican doctrine."[34] This understanding of doctrinal authority had, however, been increasingly called in question since the rise of biblical criticism. Both the content of Scripture and the classical formulations of doctrine were coming to be seen as conditioned by the

34. See above. He writes: " Without an appeal to official Anglican doctrine the Church of England will never be able to command the confidence of her children or recover real internal unity and concord. The Commission ought to have re-echoed Thomas Rogers (Bancroft's chaplain) in 1607: ' The doctrine of the Church of England is known by the Thirty-Nine Articles. Other doctrine than in the said Articles is contained our Church neither hath nor holdeth'."

historical circumstances and the prevailing cultures of their times. Credal statements are thus subject, like all other expressions of human thought, including the biblical writings, to the relativities of history. If this is so, it becomes impossible to speak in the traditional manner of " revealed doctrines."

The question was being much discussed in the nineteen-thirties whether divine revelation is communicated in propositional form. Theologians as diverse as Temple himself, Barth, Brunner and Buber were agreed that revelation is not given in such propositions as that Jesus is the Son of God, but is God's personal disclosure of himself in the events of history, in particular in the " mighty acts " to which Scripture bears witness. This in turn, however, raises other questions. It is not an event in itself (supposing a " bare " event to be conceivable) which may be revelatory of God, but an event as interpreted. What, then, is the relation, within the complex whole of a " revelatory event," between the " objective " occurrence and the presuppositions, including the religious attitude, of the experiencing and interpreting human subject? What is meant by the affirmation that a particular event is in some special sense an act of God? What differentiates such an event from other occurrences, and does the difference lie solely in the interpretation placed upon it by persons who have experienced it at first hand or heard or read about it at second hand? By what criteria, then, can claims to have experienced revelatory occurrences be evaluated? And if revelation is mediated in personal experience and apprehended by an attitude of faith, what is the relation between this faith-experience and the theological formulations which are subsequently devised in order to articulate and interpret it? What, further, is the relation between faith which encounters and apprehends revelation in certain experienced events and " the faith " as an articulated system of theological interpretations of the insights of faith? Are theological formulations, and the structured system of doctrine into which they come to be organized, to be regarded as models (comparable with those of the scientist, though used in this case not for prediction but only for analysis), serving to articulate religious experience (that is, experience as interpreted by faith) and valuable in so far as, and only in so far as, they continue to fulfil that task successfully?

If this is a true suggestion, then doctrines are human intellectual constructions which, however completely and satisfyingly they must have served to articulate Christian faith-experience in the past, must always be scrutinized and tested in every generation to discover whether they are still articulating and interpreting it successfully in new historical situations, which include changes in men's intellectual and spiritual presuppositions, or whether they need to be modified or even discarded for some other model. This applies, for example, to the doctrines of the incarnation and the Trinity. The first questions to be asked about them are exegetical and historical: What faith-experience underlay them? What did those who gradually developed them, and transmitted them to subsequent generations by a continuing process of reflection and interpretation, intend them to express? The next question has to be more complex: Can we enter into and share that original faith-experience? If so, do we find it satisfactory to express this in terms of the traditional models, or must we try to modify them or replace them, realizing that any modifications we may make to ancient models and any new models that we may construct will before long themselves be subjected to the same treatment?

If the question of revelation and its relation to Scripture and creeds has to be approached along these lines, theology becomes a search for truth, an asking of questions rather than an exposition of received answers. The theologian must take the past seriously, for the experience of human beings in the past provides his primary data and is the starting-point of his quest; but he need not be bound by the interpretations of the past that were offered by his predecessors. There is still a clear distinction between Christians and those who either do not have faith in God or whose faith-experience of God does not have Jesus as its focus and primary reference-point; there is a distinction between good theology which satisfactorily articulates and interprets the data of experience and bad theology which does not; but Gore's condemnation of Major and Rashdall as " formidable heresiarchs " becomes meaningless, for within the area of Christian faith the concept of heresy disappears. It is in the light of this that the practical question which also confronted the Commission has to be considered: whether the open-ended search for truth, for which no particular assured results can be predicted, can properly be engaged in by the clergy as theologians, or whether as the Church's accredited teachers they should regard themselves as commissioned, rightly or wrongly, to pursue theological speculation only as far as the limits prescribed by a received tradition or party line.

These are among the far-reaching questions which doctrinal controversies had put on the Commission's agenda—and perhaps one should add the yet more fundamental question of the grounds for belief in God. It comes, then, as a surprise to find " The Sources and Authority of Christian Doctrine " placed under the heading " Prolegomena," and to read in the Chairman's Introduction that they began their proceedings by discussing the grounds of belief to enable them to come " to know one another and to establish a spirit of confidence before we approached the more sensitive points of discussion." These fundamental problems, in other words, provided them with a kind of limbering-up exercise for the real slogging match over the ministry and sacraments.

Yet within thirteen pages a good deal is achieved.

Belief that the Bible is " the inspired record of God's self-revelation to man and of man's response to that revelation " is not an *a priori* dogma but a conclusion drawn from the spiritual insight displayed in its contents. The tradition of its inerrancy " cannot be maintained." The working of the divine Spirit, recognized in the work of biblical authors, editors and revisers, and in the formation of the Jewish and Christian canons, is also to be traced outside the limits of Israel and Christendom; but the inspiration recognized in the Bible is unique inasmuch as it is related to the special and primary operation of the Spirit in the fellowship of Christian believers. The authority of the Bible resides in its being the record of God's self-revelation in history, culminating in Jesus, and the source and primary criterion of the Church's teaching and life. It does not prejudge the conclusions of any historical or scientific investigation, including biblical criticism itself; Christian thinkers are not bound to biblical thought-forms; the spiritual value of the various parts of the Bible is not equal, and it has to be judged in relation to the mind of Christ as disclosed to Christians by his Spirit. The recorded teaching of Jesus was conditioned by the thought-forms and circumstances of the time (and what is recorded is by no means always to be regarded as reproducing the actual words of Jesus). Yet the Gospels faithfully convey " the impact made upon the Apostolic Church by the mind and personality of Jesus, and thus possess supreme authority."

This short but quite profound discussion of Scripture is well worth study today, when biblical fundamentalism is more prevalent than in 1938. It contrasts well with the one or two cursory and uncritical sentences devoted to the authority of Scripture by the Anglican–Roman Catholic International Commission.[35] The Report, however, is very thin where the basic question of revelation is concerned.

35. *Authority in the Church*, paras. 2, 15, 18.

It tells us that " there is a revelation of God in nature, but beyond this God reveals himself in varying degrees in the course of historical events and in the experience and character both of nations and of individuals," and that " the process of Divine self-disclosure in the history and religious experience of Israel . . . culminates in Jesus Christ "; but this leaves the fundamental problems untouched. It recognizes that great changes had taken place in science and philosophy during the period of the Commission's work. " An astonished public has been made aware that some leading students of physics consider that the knowledge gained by their studies is schematic only and not a knowledge of reality." Yet the Commission do not face the question whether the content, and even the concept itself, of revelation can remain unaffected by this revolution. Sometimes they seem to see their task as one of translation or re-presentation only: " to set forth the truths of the Everlasting Gospel unchanged in sub-stance " for the fact that there may have to be changes in the intellectual formulation of revelation " does not mean that there is any change in that which has been revealed." It is very questionable whether such a simple and tidy distinction can be maintained.

On the other hand, the Report is clear that neither the meaning nor the actual language of credal formulations is unalterable. They are " classical " and have peculiar authority for the Church; yet it may become necessary to associate with a traditional phrase " a meaning not originally connected with it," and there may come a point at which the moral judgement of the community may decide that " a changed interpretation ethically demands a change in the phrase used." " The apprehension of Revelation by the human mind must needs find expression in the form of propositions, but no such formulations are to be regarded as being, in principle, irreformable." If any formulations are " final," this is not because " they are exempt from examination, but in the sense that

examination invariably leads to their re-affirmation." As
for specifically Anglican formulations, it is clear that they
are subject to the relativities of history. The Articles are
" a declaration of the position adopted by the Church of
England at a critical moment in relation to the chief
controversies of that moment." However, " if an
Anglican theologian thinks a particular formulary not
wholly adequate, he must try to preserve whatever truth
that formulary was trying to secure and to ensure that
whatever statement he puts forward as more adequate
does in fact secure this." In general, " acceptance of the
Church's authority by the individual must always rest on
his own judgment."

The Commission do not always act on their own
principles. In one place absolute authority seems to be
attributed to the Catechism. The view that sacraments
are efficacious means of grace, in the sense that they
produce certain dispositions in the recipients which enable
them to receive grace, is criticized on the ground that such
dispositions might equally be produced by other means,
and that this would be incompatible with maintaining,
" as Anglican formularies *require*,"[36] that Baptism and the
Eucharist are " generally necessary to salvation." Nevertheless, this part of the Report is a remarkable achievement, not least for the unanimity with which Anglicans
from very different party traditions endorsed a strongly
liberal attitude towards the authority of Scripture,
Church, creeds, councils and formularies, and by implication pointed to the possibility of more profitable forms of
theological dialogue than the futile sequence of *gravamina*
and " reaffirmations."

Today the Commission's belief seems strange that the
doctrines of the Holy Spirit and the Trinity " are not the
source of any tendency to division in the Church of
England "; they were therefore left as another item of

36. My italics.

unfinished business. The much fuller section on Christology, however, is worth close attention. It outlines the approaches to Christology characteristic of Alexandria and Antioch: the one starting from the conviction that Jesus is personally God, the other from the historic figure and human experience of Jesus, in whom is found a revelation of God which supersedes all others. Christ's " sinlessness " means that the result of his impact upon men is to evoke penitence, while of this there is no trace in his own consciousness; in speaking of this we are not concerned with an inductive inference from single actions but with the total impact of a character wholly given to and united with God. It is clearly stated that pre-existence is not predicated by orthodox theology of Jesus as man; but no attempt is made to explain or defend the concept of the pre-existent Word or Son, apart from the comment that the doctrine of Christ as the eternal Word implies that the creation, redemption and consummation of the world are all activities of the one God. Christ is in the full sense man and in the full sense God; this truth is what the doctrine of the incarnation signifies. The Commission do not ask whether that doctrine in its traditional form is the only or the best way of articulating that truth.

Much less satisfactory is the treatment of the controversial subjects of the virgin birth and the resurrection. If the former is claimed to be an historical event, the grounds for believing it must be historical evidence. But since the evidence in this case can only be inconclusive, the Report offers " grounds on which the doctrine is valued " that in Christ " humanity made a fresh beginning " (which seems hardly compatible with the belief that he truly was " made man " with the same nature as our own); that it coheres with the supernatural element in the life of Christ; that it expresses the response of the human race, through Mary, to God's purpose. So " many of us " hold. On the other side " some among us " think that it mars the completeness of the belief that in the incarnation God revealed himself at every point in and through human nature. The question is thus treated as theological rather than historical; and both attitudes are said to be consistent with belief in the incarnation. The resurrection is treated on similar lines: the story of the empty tomb is " the symbol " of the victory of Jesus; yet the majority of the Commission hold it to be literally true. An appended note on the historical evidence gives an interesting insight into the Commission's methods of exegesis and interpretation. It is worth noticing that they are unanimous in interpreting the ascension symbolically.

It was unfortunate that Temple introduced into this context another controversial issue: the question of the liberty of the Church's official teachers to criticize its traditional teaching. " I fully recognize," he said in the Introduction, " the position of those who sincerely affirm the reality of our Lord's Incarnation without accepting one or both of these two events as actual historical occurrences "; yet " in view of my own responsibility in the Church I think it right here to affirm that I whole-heartedly accept (them) as historical facts." This is confusing. If they are *historical* facts, only historical evidence can lead anyone, whatever his responsibility in the Church, to accept them; Temple's responsibility, moreover, was surely to seek truth himself and promote the quest for truth in the Church. " Why," asked the Bishop of Durham (Hensley Henson), " should his Grace's position in the Church make it right to do this? It is presumably because his Grace is a teacher . . . but he is only a teacher . . . and what I . . . wish to stand out against is the double standard of truth. It must not be implied that the teachers can publicly affirm one thing and that others can take a larger liberty than the teachers. I believe this is unchristian and that the general intention of the report is otherwise."[37] Temple's disclaimer was

37. Speech in York Convocation, 2 June 1938.

certainly strangely inconsistent with the Report's full acceptance of biblical criticism, its clear assertion of the reformability of credal formulations, and its general presupposition that such questions as these are open to free enquiry.

The reception of the Report was both varied and predictable. Temple defended it at the outset against criticism that its unanimity was bogus: it had been achieved only by including frequent and important expressions of differences within the body of the document. " Where disagreement remained," he asserted,[38] " we have tried to secure that each view is expressed, not in the language beloved by its adherents but feared or hated by others, but in the language which may show to those others its positive spiritual value. . . The aim has been to set the points of difference against the background of relevant agreement, so as to make it apparent that those who differ are not opposed in fundamental belief, but in their way of apprehending and expressing a fundamental belief held by all alike." The well-known " High Church " parish priest, Canon Peter Green,[39] maintained that doctrinal differences, which have always existed within the Catholic Church, are to be welcomed; only by their interaction can the truth be kept alive and healthy. He made two important points: alongside the Church's official teaching there has always been an " unofficial view " on many important doctrinal issues; and even when modern Christians believe in historic facts related in the New Testament, they necessarily interpret them very differently from the early Christians—the ascension being a case in point.

Although critical in detail, the Bishop of Gloucester (A. C. Headlam)[40] claimed that the Report " expresses our

38. Presidential Address to York Convocation, 19 January 1938.
39. *Church Times*, 29 April 1938.
40. *Church Quarterly Review*, April–June 1938, pp. 83-94.

inherited Christian belief in a manner which thoughtful people of the present century can understand and accept, and removes much that is not, and never has been, an essential element in the Christian belief." It shows that " the great body of Christian doctrine wisely stated is what all parties of the Church accept, although there are on each side some points which are rejected or held only by a particular school of thought. . . The limits have not yet been settled, nor is it desirable that the limits of freedom should be too carefully marked out. . . A very strong and wise exposition of Christian theology is given."

Professor J. M. Creed[41] defended the Report in respect of its very different approach from that of contemporary Continental dogmatics. " Yet in so far as those movements testify to a recovered consciousness of the divine transcendence . . . their temper is not uncongenial to many members of the Commission, and in the sections which deal with the doctrines of God, the Church and the Last Things a kindred spirit may be detected. Yet nowhere is this doctrine of transcendence so asserted as to seem to confound the testimony of the reason and conscience of mankind. Rather does the Report encourage the belief that it is through reason and conscience that God must be apprehended if He is to be apprehended at all."

H. D. A. Major, however, warned[42] that traditionalist opposition was taking two forms: suggestions by some that " the report itself is of no real significance—the lucubrations of a small group of ecclesiastical theorists," and that its contents may therefore be ignored; and a call from others for its specific condemnation and official rejection. The latter, in fact, took the form of a petition to the Convocations of Canterbury, signed by 6338 clergy, and York, signed by 1868. As any student of church history could have predicted, the " Catholic-Evangelical "

41. Speech at the annual meeting of the Modern Churchman's Union, 18 May 1938.

42. *The Modern Churchman*, 28 May 1938, pp. 57-64.

axis had gone into action. A covering letter to the Canterbury petition was signed by the chairmen of the Oxford Evangelical Conference, the Executive Committee of the Church Union, the National Church League, the Executive Committee of the Central Evangelical Council, the Federation of Catholic Priests, and the Superior General SSJE; a similar letter to York was signed by leading Anglo-Catholic and Evangelical clergy.

This petition was yet another exercise in reaffirmation: of " the assent given by us at our ordination to the truths (1) of the Virginal Conception of our Lord Jesus Christ by the direct operation of the Holy Ghost, and of His Incarnation thereby of the Virgin Mary His Mother, without seed of man; (2) of His Bodily Resurrection from the tomb on the third day; and (3) of His Ascension in the Risen Body to the right hand of the Majesty on high." In view of " the clamant need for certitude in matters of faith we note with all the graver concern that the inerrancy in spiritual things which belongs to the Incarnate Son of God is being impugned by much modern teaching." A declaration was asked for that the doctrine set forth in the Book of Common Prayer and the Articles remains the authentic teaching of the Church of England, and that the Church of England holds and teaches the Nicene Creed " in that sense only in which it has ever been held throughout the history of the Church, and that her ministers cannot rightly claim a liberty to set aside by private interpretation the historic meaning of those clauses which state the events of the earthly life of our Lord Jesus Christ."

Another broadside was fired by the Catholic Advisory Council, representing the main Anglo-Catholic societies and the Superiors of the Cowley, Kelham, Mirfield and Nashdom communities. Its effect was dissipated by its being aimed simultaneously, not only at teachers who depart from the doctrinal standards of the Prayer Book and from the Church of England's reverence for " the

Bible as the written Word of God," but also at the recognition of non-episcopal ministries and the use of them for the reception of the sacraments, the possibility of the admission of women to holy orders, the policy of many bishops in their dealings with divorced persons who have been "remarried" and in their toleration of contraceptives, the proposals for union in India, and the regulations concerning deaconesses, "together with such accomplished facts as the open Communion service recently held at Oxford."

The Report was debated by the Convocations in June 1938. It was cordially welcomed, and although, inevitably, a "reaffirmation" was added, this was in moderate and sensible terms, ignoring the reference in the Petition to "that sense only in which [the Nicene Creed] has ever been held and its demand for the foreclosing of critical enquiry into the historical clauses." The resolution ran: "That this House welcomes the report . . . as a survey of the currents of thought and belief within the Church, a statement of the agreement and disagreement actually existing, and a contribution to the understanding and appreciation of one another on the part of those who differ; recognises that the report neither is nor claims to be a declaration of the doctrine of the Church—a purpose lying outside the Commission's terms of reference, and one for which no commission appointed as this was could be competent; desires that the report may be widely studied in that spirit of open-minded devotion to truth and readiness to learn from every tradition of Christian thought which is characteristic of the report itself. Further, inasmuch as many have misunderstood the function of the Commission as explained above, this House, while recognising the reality of the problems which scholars and theologians are handling and desiring to maintain in the Church the fullest freedom of inquiry which is compatible with spiritual fellowship, thinks it well to state that the doctrine of the Church of England is now, as it has been in past time, the doctrine set forth in the Creeds, in the Prayer-book, and in the Articles of Religion."

The Dean of York (H. N. Bate)[43] welcomed the Report in the Lower House of York " for what it is: not as a doctrinal formulation but as a cross-section . . . of the present adventure of thought within the Church of England." His speech ended optimistically, though with a sting in its tail: " Our Church has rendered an almost unique service to Christendom and . . . has gained enormously in robustness and strength, by its obvious fearlessness. . . It is in this spirit that I myself can welcome the report of the Commission with all that is disquieting in it."

In the Upper House of Canterbury an effusion of optimism from Winnington Ingram contributed light relief to a rather unremarkable debate: " To my mind the most wonderful thing about it is the agreement between twenty men of such different schools of thought. . . The Virgin Birth and the Empty Tomb are parts of the original Gospel which we are bound to hold, and I believe that the modern doubts about these matters are due to a Victorian philosophy which is out of date. I happen to know one very leading radiologist who said to me the other day: ' They used to believe differently in the Victorian days, but we now know that matter is nothing in itself and spirit is everything '." To this the Bishop of Birmingham (E. W. Barnes) rejoined: " I hope that the statement made by the Bishop of London on the authority of one whom he described as a distinguished radiologist will not be accepted . . . without challenge. . . We all regard the supremacy of the spiritual as ultimately the supreme fact of the Universe. But we cannot affirm such non-existence of the material as appeared to be involved

43. His speech was reprinted in *Theology* 37, September, 1938, pp. 134-41.

in the statement: ' Matter is nothing; spirit is everything.' It is true that matter appears to have been dissolved into electrons and . . . protons, and that possibly these particles are merely manifestations of energy; but energy most definitely belongs to the material world and has an existence which cannot properly be described as non-real."

Although the Upper House of Canterbury approved the motion unanimously, the Lower House added a request that the Upper House should " express itself further in the matter of Church doctrine in accordance with the terms of the Petition." Nothing further was in fact done.

A distinguished Unitarian critic, Laurence Redfern, himself a focus of controversy in 1933 when he accepted an invitation to preach in Liverpool Cathedral,[44] asked:[45] " Will the Anglican Church remain where it now stands, offering an embarrassing choice of doctrines to its adherents? Will this Report be the sealing of a final pact between Reason and Belief? We do not think so. . . Certain it is that the demand for intellectual liberty is coming in like the tide. And this Report . . . marks the position of King Canute's chair in the present year of grace." However that may be, the Church, at any rate when another tide, the upsurge of " biblical theology " and neo-orthodoxy, had ebbed, had no option but to embrace a doctrinal pluralism.

In the increasingly polarized intellectual state of the Church of England in the nineteen-sixties and seventies, doctrinal division extended more widely and deeply into those matters which had been left by the Commission as unfinished business. Any idea of following up the plea of W. R. Matthews in 1938 for a revision of the Articles was rejected as both undesirable and impracticable. A short study of this question was made by Archbishop Ramsey's Doctrine Commission. The main task given to us, how-

44. See F. W. Dillistone, *Charles Raven* (Hodder & Stoughton 1975), pp. 163-5.
45. *Inquirer*, 5 February 1938.

ever, was to report on " The Nature of the Christian
Faith and its Expression in Holy Scripture and Creeds."
This time the membership represented the whole spectrum
of Anglican theology; all but one of the seventeen
members were clergy, but none at the time parish priests;
all, as in 1922, were men. Four typical attitudes towards
creeds were identified: some hold that the creeds are a
norm, and that adherence to them is by Anglican standards
essential; others wish to identify themselves with the
general faith of the Church, expressed in creeds, while
having difficulties and reservations concerning individual
clauses; the allegiance of others is to the continuing
Church rather than to any past beliefs, which they regard
as relative to the culture of their times, so that they can
neither affirm nor deny the creeds; for yet others com-
mitment to God and to Jesus is more important than
" provisional " assent to any credal propositions. Between
these groups there is tension, but this should be creative—
not a state of non-communication between mutually
embattled groups, but one of constant dialogue. The
creeds should be left in the kind of doctrinal position
which they currently enjoy, but " dialogue " should be
made a reality by acknowledging that free and responsible
debate about their contents is not disloyal to the Christian
cause.[46]

This plea for coexistence, not out of keeping with the
spirit of 1938, was signed unanimously. The 42 pages of
agreed report, however, were supplemented by more than
twice that number in the form of individual essays
illustrating the great variety of ways in which Anglican
theologians today actually go about their business. Had
space permitted there could have been as many distinctive
individual essays as there were members of the commission.
The report strikingly demonstrates the " choice of
doctrines " now offered by the Church of England to its

46. *Christian Believing*, pp. 36-42.

adherents. It suggests that unity in the future will be a unity (within the brotherhood of a common basic belief in God, centred on Jesus) in asking questions rather than in agreeing to answers.

Unlike the 1938 Report, *Christian Believing*, though published with a kind word of commendation from Archbishop Coggan and greeted with a little publicity and some reviews, was never passed to the General Synod for discussion or officially commended to the attention of the Church. It was, on the contrary, quietly and rapidly buried.

Of its much more ambitious predecessor, however, the words of the Bishop of Manchester (F. S. Guy Warman)[47] remain true: " It will be for a very long while a book which will help those who study it to reassert the Faith and to exercise considerateness in so doing, and at the same time to preserve that freedom of thought and enquiry which has always been part of the Anglican tradition." Now, as when it was first published, it addresses itself, as Temple said in his Presidential Address at York, neither to the expert theologian, nor to the general public, but to " that large body of persons who, without being systematic students of theology, take a serious interest in the problems of the Christian religion; for it is upon their thought, in the long run, that the growth of unity in the life of the Church depends."

47. Upper House of the Convocation of York, 2 June 1938.

CHAIRMAN'S INTRODUCTION

MY colleagues on the Commission have asked me to write an introduction, traversing the ground covered by the whole Report of the Commission, and supplying an interpretation and a commentary, which aims at being fair to the intent of the Commission but is avowedly individual and personal. What I offer has been seen by all members of the Commission, and many have made comments; to these comments I have paid most careful attention, but for the result I am wholly and solely responsible.

THE SPIRIT OF OUR GATHERINGS

I would begin by emphasising what is said in the Introductory Chapter of the Report itself about the spirit in which our discussions have been conducted. We have become a company of personal friends. That fact is closely connected with the measure of agreement that we have reached. It is a sad reflection upon the sincerity of Christian discipleship that so often in the history of the Church controversy has been conducted with bitterness and has been associated, as both cause and effect, with personal animosity. It is truly said that to become bitter in controversy is more heretical than to espouse with sincerity and charity the most devastating theological opinions; and by this standard the " orthodox " are condemned as grievously as their opponents. Progress in apprehension of the truths of the Gospel must chiefly come by the intercourse of minds united in friendship, so that they can do that most difficult thing to which St. Paul refers as though it ought to come naturally—" speaking the truth in love." We have been very frank in our comments to one another; brutally frank at times, were it not for the friendship which secured us against all risk of being " wounded " or " hurt." We escaped early from that false responsibility which consists in a sense that a man "represents" some section of ecclesiastical opinion. We were drawn from most of the existing "schools of thought" in the Church, and had our own several apprehensions of the truth as it is in Jesus Christ; but our minds moved freely, at times even playfully, in the intercourse of friends, and each both learnt and taught as our work advanced.

Behind the friendship and the laughter were the steady purpose to pursue the truth, and the common devotions in the Chapels of the Colleges where we met. Each morning the Chairman celebrated the Holy Communion, and the daily Offices were duly said. In our prayer together and in our Communions we found the direction for our common effort. The memory of our meetings is associated in my mind with the description of the mingled devotion and hilarity of "the Holy Party," which Scott Holland gives in his charming biographical sketch of Francis Paget (*Bundle of Memories*, pp. 64-65).

We have avoided the method of decisions by a majority, except in questions of procedure. We have tried by conference to reach real agreement; where this has proved impossible, we have set out the divergent views that are still found to be held among us. Sometimes we have stated our conviction that these should all be regarded as permissible in the Church of England; but we have considered that our function is to elucidate doctrine and doctrinal tendencies, not to declare principles of discipline except so far as these are themselves doctrinal. The last point may be illustrated by our conviction that the authoritative value of agreement or *consensus* in doctrine depends upon the freedom of those who agree, so that the utmost liberty of thought compatible with maintenance of spiritual fellowship should be secured. But what is the precise point at which the spiritual fellowship is endangered, and by what methods those who endanger it should be restrained, are questions that lie outside our province. Similarly we have not been concerned with questions of pastoral expediency. For instance, we have affirmed our belief that when Holy Communion is administered by means of the Reserved Sacrament the same gift is offered to the recipient as in the open service. But we have not considered whether, or in what circumstances, it is expedient to provide that means of administration.

Our terms of reference, as set out in the letter of Archbishop Davidson to Bishop Burge, did not include the question what varieties of doctrine or of interpretation are to be regarded as permissible in the Church of England. At some points we have expressed our conviction that various types of doctrine are permissible; and at others we have indicated a clear line beyond which any doctrine or interpretation would seem to us not permissible. Here and there a member or members of the Commission may doubt or even deny that the view held by one or more of his colleagues can be regarded as theologically compatible either with Catholic doctrine or with the tradition of the Church of England, and such a situation is apparent at some points in the Report. It is therefore important to emphasise the distinction between the judgment that such-and-such an opinion is incompatible with the Christian faith or the Anglican tradition, and the judgment that such-and-such a person, who holds an opinion thus condemned, should be excluded from the exercise of office or of membership in the Church. The latter is a judicial and administrative decision, which must be based on other considerations as well as on those of theology; the former is a theological verdict, with the practical results of which the theologian as such is not directly concerned. We have interpreted our function as solely theological and not in any sense judicial.

When a group of men have met together regularly for a dozen years and more, in order to discuss their various interpretations of something which they hold in common, they inevitably form a common mind which finds expres-

sion in the language that they use. It may easily result
from this that they use terms with a suggestion of meaning
not commonly associated with those terms, so that the very
process whereby they have become so intimately associated
with one another causes them to be unintelligible to anyone else.

This peril is increased when they have sought to express
their common mind in brief statements which are accepted
by all of them. In the fashioning of such statements many
phrases are proposed and rejected before the generally
acceptable expression is found. The precise *nuance* of the
phrase adopted can then be appreciated only by those who
will think of all the possible alternatives, and what may
have been the grounds for the preference shown. No
reader can be expected actually to do this, so that the extent to which the expressions used convey the full intention
of their authors must be in some measure accidental.

The Scope of the Report

Readers of the Report who wish to estimate its significance accurately must keep in mind the limitation of scope
implied in the circumstances of the Commission's appointment. It was not appointed in order to survey the whole
field of theology and produce a systematic treatise in which
the space allotted to any subject would bear some appreciable
relation to the inherent importance of that subject. The
Commission was appointed because the tensions between
different schools of thought in the Church of England were
imperilling its unity and impairing its effectiveness. Consequently those subjects (on the whole) receive most attention in the Report which are at this time, or have been
during the period of the Commission's labours, occasions
of controversy within the Church of England or sources of
confusion in Anglican practice.

These are not the same as those which cause most concern to Continental theologians. If any such honour us
by reading this Report they will be startled to find so little

said about the Fall; about Freedom, Election, and Pre-destination; about Justification by Faith; about the Order of Creation and the Order of Redemption; about the possibility of Natural Theology. They will be filled with astonishment at the brevity of our treatment of Divine Grace under that title. Our reply that almost the whole of our Report is concerned with Divine Grace in its various manifestations would do little to diminish their bewilderment.

That is one illustration of the difference of habit in theological thought as this has developed under the different conditions prevalent in our own country and on the Continent. This difference has many causes; among these may be the constant stream of Platonism which Dr. Inge claims to have been a special characteristic of English thought; but certainly we must reckon among the special determinants of English theology the fact that our Reformation Fathers appealed so largely to the authority of Patristic, and especially of Greek Patristic, writings. They were at one with the Continental Reformers in their indebtedness to St. Augustine; but to a greater extent they paid regard also to the works of Origen, Athanasius, Basil, and the two Gregories. In these the distinctive doctrines of St. Augustine, which he developed in his controversy with Pelagianism, are (naturally) not to be found. The heirs of Luther's Augustinianism are apt to' accuse English Christianity as a whole of Pelagianism; and it must be admitted that we have a perpetual tendency in that direction. As I regard Pelagianism as of all heresies spiritually the most pernicious, I share in some degree the Continental anxiety concerning our habitual inclination towards it. Yet I am glad that we have not been lastingly subjected to the distinctively Augustinian doctrine of the Fall, but can balance this with the very different doctrine of some of the Greek Fathers.*

* See N. P. Williams, *The Ideas of the Fall and of Original Sin,* pp. 189-314.

In recent times the great influence of Westcott and of the *Lux Mundi* school has strengthened the dependence of Anglican theology upon the Greek as contrasted with the Latin Fathers. In the result there is found to be a closer relationship in theology between the Orthodox Churches of the East and the Church of England than between the former and either Rome on the one hand or Wittenberg or Geneva on the other.

Our Report must be read in the context of the thought of our time and with regard to its constant changes. Even during the period of our labours great fluctuations of mental habit have been apparent in the spheres of secular science and philosophy. An astonished public has been made aware that some leading students of physics consider that the knowledge gained by their studies is schematic only and not a knowledge of Reality. In the political world the ideas of freedom and fellowship are passing through readjustment and revaluation. And in our own sphere, that of Theology, the work of such writers as Karl Barth in Europe and Reinhold Niebuhr in America has set many problems in a new perspective. It has not been our task to comment on these variations in the intellectual atmosphere; but if what is either preached or written is to be understood, its expression must be adapted to the minds which may hear or read. Our task has been, so far as we were able, to discuss the unchanging truths of the Christian revelation, and the various interpretations of these current in the Church of England, in such a way as to be intelligible to those of our contemporaries who have some acquaintance with theology. But it has always been our desire to set forth the truth of the Everlasting Gospel unchanged in substance. Indeed, we believe that its permanence amidst the welter of modern theories, which seem to succeed each other with kaleidoscopic inconsequence, may be one of its chief means of drawing to itself the attention of a bewildered generation.

Our aim, however, is not specifically to commend the

doctrine of the Church, but to examine the differences of interpretation current in the Church of England and to elucidate the relations of these one to another. If in so doing we have commended to any perplexed minds the Gospel itself or have removed obstacles to belief, we are thankful that our work should have this result. But that is a different function from ours, and, doubtless, a higher. Our function, allotted to us by those who called us into existence as a Commission, is what we have described. This accounts for, and as we hope justifies, the rather detached and academic quality of our work. There is in the Church of England a rich treasury of spiritual experience, a living tradition of personal devotion and freely moving thought. The same is true of every one of the schools of thought within it. The examination of these, and discussion of their inter-relations, cannot have the vitality and richness characteristic of the traditions themselves which are thus discussed. The fault of detachment, if any regard it so, is inseparable from the particular service which we were asked to render.

THE SCHEME OF THE REPORT

What has been said concerning the contents of the Report applies equally to the order in which these are presented. We have not followed the natural order of theological exposition, such as would be appropriate to a *Summa Theologiæ*; nor have we followed the order of discovery or appropriation, such as would be appropriate to an educational textbook. Our subjects of concern are supplied to us neither by the orderly sequence of theological science nor by the psychological sequence of personal apprehension, but by the contemporary situation within the Church of England. This fact makes it incidentally the more important to remember that, even so, we are not concerned with matters of discipline or of pastoral expediency. The practical problems must be handled by the proper authorities; but these arise in part from theological divergences or misunderstandings. It is with the underlying theology, not with the practical problems, that we are concerned. Having thus a selection of themes rather thrust upon us than chosen by us, we have sought to arrange these in the order that may make our treatment of them most intelligible and easiest to follow.

We began our proceedings by discussing the Grounds of Belief. This was of special value inasmuch as most actual divergences between English Christians were thus handled, or at least glanced at, by implication, yet the party alignments familiar in our more frequent controversies were irrelevant. Thus we came to know one another and to establish a spirit of confidence before we approached the more sensitive points of discussion. But it was never intended that we should embark on an adequate treatment of the Grounds of Belief; that would require a complete philosophical treatise, such as this Commission was neither commissioned nor specially qualified to undertake. Accordingly that section of our Report appears as a preliminary collection of Prolegomena, indicating the temper and governing principles of our approach to what was more definitely our concern.

I would here point especially to what is said about the Authority and Inspiration of Scripture, and about the Authority of Anglican formularies. We fully acknowledge the supremacy of Scripture as supplying the standard of doctrine; and we try to indicate how Scripture should be regarded in this connexion: everyone knows that it is possible to quote texts which, torn from their context, may be presented as supporting entirely un-Christian opinions. Short of that, everyone knows that most heretics have been convinced that they were conscientiously following and interpreting Scripture. Our attention must be fastened on the trend of Scripture as a whole and upon its climax in the record of the Word made flesh, by the light of which all the rest is to be interpreted; in that concentration of attention and in that interpretation, our best guide is the continuous stream of universal Christian tradition.

Some will be surprised that we have not given a greater prominence to the Anglican formularies and, in particular, the Thirty-Nine Articles. There is much ignorance and much confusion of mind about the Articles. They have not, at any rate from the early seventeenth century onwards, taken in our system the place occupied in the Lutheran system by the Augsburg Confession. They are, indeed, too short for such a purpose. They are not a complete confession of faith, but a declaration of the position adopted by the Church of England at a critical moment in relation to the chief controversies of that moment. A clergyman wishing to instruct in the Christian faith the communicants in his parish, or the candidates for confirmation, seldom has occasion to refer to the Articles; he is guided by the Catechism and the other parts of the Prayer-Book. Moreover, the Articles are, in their influence upon the life and thought of the Church, inevitably far less formative than the Prayer-Book; for the constant worship of any group of Christians must exercise upon them a far more pervasive and penetrating influence than that of any formula to which the worshipping congregation has no frequent occasion to refer, especially when that formula is found to be largely concerned with questions no longer foremost in our minds.

The Church of England is a living community, moving, as we trust, under the guidance of the Holy Spirit. We have, therefore, not supposed that it could be the function of a Commission, appointed as we were, only to see what bearing the Articles or even the Prayer-Book might have on the questions that chiefly divide Anglicans, but rather that we were called upon to handle these questions as best we could in the light of reason, of modern knowledge, and of that universal Christian tradition to which our Reformers themselves appealed.

The Church of England has no official Philosophy and

it certainly was not our desire to provide one for it. There is need of Christian philosophers, who set out the map of the world as it is seen in the light of Christian faith. But the value of their work depends upon their intellectual freedom and independence. An official philosophy is a *monstrum horrendum*. But if we were not to offer a philosophy our treatment of some great subjects must needs be brief. So, for example, many may be surprised that our section dealing with Miracle is so scanty, though the subject is certainly one which occasions divisions in our Church. But anything resembling an adequate treatment of it would of necessity carry us into philosophy. Theology is interested in the question whether or not God is limited in His own activity by the uniformities of the physical world. On the question whether or not events occur which are strictly miraculous, the Commission is divided; but the reluctance of some to admit miraculous events, or the strictly miraculous character of events admitted, is based on the supposition, not that God *could* not do such works, but that He *would* not. To some of these it seems "more congruous with the wisdom and majesty of God that the regularities, such as men of science observe in nature and call Laws of Nature, should serve His purpose without any need for exceptions on the physical plane." Others are affected by hesitations arising from consideration either of the nature of human testimony in general or of the evidence for particular miracles; or, again, by the absence at the present day of miraculous divine intervention at times when such intervention might seem morally desirable. It is admitted, then, that God *could* work miracles if He pleased. To go beyond this in one direction is to embark on a purely philosophical discussion about the relation of spirit to matter or of the Transcendent to the Immanent; while on the other side the discussion turns to particular recorded events and asks both whether they took place, and if they did whether they are properly called miracles. Our short statement, therefore, seemed to us to cover the ground which is our proper field of interest, so far as the general question of Miracle is concerned.

In this statement we have an illustration of the method adopted by the Commission. Some members, including myself, would repudiate with vehemence the opinion that "it is more congruous with the wisdom and majesty of God" that He should never vary the regularities of Nature; for the exquisitely subtle adaptations of method in the pursuit of an unswerving purpose seem to us still more expressive alike of wisdom and of sympathy; and we see no strictly religious interest in what we should rather regard as a monotonous uniformity. But some of our colleagues hold that view and find that the grounds for it in their minds are such as constitute a religious motive; and we have readily concurred in recognition of this fact.

After a section of Prolegomena, dealing with the Sources and Authority of Christian Doctrine, our Report deals, within the limits already outlined, with the Doctrines of God and of Redemption. This section opens with some of the fundamental elements in the Doctrine of God, but pauses to discuss the Fact of Sin. Here we have gone into greater detail, because it seemed to us that there is great confusion of thought on the subject, especially as regards the distinction marked technically by the terms Formal Sin and Material Sin, and because greater precision of thought than is common among either clergy or instructed laity is needed, if the increasing practice of spiritual consultation and direction is to be fruitful.

The preliminary statements on the Doctrine of God and the discussion of the Fact of Sin prepare the way for our treatment of the pivotal theme, Redemption in Christ. Here emphatically our allocation of space is determined by present tendencies to division in the Church of England, for we have given relatively large space to Christology and relatively small space to the Atonement. On the general relation of these two in the Christian theology of our time I shall offer an observation among the general comments at the close of this Introduction. But it is certainly a fact that differences concerning our interpretation of the Person of Christ have lately tended to division in our Church as differences concerning the Atonement have not. This would not have been true fifty years ago; perhaps it will not be true twenty years hence. But at the present time, though there are, no doubt, real divisions in the Church concerning the doctrine of the Atonement, this has not been in the forefront of theological controversy. Accordingly we have set out a brief statement on this subject which we hope may be of value to those who will give it careful attention; and in another connexion we have given much space to the doctrine of Sacrifice. But the problem of Christology we have discussed much more fully.

Having thus set forth once more the Church's doctrine of the Person of Christ in terms which may (we hope) commend the constant teaching of the Church to people whose minds are fashioned by the habits of thought current to-day, we go on to speak of the great credal affirmations. Here it is inevitable that we should in some measure reproduce the divergences that mark the thought of scholars and theologians of our generation. In view of my own responsibility in the Church I think it right here to affirm that I wholeheartedly accept as historical facts the Birth of our Lord from a Virgin Mother and the Resurrection of His physical body from death and the tomb. And I anticipate, though with less assurance, that these events will appear to be intrinsically bound up with His Deity when the relations between the spiritual and physical elements in our nature are more completely understood. But I fully recognise the position of those who sincerely affirm the reality of our Lord's Incarnation without accepting one or both of these two events as actual historical occurrences, regarding the records rather as parables than as history, a presentation of spiritual truth in narrative form.

In connexion with the Resurrection we have included a section illustrative of the process of enquiry and of balancing different types of consideration which has, in fact, preceded the formulation of nearly all our findings. We have not in other connexions given such an outline of the process of our thought for fear of over-weighting the Report. But we have tried in all cases to make that process thorough. Individual members have on various occasions prepared for us memoranda of considerable length; indeed, one of these became so extensive that it was published as a book—Canon Mozley's *The Impassibility of God*. In that case a very brief passage in our Report serves as the summary of a very long discussion. It seemed to us well that our process of thought should be illustrated on one occasion, and that no occasion could be more appropriate than the cardinal doctrine of the Resurrection.

Our discussion of the Credal Affirmations concerning our Lord is followed by a section on the Holy Spirit, and the whole treatment of the Doctrine of God and Redemption is summed up in the Doctrine of the Trinity. Here once more (as in the first and fifth of the Thirty-Nine Articles) there is a brevity altogether disproportionate to the greatness of the theme, but these doctrines are not the source of any tendency to division in the Church of England to-day.

On reaching the Doctrine of the Church we somewhat changed the style of our Report. Here the subjects of most lively controversy are close at hand. We are aware that our approach to this doctrine through the Old Testament and the reiteration of its phrases in the New Testament is uncongenial to many non-theologically-minded enquirers to-day. But we are not writing chiefly for the general public, though we are glad if we can give help in any quarter. Our concern must be to set out the true doctrine as we understand it in the hope that others, who gain suggestions from us for their teaching work, may interpret this to those with whom they deal. The same considerations governed our treatment of the Ministry and Sacraments. In reading the section on the Ministry it should be borne in mind that many members of the Commission would make affirmations going far beyond what we have set forth. But we think it significant and important that, coming from schools of thought so different, we have been able to agree in this statement; and we are not without hope that a statement of this kind may help to commend the traditional order of the Church to the acceptance of our Christian brethren of the Free Churches. But it was with no such object that it was drafted. We thought of nothing else in drafting it except what we as loyal sons of the Church of England could conscientiously agree in setting forth as the truth.

We were still further encouraged by the measure of our agreement upon the Doctrine of Sacraments. Here there are wide divergences within our Church. But to a great extent they are divergences rather of emphasis than of substance. During generations of controversy certain words and phrases have gathered associations which are different for different parties and so become a source of confusion. Further, even where there is substantial agreement concerning the truth, it is found that one party regards as more perilous the error on the right hand, so to speak, and others regard as more perilous the error on the left. Then they start building fences at what seems a safe distance from the precipice, and so cut down the standing ground which both are prepared to occupy if only they can do so with safety from the peril that each especially dreads, and each resents and resists the activity of the other in this respect.

In our handling of some of the more debated parts of Eucharistic doctrine, where the sharpest controversy arises, we have gone back to the roots of the conceptions employed. Thus we have sketched the idea of Sacrifice from the impulse to offer it which arose from the awe-struck gropings of man's primitive mind in face of the riddle of existence. As with the Church, we found that from the dawn of history there has been a society conscious of a

divine commission, at first a national society, but converted into a world-wide fellowship through the advent of
Him who alone truly fulfilled the commission; so in the
case of Sacrifice, we trace the story of spiritual growth
from a barbarous practice down to the spiritual self-offering which alone represents the core of truth in that earlier
ritual. In both cases the decisive moment is the Death of
Christ upon the Cross wherein the Church of God was re-
constituted and Sacrifice was once for all perfected.

It has been said that the Doctrine of the Eucharistic
Sacrifice makes the Holy Communion a smaller thing than
a doctrine which concentrates all attention upon the Sacramental gift; for the former, it is said, makes the meaning
of the service something that we do, while the latter finds
it in something that God does. We are bold enough to
hope that our exposition of the doctrine of the Sacrifice
overcomes this difficulty; for it is not we who offer the
Sacrifice; Christ is the Priest as well as the Victim; and in
the Eucharist He unites us to Himself in His self-offering
to the Father, as we feed upon Him in our hearts that He,
who came to do God's will, may become the very life of
our souls.

In connexion with the doctrine of the Eucharist we have
included more technical discussion than elsewhere, partly
because it is through exact thinking that we may most
hopefully advance towards unity, but partly also because
the mere technical discussion illustrates the difficulties con-
fronting those who would penetrate into this mystery, and
may thus deepen our humility in any controversial statement of our own views or reflection on the views of others.

To our treatment of Sacramental Doctrine, both in
general and in relation to Baptism and Holy Communion,
we have added some notes on the " five commonly called
Sacraments." It was a special satisfaction to us, and we
hope it may be of service to the Church, that we are able
to present an agreed statement on Confession and Absolution, even if here again individual members would wish

to add to what is said. Here much turns on the distinction drawn in the Report between Forgiveness, understood as the restoration of personal relationship, and Pardon, understood as the formal proclamation of this either to the penitent privately or before the Church.

Our Report closes with a section on Eschatology. We are not aware of serious divisions within the Church as a result of divergent views at this point. But there is great confusion in the public mind, largely arising from a tendency to interpret as statements of future facts the great symbolic images in which the writers of the New Testament, and especially of its last Book, portray the eternal realities.

To reach a well-grounded doctrine about the Last Things is of supreme importance. Some are still either unreasonably confident or unreasonably bewildered in relation to the apparent predictions of *Daniel* and *Revelation*, while others tend to reject the Gospel as a whole because they cannot believe in a Second Advent as conventionally portrayed. It may be that the course of history is about to afford a lurid illustration of the place of Eschatology in a complete religious faith.

As I review in thought the result of our fourteen years of labour, I am conscious of a certain transition of interest in our minds, as in the minds of theologians all over the world. We were appointed at a time when theologians were engaged in taking up the prosecution of the task which the war had compelled them to lay aside. Their problems were still predominantly set by the interest of "pre-war" thought. In our country the influence of Westcott reinforced by that of the *Lux Mundi* school had led to the development of a theology of the Incarnation rather than a theology of Redemption. The distinction is, of course, not absolute or clean-cut, but the tip of the balance makes a vast difference not only in presentation but in direction of attention and estimate of relative values. A theology of the Incarnation tends to be a Christocentric metaphysic. And in all ages there is need for the fresh elaboration of such a scheme of thought or map of life as seen in the light of the revelation in Christ. A theology of Redemption (though, of course, Redemption has its great place in the former) tends rather to sound the prophetic note; it is more ready to admit that much in this evil world is irrational and strictly unintelligible; and it looks to the coming of the Kingdom as a necessary preliminary to the full comprehension of much that now is.

If the security of the nineteenth century, already shattered in Europe, finally crumbles away in our country, we shall be pressed more and more towards a theology of Redemption. In this we shall be coming closer to the New Testament. We have been learning again how impotent man is to save himself, how deep and pervasive is that corruption which theologians call Original Sin. Man needs above all else to be saved from himself. This must be the work of Divine Grace.

If we began our work again to-day, its perspectives would be different. But it is not our function to pioneer. We may call the thinkers and teachers of the Church of England to renewed devotion of their labour to the themes of Redemption, Justification, and Conversion. It is there that, in my own judgment at least, our need lies now and will lie in the future. To put the matter in another way: theology in the half-century that ended with the war was such as is prompted by and promotes a ministry mainly pastoral; we need and must work out for our own time a theology such as is prompted by and promotes a ministry at least as much evangelistic as pastoral.

As that work proceeds new problems will arise and new divisions cutting across all existing party-cleavages. Then our successors in another doctrinal commission may attempt the reconciling work that in our own field was committed to us. We have tried to discharge our own commission faithfully, and commend our work to God with the prayer that He will render ineffectual whatever in our work is due to our blindness or prejudice, and prosper with His blessing whatever has been directed by His Spirit, so that the result of our labours may be the peace of His Church.

WILLIAM EBOR:

October 1, 1937.

INTRODUCTION

THE Commission was appointed at the end of the year 1922, its terms of reference being contained in the following letter from the Archbishop of Canterbury (Dr. Davidson) to the Bishop of Oxford (Dr. Burge):

LAMBETH PALACE, S.E.
December 28, 1922.

"In pursuance of my letter of September 8 and of your subsequent letter of November 29, I write on behalf of the Archbishop of York and myself to say that it is our wish to nominate those whose names I append hereto to act as a Commission with the following reference:

> To consider the nature and grounds of Christian doctrine with a view to demonstrating the extent of existing agreement within the Church of England and with a view to investigating how far it is possible to remove or diminish existing differences.

"We note and approve your proposal that the Report of the Commission should not be an authoritative statement, but that it should, when prepared, be laid before the Bishops for them to consider what further action (if any) should be taken."

The story of the events leading up to the appointment of the Commission is set out in full in Dr. Bell's *Randal. Davidson*, pp. 1139-1150.

The Commission, as first constituted, consisted of the following members:

The Bishop of Oxford (Dr. Burge).
The Bishop of Manchester (Dr. Temple, now Archbishop of York).

The Dean of Bristol (Dr. Burroughs, afterwards Bishop of Ripon).

The Rev. F. R. Barry (now Canon of Westminster).

The Rev. Preb. E. J. Bicknell.

The Rev. J. M. Creed (now Ely Professor of Divinity at Cambridge, and Canon of Ely).

The Rev. Canon J. R. Darbyshire (now Bishop of Glasgow and Galloway).

The Rev. C. W. Emmet.

The Rev. H. B. Gooding.

The Rev. L. W. Grensted (now Nolloth Professor at Oxford and Canon Theologian of Liverpool).

The Rev. W. L. Knox (now Canon of Ely).

The Rev. W. R. Matthews (now Dean of St. Paul's).

Professor W. H. Moberly (now Sir Walter Moberly).

The Rev. J. K. Mozley (now Canon of St. Paul's).

The Rev. Canon O. C. Quick (now Professor and Canon of Durham).

The Rev. A. E. J. Rawlinson (now Bishop of Derby).

The Rev. E. G. Selwyn (now Dean of Winchester).

The Rev. C. J. Shebbeare.

Mr. Will Spens (now Master of Corpus Christi College, Cambridge).

The Rev. Canon V. F. Storr (now Sub-Dean of Westminster).

The Rev. Canon B. H. Streeter (afterwards Provost of The Queen's College, Oxford).

Professor A. E. Taylor.

The Rev. L. S. Thornton, C.R.

Professor C. C. J. Webb.

The Rev. Canon H. A. Wilson (now Bishop of Chelmsford).

The Commission was deprived after only two full sessions of the leadership of its chairman, Bishop Burge. But in that short time he had effectually set the tone and temper of its discussions. By his width of sympathy, and

his capacity not only to understand those with whom he
disagreed but also to interpret to one another those who
were involved in mutual misunderstanding, he was able to
give to the sessions of the Commission a quality of spiritual
and intellectual fellowship which has been the source of
any success achieved. His death in 1925 was a grievous
loss to the Commission. His place as chairman was taken
by Dr. Temple, then Bishop of Manchester, now Archbishop of York.

The Commission has suffered other losses by death
and one by resignation. The Rev. H. B. Gooding resigned
his place almost at once on account of departure from
England. The Rev. C. W. Emmet died before the first
full session of the Commission; in his place was appointed
the Rev. C. F. Russell, then Headmaster of King Edward
the Sixth School, Southampton, and now of Merchant
Taylors' School, Crosby, Liverpool. Bishop Burroughs
and Prebendary Bicknell died when the work of the Commission was far advanced. Both had made most valuable
contributions to its progress. In September, 1937, shortly
before the end of its labours, the Commission lost one of
its most active members, B. H. Streeter, Provost of The
Queen's College, Oxford. He brought to our discussions
that keen penetration and wide outlook which won for him
the confidence and admiration of so great a number of
thoughtful people of all ages in many countries. We owe
much both to his stimulus and to his criticism. We have
every reason to believe that he was ready to join his colleagues in signing the Report.

While Dr. Burge was chairman, Prebendary Rich acted
as Secretary and gave great help while the enterprise was
being launched; and during several years the Commission had the advantage of the presence at its sessions of the
Rev. Geoffrey F. Allen, Fellow and Chaplain of Lincoln
College, Oxford, whose assistance as an untiring worker
in the multiplication of documents and in other modes of
service was invaluable in facilitating the despatch of busi-

ness. His departure to Canton when the work of the Commission was nearing completion deprived its members of an unofficial colleague towards whom all acknowledged an obligation of gratitude and a bond of friendship.

The Commission met for its first session at University College, Oxford, in September, 1923. Since then it has met each year from a Monday till the following Saturday in September, and in 1934, 1935 and 1936 met also for a similar period in March. Between the full sessions Groups have worked upon material assigned to them, and have presented reports for the consideration of the whole Commission. At first a special Group was constituted for each subject assigned. But since 1925 the Commission has been divided into three Groups formed on geographical lines—the Oxford Group, the Cambridge and London Group, and the Northern Group—which were found to contain in each case representatives of various schools of thought. Each Group has met at least twice during the year, often for two or more days. There has thus been an abundance of discussion.

The findings of the Commission are in the form of statements which have been scrutinised first in one or more Groups and finally in the whole Commission, and in every case (except where specially stated) the finding represents a unanimous consent. Sometimes the finding itself indicates different views.

This consent must not be taken to imply that individual members of the Commission might not have preferred in certain cases a somewhat different treatment. We have not adopted the method of voting, and where there was difference of opinion on major points we have tried to represent this.

In addition to the actual findings of the Commission certain Appendices are included, which either give expression to views held only by small groups of members or else give to views expressed in the main body of the Report a degree of articulation disproportionate to the general structure of the Report.

In the years of our labour we have naturally come to understand each other; the Commission has become a company of friends, and on that basis complete frankness has prevailed in our discussions. Each has expressed his own view with candour, both trusting the sincerity of his colleagues, and knowing that they trusted his. This is the only basis on which the discussion of Christian theology can be fruitful. If God is Love, it is only among people animated by mutual love that understanding of Him can be advanced. To admit acrimony in theological discussion is in itself more fundamentally heretical than any erroneous opinions upheld or condemned in the course of the discussion.

The members of the Commission were chosen as representing different traditions or points of view. But there have been no clear lines of division. It has often happened that the chief champion of some part of a tradition has been one not reckoned as belonging to the school chiefly attached to it. This has been due in part to the fact that all members adopt in varying ways the critical method and outlook. This is not a negative method, nor necessarily sceptical in temper or result; rather it is the positive determination to test to the utmost whatever is offered for acceptance, and to exercise judgment upon it, whatever the source from which it is derived, and also to seek the truth that is present in every conviction sincerely and persistently held among Christian people. It has been our steady assumption that the convictions by which men live must enshrine truth, even when the traditional statement of that truth current among those who have upheld it is unacceptable.

One difficulty which attends all such discussion is the interconnexion of all parts of Christian doctrine. It is impossible to deal adequately with any one part if other parts are excluded. Consequently there must be much interlocking of themes, and the treatment of one considered later may involve modification in what was said about one considered earlier. This has been a main cause for the slowness of our progress.

But our slowness is also to be accounted for by consideration of the special task allotted to us. We were appointed to consider existing agreement within the Church of England and the removal or diminution of existing differences. For this reason representatives of a variety of schools of thought were chosen to constitute the Commission. Our method has been largely determined by the variety of views actually represented amongst us. Accordingly we have given most attention and the largest space, not to the subjects which are the most important for faith or for theology, but to those on which we have found most divergence of opinion. That is characteristic also of many other theological documents, as, for instance, the Thirty-Nine Articles. But beyond this, the fact that we were directed to investigate differences of view has dictated to us an inductive, or more properly a synthetic, method, which could only attain to full logical coherence if it were carried to perfection. Obviously our work makes no pretensions to such an achievement. Indeed it must be the task of many generations to work out that synthesis of different apprehensions of the one revelation of God in Christ towards which our undertaking points. But we are persuaded that out of such a process of co-operative thought there may be fashioned at last a Christian theology more adequate than any that has preceded it. Certainly we have found that so soon as both parties to any controversy set themselves to find other expressions than those which have been traditional among them, they discover a far greater measure of substantial agreement than they had anticipated.

Our Report has not been composed primarily for expert theologians. We have tried to express ourselves in such a way that any who have paid serious attention to the problems of religion can follow our statement and understand it. In one or two cases, where the difference between popular interest and scientific arrangement is specially marked, we have taken first the aspect of the subject most prominent to thoughtful but inexpert Christians; in many cases we have avoided or paraphrased technical terms which convey their meaning only to the expert. We believe this method to be justified, because our aim is not to compose a new *Summa Theologiæ*, but to promote unity and mutual appreciation within the Church of England, partly by the interpretation of one school of thought to another, and partly by pointing to the fulness of a truth diversely apprehended in different quarters.

If this Report is to render the service for which it is designed, the purpose and method of its composition must be borne in mind. As we have already indicated, it is in no sense the outline of a systematic theology; that is something in one way more, but in another less, ambitious than what we have attempted. For a systematic theology proceeds from premises regarded as assured, and from these builds up its fabric by continuous reasoning. There are systems of Catholic Theology and of Protestant Theology. To them we have, of course, owed much. But there is not, and the majority of us do not desire that there should be, a system of distinctively Anglican Theology. The Anglican Churches have received and hold the faith of Catholic Christendom, but they have exhibited a rich variety in methods both of approach and of interpretation. They are the heirs of the Reformation as well as of Catholic tradition; and they hold together in a single fellowship of worship and witness those whose chief attachment is to each of these, and also those whose attitude to the distinctively Christian tradition is most deeply affected by the tradition of a free and liberal culture which is historically the bequest of the Greek spirit and was recovered for Western Europe at the Renaissance.

The removal or diminution of differences within the

Church of England can only be rightly effected by the discovery of the synthesis which does justice to all of these; and this is a task, not for a Commission, even though it sit many years, but for several generations.

Accordingly what follows must be taken only as a contribution to this task, and not as more than this, even in the judgment of its authors.

NOTE.—Quotations from the Bible in the Report usually follow the Revised Version. Sometimes, however, the Authorised Version has been preferred; and, very occasionally, the Commission has adopted for some special purpose a literal rendering of the original which is neither that of the Revised nor that of the Authorised Version.

PROLEGOMENA: THE SOURCES AND AUTHORITY OF CHRISTIAN DOCTRINE

THE faith and doctrine of Christianity are handed down to us in the context of a living fellowship. In its widest sense this fellowship is that of the Church Universal; to us as Anglicans the tradition is handed down through the Anglican Communion as a part of Western Christendom. This involves for us two consequences. The first is that in interpreting our own tradition we must give attention to the background of the universal tradition of Christendom. The second is that in discussion of doctrine to-day we are bound to consider its historical sources and the authority which these should carry.

The Christian religion is founded upon a specific revelation of God in history. To this revelation Scripture and the Church alike bear witness. But the Church has always claimed that its doctrine is based on Scripture. It is to Scripture, therefore, that we first turn in considering the sources and authority of Christian doctrine, though we proceed to offer also some observations upon the authority of the Church, and have appended further a brief note on Anglican formularies.

(A) SCRIPTURE

I. ITS INSPIRATION

Belief that the Bible is the inspired record of God's self-revelation to man and of man's response to that revelation is not for us a dogma imposed as a result of some theory of the mode of the composition of the books, but a conclusion drawn from the character of their contents and the spiritual insight displayed in them.

The Bible is more than a collection of utterances, some of which are "inspiring and therefore inspired." It makes its special appeal partly in virtue of its unity as a whole. This unity consists in the presentation of a self-revelation of God through history and experience—a self-revelation which develops in relation both to the response and to the resistance of man to the Divine initiative, and which culminates in the Incarnation.

Thus the theme of the Bible as a whole is GOD, though the working out of this theme is in parts obscure. At times the limitations of the human writer and his age distort for us the presentation of this central theme, as when vindictiveness is attributed to God; but the theme itself is never wholly obscured, and in its completeness the Bible produces the conviction that it is not only about God but that it is of God. God speaks to men through the Bible, which may therefore be rightly called "the Word of God."

From the Christian standpoint the Bible is unique, as being the inspired record of a unique revelation. It is the record of the special preparation for Christ, and of His direct impact upon men, through His Life, Death, and Resurrection. It sets before us that historical movement of Divine self-disclosure of which the Gospel is the crown.

Thus while rejecting the view that all parts of the Bible stand on one spiritual level, we also repudiate any effort to concentrate all attention on the directly edifying passages. Those which in themselves are on a lower spiritual level have their place in the whole, which derives part of its power from the universality of its range and part even from the intractability* of some of its material.

* This term is intended to cover, for example, the genealogies, or the lying spirit of Micaiah's vision, or other elements which in isolation convey little that is of spiritual value, but form part of the whole story through which the revelation came; or, again, the elements which to a modern mind seem uncouth (*e.g.*, much apocalyptic imagery).

Our sense of the Inspiration of the Bible is deepened when we recognise its sincerity as the record, through many generations, and despite the ebb and flow characteristic of this as of all spiritual movements, of higher conceptions of God supervening upon lower ones, through the continual communion and conflict between the spirit of man and the Spirit of God.

The tradition of the inerrancy of the Bible commonly held in the Church until the beginning of the nineteenth century (though often held in association with allegorical or other interpretations which profoundly modified its significance)* cannot be maintained in the light of the knowledge now at our disposal. It will already have become apparent that this belief in its inerrancy is in our judgment in no way necessary to a full acceptance of the Bible as conveying to us God's revelation of Himself. Again, in the past, as a part and consequence of the then current view of Scripture, emphasis was often laid on detailed prediction of facts, especially as concerns the life of Christ. We cannot now regard as a principal purpose or evidence of Inspiration the giving of detailed information about the future; but we recognise, as a consequence and evidence of Inspiration, such an insight into the Divine Mind and Will, and therefore such a general apprehension of the course of events to be expected in a world ruled by God, as in particular cases resulted in the prediction of events which subsequently came to pass. Nor do we rule out, as possibly a concomitant of Inspiration in certain cases, a direct prevision of detailed events, though it is not on such prevision that men should base their belief in the Inspiration of Scripture.

* *Cf.*, for example, St. Augustine's view that the Seven Days of Creation are "one day represented in a sevenfold aspect." So "the distinction of days denoted the natural order of the things known, and not a succession in the knowledge acquired or in the things produced" (St. Thomas Aquinas, *S.T.*, Part I., Q. LXXIV., A. 2, commenting on Augustine, *Gen. ad. lit.*, IV.).

Hitherto we have been mainly concerned with the grounds on which we recognise the Inspiration of the Bible rather than with the nature of that Inspiration itself. Here we have first to remember that the books of the Bible, though received as the oracles of God, were written within, and accepted as canonical by, a living and worshipping society. They can only be fully understood in relation to that society and its life. Moreover, the Bible is the work of many writers—original authors, editors, and revisers—and its final form is due to the selective judgment of the Jewish and Christian Churches. It is in this process as a whole that we recognise the working of the Divine Spirit.

The Inspiration of the Bible as a whole, or of any particular book within it, may consist either in the inspiration of individual authors or in the inspiration of those who selected, interpreted, and used already existing material. If it is contended that the latter were divinely guided rather than inspired, we would reply—first, that this distinction between God's ways of working upon or through the minds of men cannot ultimately be maintained, but also that even if it could the term Inspiration would rightly be retained for work which is truly creative, though it incorporates material already in existence.

Inspiration is not to be thought of as analogous to "possession," in which the personality of the possessed is superseded; nor does it appear that its nature can be illustrated by reference to those "psychical phenomena" which have recently attracted great interest in many quarters. The truly inspired are those whose response to the Spirit of God has issued in a free surrender to His guidance. In this surrender all individual characteristics of mentality, temperament, knowledge, and the like remain, and when Inspiration issues in writing these characteristics appear in what is written.

While the Bible supplies an example of Inspiration to which no exact parallel can be shown, the activity of the

Divine Spirit is to be recognised over a much wider field. In the Christian Church it appears in men's response to the revelation given in the Bible and supremely in Christ. According to the teaching of the New Testament, that is to be regarded as a work of the Holy Spirit which is in harmony with the mind of Christ and deepens our apprehension of Him. In the light of the Christian experience of the Holy Spirit and His work we can trace the activity of the same Divine Spirit in various degrees outside the limits of either Israel or Christendom. But (as stated in the following section on the Holy Spirit) "it is important to emphasise the fact that the Holy Spirit in the New Testament is spoken of primarily as the power known by experience to be at work in the fellowship of Christians—that is, of those who have received the Gospel—rather than as a Divine energy diffused throughout the Creation."* The unique character of the Inspiration recognised in the Bible is bound up with its relation to the Christian fellowship in this sense.

II. Its Authority

The Bible as a Whole.

The Bible possesses authority for Christians on the ground that it is the classical literature of that progressive self-revelation of God in history which culminated in Jesus Christ.

The Bible has been and is for the Christian Church the primary criterion of its teaching and the chief source of guidance for its religious life.

It further vindicates its authority by continuing to mediate to individuals the revelation which it records and by nurturing their spiritual life.

The fact that the Church has accepted this particular body of literature as canonical Scripture invests it as a whole with an authoritative character for all its members.

* *Cf.* p. 95.

Nevertheless, the use made of the Bible as an authoritative source of teaching should be controlled by the following considerations:

(1) The authority ascribed to the Bible must not be interpreted as prejudging the conclusions of historical, critical, and scientific investigation in any field, not excluding that of the Biblical documents themselves.

(2) Christian thinkers are not necessarily bound to the thought-forms employed by the Biblical writers.

(3) The Biblical writings display a wide variety of literary type. In using the Biblical books as a standard of authoritative teaching, these facts must be taken into account. The supreme spiritual value of some parts of the Bible is not shared by all.

(4) In estimating the relative spiritual value of different portions of the Bible, the standard is the Mind of Christ as unfolded in the experience of the Church and appropriated by the individual Christian through His Spirit. That is to say, the stages of the Biblical revelation are to be judged in relation to its historical climax.

The Teaching of Our Lord.

Within the body of Scripture as a whole a special authority has always been attached to the recorded teaching of our Lord as contained in the Gospels.

The Christian Church rests on the belief that in Jesus Christ there is given to mankind the supreme revelation of God. This revelation is given through all that He was and did, and thus includes but is not limited to His teaching.

In accepting the authority of His recorded teaching the following considerations must be borne in mind:

(1) The actual teaching itself was called forth by particular occasions and was conditioned by the thought-forms and circumstances of the time.

(2) The record cannot be accepted as always reproducing the *ipsissima verba* of our Lord.

In the latter connexion the following points may be mentioned :

(a) In any case, the words spoken have been translated into another language.

(b) The occasions with regard to which the teaching was originally given are not always set forth.

(c) There is some reason to think that in some cases the words attributed to our Lord reflect rather the experience of the primitive Church, or the utterances of Christian prophets, than actual words of Jesus.

(d) What appear to be the same sayings are sometimes recorded in different forms and contexts.

But when all allowance is made for possible divergences between the records as they stand and the historic facts behind them, it remains true that the religious and moral teaching of the Gospels conveys faithfully the impress made upon the Apostolic Church by the mind and personality of Jesus, and thus possesses supreme authority. Accordingly, the body of teaching in question provides a standard by which to judge the claim of subsequent developments to be true to the authentic spirit of the Christian Gospel.

It follows from what has been said above that the method of direct appeal to isolated texts in our Lord's teaching, in so far as it ignores the controlling considerations which have been set forth, is liable to error.

It is the duty of the Church and of the individual to undertake, under the guidance of the Holy Spirit, to interpret Christ's teaching and to apply it to the particular problems in every age.

APPENDED NOTE

On the General Use of Traditional Images and Phrases.

Because Christianity is supremely a historical religion, its classical Scriptures have a position that nothing else can challenge. Scriptural phrases and images have, therefore, peculiar authority for the Church, and their use in worship, especially public worship, has a unique appropriateness. The same principle applies to the classical formulations framed in the formative period of the Church's history and subsequently incorporated into its traditional forms of worship.

In some cases these phrases and images seem unnatural in the present day. But it is better for us to learn to use them with an interpretation according to our needs than to discard them for others more obviously expressive of present habits of thought. For (a) only Scripture carries us back to the concrete richness of the facts in which our religion is grounded; (b) any expressions designed to represent our own thinking are likely to miss those elements which are not naturally prominent in our minds, so that we fail to transmit the suggestion of those elements to our successors and reduce our opportunity of becoming sensitive to them ourselves; and (c) traditional phrases lay less stringent fetters in practice upon the free play of thought than any constructed to express the mind of the moment.

The interpretation spoken of above may include the association with a phrase of a meaning not originally connected with it, but far more often it will mean the recovery of the significance of the phrase as used by Apostles, Evangelists, or Fathers, and the translation of this into the intellectual context of the present.

In some cases the use of traditional phrases is censured as dishonest. This charge could only be sustained if the traditional phrase is being used in a sense wholly different from that originally conveyed by it. That it should be used to represent a meaning partly identical with, and partly different from, that which was in the mind of those who first employed it is simply what happens to some extent with all language as the context of thought is altered from one generation to another. The reason for the continued use of such phrases is that there is a core of identical meaning.* At what point a changed interpretation ethically demands a change in the phrase used is a question to be settled by the moral judgment of the community concerned; it cannot be determined in advance.

In addition to the considerations already mentioned, it is always to be remembered that the appropriate language of devotion is more nearly akin to poetry than to science, and that there are some religious conceptions (such as Heaven) which cannot be expressed by any scientific formulation but only in symbolic language.

(B) THE CHURCH

The authority of the Church in the realm of doctrine arises from its commission to preach the Gospel to all the world, and the promises, accompanying that commission, that the Lord would always be with His disciples, and that the Holy Spirit would guide them into all the truth.

The Church's understanding of the Gospel is continually renewed by its experience of communion with God through Christ; and the authority of its doctrinal formulations ought always to be interpreted as resting, at least in part, upon the acceptance of these by the whole body of the faithful. This authority, in so far as it is derived from such a *consensus fidelium*, rests upon the range and quality of the manifold experience which that *consensus* gathers up, and upon the witness which, alike in the devotional and other practice of Christians generally and in the doctrine of the theologians, it bears to the truth of the Gospel. The weight of the *consensus fidelium* does not depend on mere numbers or on the extension of a belief at any one time, but on continuance through the ages and the extent to which the *consensus* is genuinely free.

* *E.g.*, everyone speaks of sunrise and sunset without either feeling committed to a geocentric astronomy or feeling guilty of dishonesty.

All Christians are bound to allow very high authority to doctrines which the Church has been generally united in teaching; for each believer has a limited range, and the basis of the Church's belief is far wider than that of his own can ever be. An individual Christian who rejects any part of that belief is guilty of presumption, unless he feels himself bound in conscience so to do and has substantial reasons for holding that what he rejects is not essential to the truth and value of Christianity.

At the same time, belief resting on external authority alone cannot have the full value of faith, since faith requires a personal appropriation of what is believed in. Therefore, every individual ought to test his belief in practice, and, so far as his ability and training qualify him, to think out his own belief, and to distinguish between what he has accepted on authority only and what he has appropriated in thought or experience. But he must recognise that it is only in the fellowship and worship of the community that he can come fully to appreciate and accept.

Acceptance of the Church's authority by the individual must always rest on his own judgment, though where he has been brought up as a believer the transition to any deliberate acceptance may be gradual and almost unconscious.

The Church should also recognise as necessary to the fulness of its own life the activity of those of its own members who carry forward the apprehension of truth by freely testing and criticising its traditional doctrines.

(C) ANGLICAN FORMULARIES

Anglican formularies represent the doctrinal ecclesiastical and historical position of Anglicanism in relation to the rest of Western Christendom in the sixteenth century, and the position of the Church of England in relation to other Christian bodies is still defined by the retention of those formularies.

These formularies should not be held to prejudge questions which have arisen since their formulation or problems which have been modified by fresh knowledge or fresh conceptions.

Nevertheless, if an Anglican theologian thinks a particular formulary not wholly adequate, he has a special obligation to preserve whatever truth that formulary was trying to secure, and to see to it that any statement he puts forward as more adequate does in fact secure this.

APPENDED NOTES

On the Application to the Creeds of the Conception of Symbolic Truth.

The general acceptance of formulations drawn up in another age and another context of thought gives rise to special problems, especially when some of the phrases used are indisputably symbolic, and no clear distinction is drawn, or (perhaps) can be drawn, between these and others.

The purpose of credal statements is to affirm the truths on which the Gospel of the Church and the religious life of Christians are based. It is not their purpose to affirm either historical facts or metaphysical truths merely as such. It is as expressions of the Gospel and of the presuppositions of the Christian life that the statements of the Creeds, whether in the sphere of history or in that of philosophy, have permanent truth and value. In this sense every clause in the Creeds is of necessity " symbolic."*

But the word "symbolic" is ambiguous. Statements affirming particular facts may be found to have value as pictorial expressions of spiritual truths, even though the supposed facts themselves did not actually happen. In

* It may be well to point out that the Commission is not using this word in the sense in which Symbolic Theology is a technical equivalent of Credal Theology.

that case such statements may be called symbolically true in a different sense. It does not appear possible to delimit with finality or precision the extent to which symbolic elements of this latter kind may enter into the historic tradition of the Christian faith. The possibility cannot be excluded that in this sense also a symbolic character may attach to the truth of articles in the Creeds. It is not therefore of necessity illegitimate to accept and affirm particular clauses of the Creeds while understanding them in this symbolic sense. It is, however, in any case essential to hold that the facts underlying the Gospel story —which story the Creeds summarise and interpret—were such as to justify the Gospel itself.

Further, the Commission is convinced that neither can the truth of the Gospel stand unimpaired, nor can any adequate account of its origin be given unless the broad tradition concerning Jesus, to which the Gospels and the Church have borne witness through the centuries, is accepted as historical, and in particular unless it is possible for the Church to proclaim that in the historical figure of Jesus of Nazareth "the Word was made flesh and dwelt among us."

On Assent.

With a view to the avoidance of misunderstanding of what is said in the above Note, and elsewhere in this Report, the Commission desires to place on record the following resolutions:

1. The Christian Church exists on the basis of the Gospel which has been entrusted to it.

2. General acceptance, implicit if not explicit, of the authoritative formularies, doctrinal and liturgical, by which the meaning of the Gospel has been defined, safeguarded, or expressed, may reasonably be expected from members of the Church.

3. Assent to formularies and the use of liturgical language in public worship should be understood as signifying such general acceptance without implying

detailed assent to every phrase or proposition thus employed.

4. Subject to the above, a member of the Church should not be held to be involved in dishonesty merely on the ground that, in spite of some divergence from the tradition of the Church, he has assented to formularies or makes use of the Church's liturgical language in public worship.

The above considerations apply to the authorised teachers as well as to all other members of the Church; but the position of the authorised teacher is distinctive, and the Church has a right to satisfy itself that those who teach in its name adequately represent and express its mind.

5 No individual can claim to receive the teacher's commission as a right, and the commission itself involves the obligation not to teach, as the doctrine of the Church, doctrine which is not in accordance with the Church's mind.

6. If any authorised teacher puts forward personal opinions which diverge (within the limits indicated above) from the traditional teaching of the Church, he should be careful to distinguish between such opinions and the normal teaching which he gives in the Church's name; and so far as possible such divergences should be so put forward as to avoid offending consciences.

7. In respect of the exercise of discipline within such limits as the above resolutions recognise, great regard should be paid to the need for securing a free consensus, as distinct from an enforced uniformity.

N.B.—Some members of the Commission, while not dissenting from these resolutions, are of opinion that No. 6 gives by implication too wide a latitude, and would press more strongly the obligation resting upon all who hold office in the Church to believe and to teach the traditional doctrine of the Church.

PART I: THE DOCTRINES OF GOD AND OF REDEMPTION

UNDER this heading we have limited our concern to those points of doctrine which are in one way or another the chief occasions for divergence in the Church of England to-day. Accordingly, after setting forth a few considerations concerning God and His relation to or dealings with the world, we turn to that fact of sin which has called forth from God His redemptive activity, and so proceed to the Person and Work of the Redeemer, and, in closing, to the Doctrines of the Holy Spirit and of the Trinity.

(A) GOD AND THE WORLD

I. WHAT DO WE MEAN BY THE WORD "GOD"?

It has been said that "God is that living Being who is at once the ultimate existence and the supreme and all-inclusive good"; and, again, that "God is that which we can, and must, worship." These two formulæ may be taken as starting-points, the one as an initial statement of what God is in Himself, the other of what God is in relation to us.

Or to follow a familiar classification, as satisfaction at once of moral, æsthetic, and intellectual aspiration, He must be perfect Goodness, perfect Beauty, and perfect Truth. As Perfect Goodness He must be the sustainer and the goal of moral effort, such effort being taken to include all effort after Beauty, Truth, and Goodness. As Holy Love He is at once infinitely exalted and completely intimate; His holiness abases us, while His love invites us to communion. It is through some inkling of His glory that all moral effort is initiated (even in atheists), and it is in finding or rather being found of Him that both achievement and reward of such effort consist.

As perfect Truth or ultimate Existence He is the ground of all that is. And inasmuch as Personality is the highest kind of existence known to us, and inasmuch as persons hold personal relationship with Him in worship and communion, God must be considered as Personal—at least in the sense that there is Personality in Him, and that the imperfect personality found in some created beings is derived from and is in its measure the image of His.

But as ultimate existence He is more than this; He is Creator—that is, not only does the existence of all that is beside Himself depend upon Him, but He is the active originator of its existence. If it be said that, being what He is, He must create, so that the world is necessary to Him, it must be replied that even if that be so (which calls for further enquiry) the ground of this necessity is in Himself, whereas the ground of the created universe is not in itself but in Him. The Laws of Nature express the observed uniformities in the behaviour of the things that He has made; these act according to their nature or, in other words, according to what He made them. Natural Science not only studies the works of God in the sense of studying things that He has made, but also in the sense that it studies the manner of His working.

The created universe is historic; that is to say it not only persists through successive moments of time, but is such that part of its significance and value depends on the process through which it develops; alike as ultimate existence and as supreme good God must be concerned with and active in this aspect of it, and therefore neither God Himself nor the temporal process should be conceived in any way which would deprive that process of ultimate significance. Any other view either makes history and the moral struggle meaningless, or else finds in them a meaning which is irrelevant to God, so that He is not, after all, the supreme and all-inclusive good. This is part of what is meant by the Hebrew insistence that God is a living God.

The thought of God as the Eternal, and the thought of Him as concerned with and about the events of history, are both necessary.

II. THE LIVING GOD

It is an essential feature of the Biblical Revelation that it presents God as indeed the living God, on whose act of will creation itself depends, and who has a purpose for mankind, to accomplish which He is Himself active in history. This conception of God stands in contrast with the leading conceptions entertained by Greek philosophers or Indian sages, who alike tend to conceive God as a Being of static perfection, abiding for ever in the fruition of His own blessedness. The Biblical conception is greatly to be preferred. It is possible by means of it to come nearer to a rational account of the universe, and for the life of religion the Biblical conception is of capital importance.

If God is the living God, whose righteous Will is the source alike of the natural order and of the moral law, as is implied by the nineteenth Psalm, it follows that worship must include as its most vital element the submission of our wills to the Divine Will, and that service of God can only be rendered through righteousness of life.

The living God is no mere ground of the Universe, or principle of its co-ordination. His purpose is indeed the principle of its co-ordination; but this is so because He has created all things, and because of His " will they were, and were created." By His unsleeping Providence He controls its course, while normally sustaining by His Will those regularities which are scientifically apprehended as Laws of Nature. He remains free to shape events as He pleases; and by that " power that worketh in us," which is known as grace, He offers to the men who are made in His image the aid and means requisite for them if they are to live in fellowship with Him. Above the turmoil of

a creation distracted by sin He "remaineth a King for
ever"; but He does not dwell apart in everlasting calm.
He dwells "in the high and holy place," but "with him
also that is of a contrite and humble spirit." More than
that, He "so loved the world that he gave his only-
begotten Son, that whosoever believeth on him should not
perish, but have eternal life."

The living God, having His purpose for the world, reveals Himself to make that purpose known. This revelation is a self-communication of the personal God to the
persons whom He has made, and it can only be received
through a personal apprehension and response. But men
are capable of that apprehension and response only as God
bestows on them, by creation and by the operation of
grace, the spiritual illumination by which to see, and the
readiness of will by which to obey, the disclosure of His
purpose, wherever and however this is effected.

The Christian faith in God as Creator carries with it
the belief that there is a revelation of God in nature, but
beyond this God reveals Himself in varying degrees in
the course of historical events and in the experience and
character both of nations and of individuals.

The process of Divine self-disclosure in the history and
religious experience of Israel, as interpreted by the
prophets and other religious guides of the people, culminates in Jesus Christ, in whom we acknowledge the Word
made flesh. This revelation is final, but its content is being
ever more fully apprehended in the life of the mystical
Body of Christ. A self-disclosure of God must also be
recognised in the religious and moral development of the
human race as a whole.

Thus revelation is to be regarded as first and foremost
the act of God, and it is by God's help that we are enabled
to apprehend it as revelation.

APPENDED NOTE

On Discovery and Revelation.

Nothing can be discovered by man about God apart from the revelation of Himself by God to man; nor can anything be effectively revealed by God to man apart from an activity of human reason in apprehending it. But a distinction may be drawn: (1) There is a factor in our knowledge of God due to reflection on the general nature of experience (though this reflection, so far as it leads to knowledge, must itself be recognised as implying the prevenience of the Divine action and the illumination of the human mind by God). (2) There is also a factor due to the apprehension of individual historical facts through which God reveals Himself to man in a special manner or degree.

The body of Christian doctrine, however, cannot be split up into two portions assignable respectively to those two factors, as though such doctrines as those of God's unity and of His moral government of the world were assignable exclusively to the first, and the doctrines of the Trinity, Incarnation, and gift of supernatural grace to the second. The two factors which we have recognised, while distinguishable, are always interdependent. Both are involved in the apprehension of every doctrine, though the one or the other may be said in any particular case to be the more obvious.

III. CREATION

Christianity is committed to the doctrine that the world depends upon God as His Creation. Historically, this has been affirmed by the Fathers in the doctrine of creation "out of nothing" ($\dot{\epsilon}\xi$ $o\dot{v}\kappa$ $\ddot{o}\nu\tau\omega\nu$), in opposition to the idea of creation out of an independent $\ddot{v}\lambda\eta$ or matter.

On the relation of Creation to the time-process three main views have been put forward:

(1) Many Christian teachers have held that the world had a beginning in time.

(2) Augustine took over from Plato's *Timæus* the suggestion that the world was created *cum tempore* —*i.e.*, that time and the world are due to a single creative act.

(3) Origen's view that Creation is an eternal process was generally rejected in the Ancient Church, but this view in a different form is now held by many Christian thinkers.

Christianity is not specially committed to any of these views.

The universe depends upon the creative will of God. Any such view as that the finite universe proceeds by emanation from the Divine nature, as opposed to the view that it originates in the creative activity of the Divine will, is non-Christian.

It is to be recognised that the Christian doctrine of Creation as thus generally stated leaves abundant room for a variety of theories as to the evolution of the world. There is in any case a sense in which, on the Christian view, the creative activity of God must be regarded as continuous. No objection to a theory of evolution can be drawn from the two Creation narratives in Gen. i. and ii., since it is generally agreed among educated Christians that these are mythological in origin, and that their value for us is symbolic rather than historical. It is to be noted that a non-literal interpretation of these chapters is to be found in some ancient Fathers.

The Christian view excludes Pantheism. That God should be all in all is in the Christian view the ultimate goal of the creative process, but this is not to be confused with any doctrine which represents finite individuality as illusory or tends to blur moral distinctions, or which, while leaving these indeed in their own sphere, declares that this sphere is part of Appearance only, and that both finite individuality and moral distinctions are lost in the Absolute.

APPENDED NOTE

Angels and Demons.

The Commission has not thought it needful to discuss in detail the variant forms of the doctrine of angels and demons which with varying degrees of explicitness have been held in the Church. The belief in such beings is an unquestioned element in the intellectual world-view of the New Testament writers, by whom it was held that there exists, in the supernatural world, a variety of spiritual agencies, both evil and good; that the Son of Man came upon earth as the Conqueror of demons and as the Deliverer of all them that were " under the tyranny of the devil "; and that there are angels who as " ministering spirits " are " sent forth to do service for the sake of them that shall inherit salvation." The Gospels present our Lord Himself as practising exorcism, and as sharing (in this as in other respects) the current beliefs of His time. Accordingly wherever Christians have held themselves to be bound to a literal acceptance in detail of the New Testament outlook, they have inevitably believed themselves bound to accept literally the above-mentioned beliefs, among others; and the fact that the beliefs in question appear to have been shared by our Lord's own human mind would seem to most Christians decisive, even to-day.

In the judgment of the Commission the beliefs under discussion have, at the very least, a symbolical value. For many of the phenomena recorded in the Gospels it is no doubt true that an alternative interpretation, based upon medical or psychological considerations, might in our time be suggested. The presentation in Scripture of our Lord's redemptive mission upon earth in terms of the idea of a conflict with the evil powers nevertheless stands for a truth. So likewise the " war in heaven " of Rev. xii. 7 ff. (the passage which forms the Epistle for Michaelmas Day) may be held to stand for the recognition of our participa-

tion, as the "soldiers and servants" of Christ, in the
struggle between good and evil upon a cosmic scale : and,
upon this ground alone, the traditional language of the
liturgy, as for example in the *Preface*, appears to us fully
justified.

There are many of us who would go further. To them
it seems unreasonable to suppose that the only spiritual
beings which exist in the universe, other than God Himself, must be human.

To believe positively, whether on the ground of Scripture, or on the ground of tradition as interpreting Scripture and as lending weight to an inherent probability, in
the existence of spiritual beings other than human is in no
way irrational.

Nevertheless the Commission desires to record its conviction that it is legitimate for a Christian either to sus-
pend judgment on the point, or alternatively to interpret
the language, whether of Scripture or of the Church's
Liturgy, with regard to angels and demons in a purely
symbolical sense.

IV. PROVIDENCE

The Christian conception of Providence is determined
by our Lord's revelation of the goodness and Fatherhood
of God, and exemplified in such sayings as " the hairs of
your head are all numbered," " not a sparrow falls to the
ground without your Father."

To believe in Providence is to believe that the whole
course of events is under the control of God. Thus,
logically, this involves the affirmation that there is no
event, and no aspect of any event, even those due to
human sin and so contrary to the Divine will, which falls
outside the scope of His purposive activity. Providence
in the sense of the controlling activity of God, appearing
in individual human lives and most clearly to many in
their own experience, is a natural interpretation of much

that appears upon the wider stage of history, in which a movement towards the vindication of moral and spiritual values may be discerned. To the Christian the Providence of God is revealed in history, and especially in the history of Israel as leading up to the Incarnation.

The relation of God's Providence to particular occurrences, especially to calamities, is variously conceived by Christians. We wish to state first certain considerations which should govern reflection on this matter :

> (*a*) The operation of constant laws leads from time to time to the occurrence of disasters and of what are popularly called " accidents." For all the purposive life of men, and therefore for the highest interests of men, the constancy of natural law is a necessary condition. " Accidents," therefore, are incidental to what is a necessary condition of man's highest interests.
>
> (*b*) Our moral discipline depends in part upon the laws of Nature not being continually modified for our special convenience; further, the possibility of accident has moral value in itself.

The foregoing considerations suggest that events, which, from our own point of view and to our limited vision, appear to be mere disasters, may nevertheless be compatible with a dispensation of Absolute Love.

Various views have been put forward by Christian thinkers, which appeal differently to different minds, with regard to such disasters.

> (1) The calamities due to natural forces or to the evil wills of men are not directly willed by God, though they are permitted by Him and are incidental to the natural and the moral order which are the expression of His will and are to be borne as part of the price of those high interests which require these as their condition.
>
> Those who accept this view argue that we cannot attribute to goodness what we see to be bad, and that especially what is done against God's will by wicked men cannot be attributed to God's will. To them it is no comfort to say, " It is the will of God," for that

makes matters worse by making Him directly will what is evil.

(2) The Providence of God so perfectly orders all things that both natural calamities and the consequences of wicked acts are to be accepted as directly willed by Him, and therefore as part of His loving care for us, even when we cannot see how this can be.

Those who accept this view agree that they cannot themselves see good in what appears to be wholly evil, yet find comfort in the thought that in the perspective of eternity many things may have a new quality. They call in their faith in God's love and power to correct their sense of the occurrence as purely evil.

These views among others have been held by Christian thinkers; a third view which commends itself to most members of the Commission is as follows:

(3) Even in regard to a wicked act with disastrous consequences for others than the doer it is necessary to hold that God wills that the consequences shall result from the act. It is not a case merely of permitting these consequences. On the other hand, the fact that the resulting of these consequences is best, and is willed by God as being best, may depend not on the immediate consequences in themselves, but on remoter consequences—as, for example, the preservation of the invariability of natural law, to the importance of which attention has already been drawn. It follows that belief that God wills the resulting of the consequences, and that therefore this must be best, does not involve the belief that in themselves and by themselves these consequences are good or that they are willed by God for their own sake. Similar considerations apply to natural disasters. Again, alike in regard to the immediate consequences of sin and to natural disasters, belief in the overruling Providence of God definitely implies belief that there is no consequence which is not capable of being made to subserve the Divine purpose through the co-operation of man with God. It does not, however, imply that particular events must be thought of as good in themselves, or even that their immediate consequences must be

thought of as good in themselves. Indeed, the whole which is good may have its perfection precisely because it involves the resolution of real "discords," and this may require the recognition of particular events as definite evils to be faced and overcome. It remains true that God's permission of evil is conditioned by His power and purpose to conquer it, and should not be separated from them in Christian thought.

Whatever view be adopted, there are dangers to be avoided. There is need to avoid any denial of either the power or the love of God; and there is need to avoid any warping of our sense of good and evil. Further, all Christians must agree that, in whatever befalls them, God has them in His keeping and overrules all things according to His loving purpose; at the same time, they are bound to consider what is required of them that they may conform to and co-operate with that purpose.

It is objected that the whole conception of Providence is incompatible with the scientific view of the world as governed by Natural Law. It is to be observed that the phrase "governed by Natural Law" admits of a variety of interpretations. What is really meant in this objection is a strict physical determinism, accounting without remainder for all events in their entirety, including the actions of human beings, so that it would have been possible for any mind of sufficient intelligence, fully acquainted with the physical antecedents, to predict any event with certainty. This view cannot be reconciled with Christianity, and is, moreover, open to grave philosophical objection. The moment any place is allowed for spiritual action of such a character as to modify physical events, it cannot be settled *a priori* what are the limits of this freedom.

V. MIRACLES

It is evident that the Christian belief in miracles is dependent on belief in God, and it must be recognised that the activity of God's purpose and power is fully present in the regularities which constitute the familiar natural order. A miracle, if it occurs, is not a breach of order, but expresses the purpose of God, which also determines the order of nature. It is therefore nothing irrational or capricious. But an event is rightly called a miracle in so far as it is a work of God's power and holiness, and cannot be co-ordinated with the general scheme of the universe by means of the ordinary categories of science alone or even of those ordinarily required for the interpretation of human action. A miracle, in the Christian meaning of the word, directly and of itself manifests to the believer the spiritual character and holiness of the power sustaining the universe, and is thereby distinguished from a mere portent.

It is felt by many that miracle has a special value, in that it is a striking demonstration of the subordination of the natural order to spiritual ends, and affords particular points at which God's activity is manifested with special clarity and directness. On the other hand, it is to be recognised that many others feel it to be more congruous with the wisdom and majesty of God that the regularities, such as men of science observe in nature and call Laws of Nature, should serve His purpose without any need for exceptions on the physical plane. It is important to notice that the motives leading to this view are not exclusively scientific, but that a religious interest also is involved.

It has to be recognised that legends involving abnormal events have tended to grow very easily in regard to great religious leaders, and that in consequence it is impossible in the present state of knowledge to make the same evidential use of the narratives of miracles in the Gospels which appeared possible in the past. This is a religious gain, inasmuch as the use of miracles to force belief appears to have been deliberately rejected by our Lord.

It must be recognised that as regards the abnormal events recorded in the Gospels, a belief as to the Person of our Lord, which must mainly be reached on other grounds, constitutes a part of the ground for belief in their miraculous character. A similar principle must be applied in consideration of other events alleged to be miraculous.

VI. GRACE

The term "grace" has a long and complex history. Its use in later Christian theology must be distinguished from, though it arises out of, the use of χάρις in the New Testament and especially in S. Paul's Epistles. S. Paul inherited from the Septuagint the term χάρις as the equivalent of the Hebrew *hēn*, meaning the personal favour of God. As a result of his own religious experience he emphasised the free and undeserved character of this grace. In subsequent theology the term has been affected by current associations of the Greek χάρις and the Latin *gratia*.

Grace has thus come to mean the will of God (which is also His love) regarded as active on behalf of and in man. It is not merely "favour" or "goodwill," but a "power that worketh in us" (Eph. iii. 20). Though the operations of grace have been distinguished for purposes of description and practical convenience, grace itself is one. For example, there is no distinction, except of mode, between "prevenient" and "co-operant" grace on the one hand, and "sacramental" grace on the other.

Grace is always prior to every good inclination of the human soul, both to that "natural" goodness which persists despite the corruption of human nature through sin, and to that "supernatural" goodness or sanctification which results from the work of the Holy Spirit in and through the Church.

The operation of grace is not opposed to the freedom of

the human will, since grace acts through the will and not externally to it. It is, indeed, only within the sphere of grace that true freedom is to be found.

The word "grace" has also been used to describe the effects of its operation in human character (*gratia habitualis; cf.* such phrases as "graces of character"). In this usage emphasis has customarily been laid upon the development in man of a "supernatural" righteousness. This conception is important, as witnessing to the distinctiveness of the Christian ideal and to the necessity of obtaining grace through Christ for the attainment of this ideal. This conception is independent of any particular view as to the way in which this grace is mediated.

We do not propose to discuss the minute distinctions as to kinds of grace elaborated by the Schoolmen. It may be noted that they are frequently expressed in language which is affected by theories of the Fall which cannot be reconciled with our historical and scientific knowledge.

It is essential to emphasise the spiritual character of grace, and in view of this physical metaphors, though admittedly inevitable, should be used with clear recognition of their metaphorical character.

VII. JUSTICE AND LOVE IN GOD

Much contemporary perplexity is due to the difficulty of relating the Justice and the Love of God. This difficulty is unnecessarily increased by a frequent acceptance of a formula of Justice much cruder than the conception of it on which men mostly act, to say nothing of the conceptions of it which may be found in the writings of philosophers and theologians. While men often seem to accept as the formula of Justice the balancing of moral action with corresponding happiness or suffering, in their treatment of individual cases they seldom apply this principle; for it is recognised that the moral worth of men who do what are in a juristic classification the same acts is not necessarily the same, and that they ought not necessarily to be treated in the same way.

Still, it may be felt that this only means that God can achieve the perfectly just correspondence between moral worth and suffering as men cannot, and if He is just this must be His act.

Now it is plain that He may in fact achieve this, even though we, with our limited range, cannot trace it. But it is urged that experience does not suggest this—in this world, at any rate, it does not happen; and there are sayings of Christ which tell the other way. It cannot be right to make this balancing of guilt with suffering the chief manifestation of any quality regarded as an attribute of God.

But this is not really the chief activity of Justice, whether or not it is one of its activities. Plato, for instance, speaks of the principle whereby like is drawn to like, so that in the end each of us would be associated with those of the same moral type as ourselves; so also there is the law that when we defy the eternal values we lose sensitiveness to them, and, conversely, that as we live by the light we have we receive fuller light. These are principles of Justice, though they are plainly distinguishable from the deliberate balancing of moral worth with happiness or suffering.

These principles are found to be supported by experience broadly regarded. And it is clear that between Justice, so conceived, and Love (ἀγάπη) there is no incompatibility, however much more may be connoted by the term Love, for Justice so conceived is free from all that is arbitrary or that is hostile towards the sinner.

Yet to say that God is Love does involve a real transcendence of the category of Justice. This does not mean that Justice has no place in God, but that it is never "mere Justice" as that phrase would usually be understood. The attitude of God towards sin as represented by the Cross includes Justice (as S. Paul insists), but is certainly not adequately expressed by that term.

The deepest human experience, with its strong sense of guilt, implies that there exists in God an antagonism against sin which is most naturally called "the wrath of God." The believer who is genuinely conscious of guilt is convinced that his own condemnation of his sin reflects the condemnation of it by God, and that God would be less than God if He did not thus condemn it.

But the Cross, which reveals what sin means to God, and therefore the opposition or antagonism of the Divine nature to sin, also reveals God showing His Love for us "while we were yet sinners," and seeking to draw men out of the sin which is the occasion of His wrath into the communion with Himself for which, as His children, He created them.

It is impossible to overstate the significance of the Christian doctrine that God is Love; but we have to be on our guard lest we associate this with a sub-Christian scale of values. God as Love always desires what is best for His children; but this may not be what they are now ready to choose, and His Love may, for Love's sake, make demands which are very exacting and insist on them with a relentless sternness. We may only be able to appreciate this as Justice; but as we rise to a fuller understanding we apprehend it as an aspect, or activity, of Love.

The Fathers assumed, partly under the influence of Greek thought, the notion of Divine impassibility. This notion is often taken to mean simply that God is incapable of suffering; but it has wider significance, and implies that God is not subject to human passions. In this sense it is a valuable safeguard against unduly anthropomorphic ideas of God, and is affirmed in the first of the Thirty-Nine Articles ("one living and true God, everlasting, without body, parts, or passions"). But Greek thinkers admired "self-sufficiency" ($a\vec{v}\tau\acute{a}\rho\kappa\epsilon\iota a$) in man, and so the notion of impassibility as an element in the Divine Majesty has sometimes been associated with a moral ideal which is less than Christian. It is true that the conception of God as Almighty implies that nothing can befall Him against His own will, and that if He suffers it is because He wills to suffer. It is also true that the revelation in Christ discloses God as taking on Himself in the Person of His Son the suffering involved in the Incarnation. We recognise that this carries with it a loftier conception of the Divine Majesty than that which would deny that suffering can enter at all into the experience of God.

Along with this goes a distinctively Christian conception of Omnipotence, which in fact avoids many of the difficulties often associated with this term. Omnipotence as mere power to do anything is a very abstract conception, but the actual exercise of power is always related to purpose; Omnipotence in God means, therefore, the power to order and control all things to the fulfilment of His purpose, which is a purpose of Love in relation to free spirits. He shows His power in the creation of free spirits; but also He shows His power in the redemption of free spirits, a redemption effected through the willing acceptance of sacrificial suffering.

(B) THE FACT OF SIN

Our consideration must now be turned to that condition of man which has called for Divine action as its remedy. There is much confusion of thought with regard to Sin, and in what follows we try to disentangle the most important threads. We consider successively Actual Sin, Original Sin, and the distinction between Mortal and Venial Sin. We append some Notes dealing with certain more detailed points which arise in connection with these.

I. ACTUAL SIN

The term " sin " in the sense of " actual " sin is used in two ways; sometimes it stands exclusively for actions done in defiance of conscience* ("formal sin"). Ethically regarded, such actions involve guilt; religiously regarded, they are acts of deliberate rebellion against the Will of God, or at least failures in obedience or loyalty to that Will. But sometimes also the word " sin " is used for all acts and all spiritual conditions that are in fact contrary to or alien from the Will of God, whether recognised to be so or not (" material sin ").

Thus sin is a term which belongs to the terminology of religion rather than to that of ethics. In a theistic religion it means that which is contrary to God's nature and impairs communion between God and man. Hence the content of the term is determined by the conception of God, and when this conception becomes fully ethical, sin comes to mean ethically bad dispositions and actions when viewed in relation to God.

In the Old Testament the idea of sin is progressively moralised, though the idea of merely ritual impurity is never wholly abandoned, and there is also an increasing recognition of individual responsibility.

In the teaching of Christ the primary emphasis is upon the positive nature of righteousness as being the expression of love to God and to man. Sin, therefore, becomes primarily a refusal of trust and of obedience on the part of His children towards a heavenly Father, or a failure of brotherly love. Sinfulness is ascribed both to individuals and to communities or classes. Sin lies in the disposition of the " heart." Its universality is assumed. It is to be noted that the commands of God are never arbitrary, but proceed from His righteousness and love, and that He always wills the highest good of His creatures.†

Thus in theory the conception of " actual sin " presents no difficulty to those who accept the belief in God as a righteous and loving Father, and allow to men some

* See Note B on the Senses Attached to the Term " Conscience," p. 67.
† See Note E on the Wrath of God against Sin, p. 70.

measure of real choice in giving or refusing a response of love and obedience. It denotes simply the doing of what is in fact wrong, or the failure to do what is in fact right.

In practice, however, the case is not so simple. Sins deliberately committed with a full knowledge of their sinfulness ("sins of malice") are not so common as sins committed either under the influence of overwhelming temptation ("sins of infirmity") or sins committed without clear realisation of their sinfulness ("sins of ignorance"). Further, it is possible to find cases where an act is committed which is sinful because it is done in defiance of conscience, although the act in itself is not actually evil but is wrongly held to be so. Hence the distinction is drawn by moral theologians between "formal sin," which covers the doing of acts believed at the time to be wrong, whether really wrong or not, and "material sin," which covers all actions which are actually evil, whether recognised as such or not.

Clearly, the degree of responsibility attaching to the wrong-doer varies in the different cases noted in the preceding paragraph. A sin of infirmity involves less guilt than a sin of malice. A common type of sins of infirmity is found in cases where a particular habit of a sinful character has been formed which the sinner finds it difficult or almost impossible to break ("habitual sins"). Such habits may have been formed with more or less ignorance of the fact that they are sinful, so that it may be necessary for the Church or the Christian minister to convince the sinner of their sinfulness as well as to point to the means of overcoming them.

It must, however, be emphasised that ignorance is only a complete excuse for wrong-doing when it is unavoidable ignorance of a particular fact or precept. It is not an excuse in so far as the particular fact or precept is one which the wrong-doer could have, and ought to have, ascertained. Further, where a moral principle is involved, ignorance is always evidence of some moral defect. It may not be a moral defect for which the sinner is responsible, since it may be wholly due to the environment in which he has been brought up—as, for example, in the case of a convert from heathenism. In the case of those brought up in more or less Christian surroundings, some degree at least of moral obtuseness is usually present in the wrong-doer, and this moral obtuseness is in itself evidence of a defective character for which he may be partly responsible, although there be also a moral defect in the environment as well.

It must further be observed that these considerations do not by any means apply exclusively to those personal vices or to that lack of personal virtue which it is common to consider as "sins." Much that is most evil in the world, and from which we most need to be delivered, consists in and arises from habits of mind or an outlook on life which is taken for granted by those who share it. The things most wrong with a man are often those of which he is least conscious. The notion that what is required of us is merely to do what we happen to regard as our duty is disastrous. A primary duty of the individual is to try to find out what his duty really is. It is equally a primary (though frequently neglected) duty of the Church to point out the extent to which mankind in general is dominated by false ideas of what duty really is, embodied in false ideals and false social conventions.

Thus while ignorance of moral principles (as opposed to unavoidable ignorance of particular facts or precepts) may to a greater or less extent diminish the personal responsibility of the wrong-doer for particular actions or attitudes of mind, it only does so (in so far as it does so) by transferring the responsibility to the society in which he has been educated and in which he lives. There are many cases in which the guilt rests in part at least upon the Church in so far as it has fostered, or at least connived at, moral ideals which are lower than the standard of our Lord Himself.

II. ORIGINAL SIN

In the section dealing with actual sin it is pointed out that the word "sin" covers not only actions done in defiance of conscience, but also "all acts and all spiritual conditions that are in fact contrary to, or alien from, the Will of God, whether recognised to be so or not." It is of special importance to remember this as we approach the conception of original sin.

It is a fact of experience that man is universally prone to sin. This is not to be understood to mean that man is "totally depraved," or is not also in many ways prone to righteousness. What is affirmed is that every man does in fact tend, in one respect or another, to be and to do what is other than perfectly good. This is, indeed, a grave understatement of the reality of human evil. But so much at least will not be questioned, and is by itself sufficient to create a serious problem for those who believe that man was created by a perfectly good God and "in his own image."

The general conception of original sin was in the first instance suggested by this fact of experience. It has been utilised in two main ways: (a) To account for the fact itself; (b) to avoid attributing to God responsibility for the fact. It is to be noted, moreover, that the universality of the sinful disposition is a truth of great practical importance, because it points to man's need of the help of God if he is to live in accordance with God's Will.

The term "original sin" is to some extent ambiguous. It stands for the sinful disposition which is in fact found in all men from a time apparently previous to any responsible act of choice; but historically it has been associated with an interpretation of this which refers it to the transgression of the first man. In any case the fact demands explanation, for it seems to reflect discredit upon the Creator. The doctrines of the Fall and of original sin, in their traditional association, have served to give recognition to the belief that a universal tendency to evil (within which must be included the tendency to seek satisfaction and rest content in anything less than perfect goodness) is inherent in our actual human nature, while they have also been valued because they have at least appeared to lift from God the burden of responsibility for evil.

Among the historic attempts in Christian theology to explain man's sinful disposition, three streams of thought are of special importance. These may be indicated by the following phrases: (*a*) Loss of communion with God; (*b*) racial depravity and guilt; (*c*) modern evolutionary theories. Each of these draws attention to important elements of the truth: (*a*) Our sinful state cannot be rightly estimated except in connexion with man's relation to God; (*b*) there is a solidarity of the race in sin as in redemption; (*c*) original sin must be related to our evolutionary inheritance.*

Evolutionary theories are often so stated as to imply that this sinful condition is held actually to consist in the persistence of certain animal instincts not yet adequately regulated by reason, or in a disproportionate development of the various instincts. But this (like the Augustinian concentration on sexual concupiscence) becomes misleading unless the fact is recognised that human nature is fundamentally spiritual, and that the seat of sin is primarily in the rational and spiritual nature itself.†

The Augustinian doctrine of original righteousness— a state of high spiritual endowment forfeited by the Fall— has not been universally held in the Church, and does not in fact appear to have found a place in Christian teaching before the fourth century. It is no necessary part of the conceptions either of original sin or of a real Fall.

The belief that the process of human generation is in

* Note C on Historical Forms of the Doctrines of Man's Universal Sinfulness and Original Sin, p. 68.

† See Appendix (p. 221): On the Psychological Aspects of Sin.

itself sinful, or that sin is conveyed to the offspring because of any sinfulness in this process, is not a necessary
part of the doctrine of original sin, and we are agreed in
repudiating it. We believe that it is wholly unwarranted,
being part of a profoundly unsatisfactory view of sex and
of sexual relations; it must be eliminated if a satisfactory
doctrine of original sin is to be reached. It arises, no
doubt, from the intimate connection which exists between
sex and shame, and from the perception that innocence in
this sphere can only be maintained or achieved by conquest. But that the sexual nature is necessarily or inherently sinful must be absolutely denied.

We are agreed in asserting that man, as known to
history, both now and throughout the ages, has been under
the influence of a bias towards evil.

In our interpretation of this fact, and in relating it to
the purpose of God, we are not agreed; but we are united
in holding that none of the views outlined below should
be regarded as illegitimate in the Church of England:

(1) Since man is by his very nature social, we are involved in some form of social solidarity, so that, evil
having beyond question found an entrance into human life,
all are brought under its influence.

> (a) Some hold that this influence of social environ-
> ment upon each individual is a sufficient explanation
> of the facts.
> (b) Some hold that, in addition to social inherit-
> ance, there is a racial inheritance of evil, a biological
> transmission of moral taint.*

* This, it is claimed, does not necessarily involve belief in the
inheritance of acquired characteristics. Just as on the physical
plane evolution by survival of the fittest produces a close imitation
of what would result from the inheritance of acquired characteristics, so it may be in respect of moral dispositions. The conception of biological inheritance is equally applicable either on the
basis of the inheritance of acquired characteristics or on the basis
of the theory that society is such as to give an advantage (from the
point of view of survival and procreation) to stocks possessed of
certain characteristics. Moreover, some who believe in the racial

(c) Some, whether accepting (b) or not, hold that more than (a) is involved, and that there is a transcendental solidarity of the human race in evil which creates or determines a proneness to sin in each individual.

(d) Some hold that the very essence of man as a finite spirit is a sufficient explanation of the facts.*

(2) In regard to the question of God's responsibility for sin.

(a) Some hold that God, having made man free, has no further responsibility for sin, which falls outside His original purpose for man.

(b) Others hold that from the beginning sin falls within that purpose, though among these, again, there would be a difference as regards the directness with which the responsibility for it is to be attributed to God.†

Questions have arisen about the "guilt" of original sin, but they seem to concern the proper use of words rather than any great matter of substance. Inasmuch as the general state of sinfulness into which we are born is something which we have done nothing to create, we are not accountable for it, and if the word "guilt" is taken to mean moral responsibility and consequent liability to

---

inheritance of evil are not thinking of biological inheritance at all, but of a solidarity in natural humanity, so that we are born into, and are as units in, a corrupted natural order.

* See Appendix (p. 223): On Finitude and Original Sin.

† It is important in this connection to be quite clear what is meant by those who assert that God so created man that sin was inevitable. Some have meant that God predestined man to sin (in the sense that, since God's purpose was, from the beginning, a purpose of redemption, this purpose must have included that from which man is to be redeemed—namely, sin); others have meant that He gave to men something which may be described as "free will," and that—given "free will"—it was so improbable that men would always choose rightly as to render wrong choice "too probable not to happen," although not, strictly speaking, necessitated by God. On the latter view such inevitability of sin is the cost of "free will" and, therefore, also of the emergence of individuals who freely choose to love God and to do His Will.

punishment, we agree that there is no guilt attaching to the individual in respect of original sin. But the word " guilt " is used in other ways. Thus (a) if it is used in a more general sense, and is regarded as applicable to a society, so that we may speak of a corporate account-ability and of a correspondingly corporate guilt, then the whole natural society of mankind is " guilty " in respect of its condition (which has resulted from past sins), and individuals, even from birth, participate in guilt in the sense that they are members of a guilty society. Similarly (b) if the word " guilt " is taken to include the taint or defilement of sin, we agree that there is guilt attaching to original sin. But many of us would repudiate one or both of these latter uses of the term " guilt."*

Whether or not the term " guilt " is fitly employed in connection with original sin, the general state of sinful-ness into which we are born involves at least partial aliena-tion from God.

What seems to be of practical importance in the con-ception of original sin may be summarised as follows:

Man is by nature capable of communion with God, and only through such communion can he become what he was created to be. " Original sin " stands for the fact that from a time apparently prior to any responsible act of choice man is lacking in this communion, and if left to his own resources and to the influence of his natural en-vironment cannot attain to his destiny as a child of God.

III. MORTAL AND VENIAL SIN

A distinction between different types of sin is found in 1 John v. 16, which speaks of a " sin unto death," so grievous that the writer does not feel able to recommend prayer for the sinner; and the expression " mortal sin " in later theology was based on this passage. The sin here contemplated was probably complete apostasy from the

* For a further treatment of this subject, see Appended Note A on Sin and Guilt, pp. 66 f.

Church. In the early centuries idolatry, murder and adultery were regarded as constituting a class of sins so grave that it was disputed whether the Church could remit them. Later the term "mortal sin" was applied to all sins of such a kind that they entailed the eternal damnation of the soul unless the sinner received formal absolution. The term "venial" was then applied to less grievous offences.

The traditional distinction of certain particular offences as in their own nature mortal from certain others as in their own nature venial cannot be upheld.

It is not possible to define any point at which an act of sin becomes mortal in the sense of being so serious as to cut off a soul from the grace of God. Nor is it possible to judge the gravity of any sin without reference to the circumstances, temptations, and character of the sinner. At the same time, it is obvious that some sins are more grievous than others. In practice the pastor is bound to have in mind a general distinction between sins which are more and sins which are less serious; but the gravity of any particular sinful act can only be estimated in the light of all the circumstances, which are known fully to God alone. But it is a special function of the pastor to assist the individual conscience to recognise the gravity of the more serious and dangerous forms of sin, whether or not these are such as to give rise to scandal.

A distinction between mortal and venial sin does, however, correspond to the facts of experience in so far as those who have fallen into sin very commonly feel, rightly or wrongly, that some of their sins are of such gravity as to cut them off from the grace of God, while others appear comparatively trifling. Their judgment on these matters may often be wrong, but the judgment itself is a fact which the pastor must take into account. It may be that the sinner has special need of pardon, or it may be that he needs fuller instruction in Christian morality; in either case his condition calls for appropriate remedy.

APPENDED NOTES

A. *On Sin and Guilt.*

In the actual experience of penitence there are discernible two elements that should not be confused. There is the sense of guilt, of responsibility, when the sinner feels that he is responsible, because he need not have done the sinful act, and there is the sense of shame, of being defiled, when the sinner realises that his character is such as to issue in such an act. These two easily coincide; but they are not identical; and the second can exist without the first. Penitence on its self-regarding side may take the form of self-condemnation or of self-loathing, or both. When they fall apart, these two call for quite distinct treatment.

With such distinctions in our minds we proceed to consider more exactly the question how far guilt is invariably a concomitant of sin.

It is clear that guilt, in the sense of accountability, always attaches in some degree to formal sin—the doing of what is believed to be wrong. In nearly all cases there is guilt attaching to habitual sin, for nearly always formal sin has played a part in forming the sinful disposition so described. But there are probably some instances of habitual sin where this is not so, and such a thing is certainly possible. It may be due to original sin and, so far as actions have contributed to it, to sins of ignorance. For such sins—*i.e.*, for sins of excusable ignorance or for his share of original sin—the individual sinner is not individually accountable; if guilt is synonymous with such accountability, then for such sins no guilt attaches to the individual as such.

But (as is said above) such sin has its source in the natural society and the wills to which in any respect its character is due: so there is a real, though less easily defined, sense in which guilt attaches to the society and to individuals as its members. Thus an Englishman to-day may feel that he has a share in the guilt of the nation which burnt Joan of Arc, or which took a leading share in the slave trade, just as in the latter case he may feel himself to share the credit which belongs to the nation which took the lead in abolishing the slave trade.

Further, there is a stain or taint (*macula*) of sin wherever there is sin, and some use the word " guilt " as including this. It is sometimes said that for this there should be shame but not penitence; others would say that, while there should be shame certainly, there should also be penitence for this (as for all sin and its effects), but not self-condemnation; for the essence of penitence is realisation of alienation from God, and desire for restoration to the Divine fellowship and for grace to continue in it.

We are all agreed that there is a distinction between stain and guilt; and we are all agreed that, since some of the sins of the past that still trouble us were not committed by ourselves, these cannot entail the kind of self-con-demnation which is appropriate to our own misdeeds. In face of the fact that theologians, both " Catholic " and " Protestant," have deliberately asserted the guilt (*reatus*) of original sin, some members of the Commission are not satisfied to attribute this fact to mere confusion of thought, but would regard it as proceeding from a truly Christian sense of the sinfulness of sin in all its aspects. Others hold that in no sense can guilt (*reatus*) be rightly attached to original sin.

B. *On Senses Attached to the Term " Conscience."*

The word " conscience," as it is commonly used by English people to-day, has at least four distinct meanings: (1) Properly, in the view of the Commission, it stands for the mind as passing deliberate moral judgments upon conduct, such as involve both some knowledge of general moral principles and the application of these to the particular case in question. (2) It may also sometimes stand for what is more correctly called "the moral consciousness"—*i.e.*, the general capacity for moral judgment—*e.g.*, it may be said that man is distinguished from other animals by possessing conscience. (3) Most commonly in general usage it stands for an immediate feeling, experienced apart from all deliberation and weighing of various considerations, that a given action or kind of conduct is right or wrong. (4) It is often used also to denote directly "the voice of God within us"—*i.e.*, God's Will as to conduct recognised as expressing itself in the human consciousness either through moral feeling or through considered judgment on a moral question.

Where the word "conscience" occurs in our Report, it is meant to be taken primarily in sense (1). Of course, if the word is taken in sense (1) or sense (4), there is no question but that defiance of conscience involves both actual and formal sin. Much confusion, however, is caused in popular thought upon this subject by a quite unjustified supposition that an immediate feeling as to right and wrong is necessarily to be identified with the voice of God within. Cases occur not infrequently where such a feeling is not endorsed by the considered moral judgment of the same individual, and, even after the action has been approved by the moral judgment and performed, an uneasy feeling that it is wrong may still persist. While fully aware of the danger of sophisticating conscience, we hold, nevertheless, that the considered moral judgment is the authoritative guide of conduct, and it is this meaning of the term conscience which we have in mind when we speak of action either in defiance of conscience or in accord with it.

C. *On Historical Forms of the Doctrine of Man's Universal Sinfulness and Original Sin.*

In the Jewish Church it was recognised that all men are prone to sin, and this was explained by the twofold imagination, good and evil, implanted by God. Later Jewish theology also, though less frequently, explained the origin of sin by reference to the story of the union of the sons of God with the daughters of men (Gen. vi.), or to the story of the eating of the forbidden fruit (Gen. iii.).

Both these latter explanations are found in early Christian theology, though, no doubt as a result of S. Paul's influence, the reference to Gen. iii. rapidly became predominant. Origen, however, developed a wholly independent theory of a pre-natal falling away of created intelligences from the creative Logos.

The reference to the fall of Adam has led to various interpretations.

(1) The Greek Fathers for the most part think of Adam's state before the Fall as one of primitive innocence, but not of high spiritual endowment. By his transgression he fell away from communion with God and forfeited the grace bestowed in that communion. The apostasy persists and is increased in his descendants.

(2) S. Augustine held that Adam's state before the Fall was one of high spiritual endowment, that this was forfeited by the Fall, and that the whole race was thereby involved in depravity and guilt. This view was re-emphasised and developed by Luther, Calvin, and most of the great Reformers.

(3) One common doctrine of scholastic theology was that, in consequence of the first man's transgression, God withdrew from man the *donum superadditum* (S. Thomas), or *dona supernaturalia* (Bellarmine), apart from which man cannot please God.

From this it is clear that the Church is not committed to any one doctrine with regard to this subject.

In our view the doctrine of a universal tendency to evil in man is not bound up with the historical truth of any story of a Fall.

D. *On the Connexion between the Fall and the Incarnation.*

Two main views have been held as to the connexion between the Incarnation and the Fall—viz. (*a*) the Thomist view that the Word became incarnate to redeem man from sin and therefore would not have become incarnate if sin had not appeared in the world; and (*b*) the Scotist view that the Word would have become incarnate in any case, His human nature being determined by the Divine Will from the beginning, though apart from sin this would not have involved suffering and the Cross.

Both views appear to have been in existence as early as the fourth century, and the Church is not committed to either of them.

E. *On the Wrath of God against Sin.*

We think it desirable to add a special note on this phrase, both in itself and as illustrative of a range of language which presents grave difficulties and has often been disastrously misunderstood, but which is deeply rooted not only in religious tradition but in the Gospels.

The " wrath of God " is a Biblical phrase expressive of the eternal antagonism of the Divine holiness towards all forms of spiritual and moral evil. In the earlier stages of Hebrew religion the going forth of " wrath " from " the Lord " sometimes appears arbitrary; at a later stage God's antagonism is only towards sin, but His dread supernatural " wrath " is still inevitably provoked by moral evil; there is a white heat of the Divine holiness, a " consuming fire " before which the sinner cannot stand.

Such language, representing an element in the distinctively religious apprehension of God's attitude towards sin and sinners which it is not easy to rationalise, may be too inexact to be incorporated as it stands into any scientific theological system, but may nevertheless be required to

supply " ideograms " (to borrow Otto's useful term) illustrating pictorially and indirectly, even if not formulating
accurately, genuine elements in the character of God.

It is to be observed, further, that in the New Testament
the " love " and the " wrath " of God in relation to sin
and forgiveness are closely connected,* and there is an important sense in which the assertion of God's " wrath "
against sin is the indispensable presupposition of any
properly Christian doctrine of forgiveness. There can be
no forgiveness where there is indifference towards either the
offender or the offence.

Even in human experience it is possible to be conscious
of the union of wrath and charity. The most intense wrath
is called forth by disappointed trust, and presupposes a
certain worth and dignity in the person against whom it
is directed. Pure hostility is cold and implacable, and
seeks the ruin and destruction of its object; but the wrath
and sorrow evoked by a traitor is different in quality.
The hostility aims at suppression; the wrath expresses condemnation, and aims at securing that the offender shall
be made to " rue his deed " and to be ashamed of himself.
But he can only do this if he is still capable of better
things; such suffering is a condition of moral recovery,
and it is what his best friend must wish for him.

" Wrath " in this ethical sense is not only compatible
with love, but in its purest form cannot exist apart from
love. Righteous wrath cannot be based on self-concern,
nor at its best is it consistent with any loss of self-control
such as characterises the primitive emotion of anger.

---

* " God commended His love towards us, in that, while we were
yet sinners, Christ died for the ungodly;" and yet " the wrath of
God is revealed from heaven against every soul of man that doeth
evil."

(C) REDEMPTION IN CHRIST

I. CHRISTOLOGY

(a) *Introductory Considerations.*

Christianity is distinguished among the religions of the world by the place which it gives to its Founder. It has regarded Jesus Christ as not merely the supreme prophet of God, but as Himself essentially one with God. It is exactly this which has given to its doctrine of God both its special content and its sharpness of outline, from which much of its spiritual power has been derived. It is this which has given to the central doctrine of the Incarnation its quality as a doctrine of Divine self-sacrifice (*e.g.*, "though He was rich, yet for your sakes He became poor," 2 Cor. viii. 9; *cf.* Phil. ii. 6-8); it is this which has given to the Cross the significance which Christian experience has always found in it; and it is in this that Christians have found the justification of their sense of personal communion with Jesus Himself, and of their conviction that it is through Him that the Holy Spirit is given.

Christians have from the beginning recognised Jesus of Nazareth as "Messiah" and "Son of God." This belief was held by those who had been in closest association with Him, and the historical evidence satisfies us that it corresponds with His own conviction as to His Mission.

Such a claim involves the belief that the creative and redemptive purpose of God for Israel and for mankind was, and is to be, fulfilled in and through Him, and that we are not to "look for another" who might bring a revelation and redemption which could supersede what has been given in Christ.

Many questions arise in the popular mind which show a true appreciation of real problems, but cannot be fairly answered in the terms in which they are stated. Such are the questions whether Jesus Christ existed before His birth, whether He was human in exactly the same sense in which we are, and so forth. Often these questions can only be fairly answered if the terms have first been analysed with great care. Moreover, it is to be recognised that there is in the whole orthodox Christian position a great difficulty in reconciling belief in the eternity of God the Son " who was made man " with the equally essential conviction, based on the Gospel narratives, of the truly human life of the Incarnate Christ. This challenge to the intellect is an inherent element in the Gospel. Whether or not the intellectual difficulty can ever be fully overcome it is our duty to be always seeking the way to solve it, provided that this is not done by neglect or obscuration of either of the contrasted elements which give rise to it.

In view of the historical development of the traditional Christology (in which discipleship and worship preceded systematic speculation as to the relation of the Divine to the Human in the Person of Jesus Christ), and of the experience of the Christian Church (in which such discipleship and worship have been the normal conditions of spiritual progress), it is manifest that failure to reach a complete solution of the intellectual problem is not a valid ground for withholding the worship which Christians have always given to their Lord. On the contrary, it is only in the spirit of such worship that justice can be done to both the essential elements in the problem, or that the Church can hope to attain to the fuller understanding which it is bound continually to seek.

(b) Christological Doctrine.

The doctrine of the Incarnation asserts that Christ is both God and Man. We do not understand this as implying that Jesus acted in two alternating capacities— now as God and now as Man—but rather that in all His actions and experiences He is both God and Man.

The Church believes that in Jesus Christ God was made man not only with a human body but also with a " reasonable soul." This implies that the whole incarnate life of the Son—*i.e.*, His whole outlook, activity, and knowledge in this life—was mediated throughout by faculties, physical, intellectual, moral, and spiritual, which were genuinely human. Full weight must be given to the statements that " Jesus advanced in wisdom and stature " (Luke ii. 52), and that He was " in all points tempted like as we are, yet without sin " (Heb. iv. 15).

The Incarnation belongs to the activity of God in history, and is therefore to be understood not only as fact, but as act. It is vital to Christianity to affirm that God acted through Christ, and that He still acts through Christ. " God was," and is, " in Christ reconciling the world unto Himself " (2 Cor. v. 19).

Throughout the history of the Church there have been two main tendencies in the effort of theologians to expound the truth of the Incarnation. One of these was represented in the patristic age by the School of Antioch, which was specially concerned to do justice to the true humanity of Jesus Christ as set before us in the Gospels; the one-sided development of this led to the Nestorian heresy. The other was represented by the School of Alexandria, which started from the conception of the Divine Logos, and was specially concerned to affirm the true divinity of Jesus Christ throughout the human ministry as well as in His risen and ascended life; the one-sided development of this led to the Monophysite heresy. Neither school intended to deny either His divinity or His humanity; what the Church condemned were theories which did less than full justice to one or the other or to the union of the two. The Church affirmed both, each in its completeness, and the reality of their union.

Among the various approaches to this problem which are attempted in our own time a similar divergence appears. One common tendency in theology is to consider Christology with primary reference to the conviction that Jesus is personally God; the difficulty then is to combine with this conviction a recognition of the limitations characteristic of the experience of Jesus as of all human experience. It is to meet this difficulty that the group of theories known as " Kenotic " has arisen. Others begin with the actual historic fact of Jesus Christ, in whom is found a revelation of God which at once takes precedence of all other conceptions of Him; in Christ, they hold, love is seen to be so pre-eminently the characteristic of Deity that other attributes, such as omniscience, sink by comparison out of sight. To many of those who thus start with the historic Figure and human experience of Jesus, as described in the Gospels, it is not natural to use such an expression as that the subject of that experience was the Second Person of the Trinity, and they are not, therefore, confronted with the difficulty mentioned above. Representatives of this school accordingly urge that such difficulty as is implicit in their view presses less heavily on the purely religious interest; but it is admitted that difficulty remains; it is the difficulty, not of understanding how God can submit to finitude, but of understanding how a finite experience can so fully mediate a revelation of God. Just as the two main tendencies in ancient theology led, if developed in a one-sided way, to different heresies, so these two tendencies in modern theology, if similarly developed, lead to heresies—the former to a kind of Docetism, through a denial of the full reality of Christ's human life and experience, the latter to a purely humanitarian interpretation of Him. Each of these is destructive of the full truth of the Incarnation.

Each type of approach leads to its own group of difficulties. In either case it is to be recognised that it is neither desirable nor possible to give an exhaustive account of the Incarnation. What is necessarily demanded of any doctrines claiming to be Christian is that such unity be affirmed between Jesus of Nazareth and the eternal God as finds expression in the declarations: " He that hath seen me hath seen the Father," and " Who for us men and for our salvation came down from heaven."

We would record our conviction that in this affirmation, based on the historic evidence concerning Jesus Christ
as interpreted by the experience of Christians, in spite of
the difficulties which we have recognised, we have the
only adequate explanation of the facts of life and of the
problem of the universe. But it is always to be remembered
that the religious value of the doctrine of the Incarnation
consists primarily in what it declares concerning God
rather than in what it claims for the historic Jesus, while yet
it was through faith in Jesus Christ that men were led to the
Christian's knowledge of God. They saw "the light of the
knowledge of the glory of God in the face of Jesus Christ."

The affirmation that Jesus was " perfect " is not to be
understood in any sense which conflicts with the scriptural
statements that He " increased in wisdom and stature "
and that He " learnt obedience by the things which He
suffered " and was " made perfect through suffering." It
must be understood as meaning that at every stage of His
development He had the perfection appropriate to that
stage. Nor, again, is it to be maintained that every sort
of human excellence is found in Christ. His mission was
that of Messiah, not that (for example) of a statesman or
of an artist, and His perfection is relevant to the fulfilment of His mission in the actual circumstances in which
He was called to fulfil it. There is no reason to attribute
to Him the special excellences appropriate to functions
which were not His. But what He revealed supplies the
principle that should govern the development of all special
excellences and the exercise of every special talent.

One form of the affirmation of His " perfection " is the
assertion of His " sinlessness "; here it is important to
avoid the suggestion that this rests essentially on an
ethical review of His recorded sayings and deeds issuing
in a judgment that none of these are open to moral
censure. The term " sinlessness," though negative in
form, is positive in meaning. It represents the facts that
the impression made by our Lord's life and character upon

the first disciples was that of Mediator to men of the Divine Righteousness; and that the result of His impact upon men has ever been to evoke and to deepen penitence, while yet there is no trace of anything like penitence in His own consciousness. He had the highest conception of the righteousness of God that has appeared among men, yet exhibited a consciousness of unbroken union with Him.

When we come to see how far the several acts and sayings are fully compatible with this view, we must remember that He is throughout presented as the Redeemer, and that in the execution of His Mission what might be out of place in another may be appropriate in Him. We are persuaded that a true reading of the Gospels presents to us the picture of a flawless character. But it remains true that our concern is not with an inductive inference from single actions, but with the total impact of a character wholly given to and united with God. The word "sinlessness," like the word "sin" (see above, p. 57), belongs to the terminology of religion rather than of ethics. The conception underlies the historical records and is vitally related to the Christian experience of redemption.

The conception of our Lord's "pre-existence" gives rise to a special group of difficulties and requires careful statement if misunderstanding is to be avoided. Christians give to Christ the worship that is due to God only. This is justifiable only if Christ is one with God in a sense not attributable to others. The coming of Jesus Christ is not the occurrence in history of a purely historical figure, but is the manifestation in history of the Word who "was in the beginning with God and was God." It is through the Incarnation that we apprehend the Word, and it is clear that we cannot fully comprehend the mode of being of the Divine Word as existing apart from the Incarnation, though it is right that we should try to understand it ever more adequately. But it is worthy of notice that to assert the pre-existence of the human soul of Jesus, far from being required by orthodoxy, is inconsistent with it. Questions such as are sometimes asked about our Lord's "memory" of His heavenly experience before the Incarnation inevitably arise in our minds, and are involved in various scriptural passages; but to expect an answer in terms of the psychology of the human mind would be to press beyond what can be warranted the analogy of human consciousness. More than one method of dealing with these difficult questions may legitimately be tried. More important, however, than their complete solution is the assertion that our Lord is in the full sense Man and in the full sense God. The Divine Word had found utterance through prophets and religious leaders; in Jesus Christ "the Word was made flesh and dwelt among us."

The union of Divinity and Humanity in Jesus Christ inaugurated a new era for mankind. It made and makes possible a new fellowship of man with God. About this S. Paul uses the language of spiritual exaltation. God has "raised us up with him, and made us to sit with him in the heavenly places" (Eph. ii. 6). There is a new spiritual manhood in Christ Jesus which Christians are enabled to share (*cf*. Col. iii. 9, 10 for the contrast between the "old man" and the "new"). He also speaks of it as a new creation: "If any man is in Christ, there is a new creation" (2 Cor. v. 17). It is this which gives to Christianity its character of finality and its note of triumph, although the created universe awaits still the fulfilment of the Divine purpose to "sum up all things in Christ" (Eph. i. 10).

By virtue of the grace and truth which came by Jesus Christ, Christians are enabled to share His life. Yet the Christian does not hope to become another Christ. For him Christ is the one, and the necessary, Mediator. Christ's access to the Father was direct; we have our access to the Father through Him. He leads; we follow. He redeems; we are redeemed. As, drawn by Him, we share His life, we can also, as members of His Body, fulfil His purpose in the world. Our hope is that we may be as Jesus, not that we may be Christs; for this hope is fulfilled only as we draw our life from Him. The true relationship is expressed in the prayer to the Father attributed by the Fourth Evangelist to our Lord on the threshold of the Passion: "I in them, and thou in me" (John xvii. 23). For the realisation of this we rightly hope, not through our achievement but through His: "We know that if he shall be manifested, we shall be like him; for we shall see him even as he is" (1 John iii. 2).

It is through the Incarnation, the union of divine and human in Christ, that there comes to men that fulness of divine power which is spoken of in the New Testament as the gift of the Holy Spirit, as conversely it is through the Holy Spirit that Christians are made partakers of the life of Christ.*

It is implicit in the doctrine of the Incarnation that the God of Redemption is not other than the God of Creation, and that the activities involved in the Creation, Redemption, and Consummation of the world are all activities of the one God. This is among the implications for Christian theology of much Biblical language which the ordinary reader finds obscure, such as the doctrine of Christ as the eternal Word, the first principle of all things, at once archetype, intermediary, and goal, of Creation— a doctrine characteristic of the theologies of S. Paul and S. John.

The fulness of the Divine life revealed in Christ cannot be adequately expressed in human language, and theological statements share the limitations of all theoretical formulæ. It must be recognised that changes in forms of thought and the progress of knowledge may necessitate changes in the intellectual formulation of the content of Revelation, though this does not mean that there is any change in that which has been revealed. The apprehension of Revelation by the human mind must needs find expression in the form of propositions, but no such

* See p. 95 (The Holy Spirit).

formulations are to be regarded as being, in principle, irreformable. It may be that there are theological propositions accepted in the Church which will always be found neither to need nor to be capable of revision, and in that sense may be " final " ; if so, they are final not in the sense that they are exempt from examination, but in the sense that examination invariably leads to their re-affirmation.

APPENDED NOTE

The Relation of Modern Christology to the Formula of Chalcedon.

The classical formula of the doctrine of the Incarnation is that reached by the Council of Chalcedon in A.D. 451. The relevant passage may be translated as follows :

> " Therefore following the holy Fathers, we confess and all with one consent teach men to confess one and the same Son, our Lord Jesus Christ, the same perfect in Godhead and the same perfect in manhood, truly God and truly man, the same of a rational soul and body, of one substance with the Father according to His Godhead, and the same of one substance with us according to His manhood, in all things like to us apart from sin, begotten of the Father before the ages according to His Godhead, and the same in the last days for us and for our salvation born of Mary the Virgin, Mother of God ($\tau\hat{\eta}\varsigma$ $\theta\epsilon o\tau\acute{o}\kappa o\upsilon$), according to His manhood, one and the same Christ, Son, Lord, Only-begotten, made known in two natures, without confusion, without conversion, without division, without separation ($\dot{a}\sigma\upsilon\gamma\chi\acute{\upsilon}\tau\omega\varsigma$, $\dot{a}\tau\rho\acute{\epsilon}\pi\tau\omega\varsigma$, $\dot{a}\delta\iota\alpha\iota\rho\acute{\epsilon}\tau\omega\varsigma$, $\dot{a}\chi\omega\rho\acute{\iota}\sigma\tau\omega\varsigma$), the difference of the natures having been in no way abolished through the union, but rather the property of each nature being preserved and meeting in one person and one hypostasis ($\epsilon\acute{\iota}\varsigma$ $\grave{\epsilon}\nu$ $\pi\rho\acute{o}\sigma\omega\pi o\iota$ $\kappa a\grave{\iota}$ $\mu\acute{\iota}a\nu$ $\acute{\upsilon}\pi\acute{o}\sigma\tau a\sigma\iota\nu$)."

The main upshot of this formula is plainly the affirmation of real and absolute Deity, and of real and absolute Humanity, in the one Christ. This affirmation it makes in the language of what was then current thought with all possible clearness and vigour. How the affirmation is to be explained, or how the divine and human elements are to be related, it does not declare. The Council gave its approval to the *Letters of Cyril*, which laid great stress on the fact that it was the One divine Person who was the Subject of all the experiences of the incarnate life. In these *Letters* the distinction between the divine and human natures of the One Christ was clearly affirmed, but it was the unity of the Person that was especially emphasised. On the other hand, in the *Tome of Leo*, which was also approved, great stress was laid on the distinction of the natures and on the activities severally distinctive of each nature, within the unity of the Person of Christ. The Council made no attempt to combine into a further synthesis the points of view characteristic of the *Letters* and of the *Tome*.

At that period, and, indeed, until quite lately, Christians did not attribute to the Incarnate Lord any limitations of knowledge, or, at any rate, any beyond the one concerning the date of the Parousia which He Himself mentioned. In this respect modern theology, by a return to the Scriptures themselves, with their evidence of real surprise and disappointment as elements in the Lord's experience, has broken fresh ground.

We believe ourselves to be affirming in our Report that which was affirmed in the language of its own time by the Council at Chalcedon. But we wish to assert that the Church is in no way bound to the metaphysic or the psychology which lie behind the terms employed by the Council.

II. THE AFFIRMATIONS OF FAITH

(a) *The Virgin Birth*.

The Church's tradition of faith in the Virgin Birth must not be taken in isolation from the totality of Christian beliefs about the Person and work of Christ. Indeed it is only in connexion with their whole faith about Christ that the Virgin Birth possesses its traditional importance for Christians. At the same time belief in it as an historical fact cannot be independent of the historical evidence, although in this case the subject is one on which the historical evidence by itself cannot be other than inconclusive.

The main grounds on which the doctrine is valued are the following. It is a safeguard of the Christian conviction that in the birth of Jesus we have, not simply the birth of a new individual of the human species, but the advent of One who " for us men and for our salvation came down from heaven." It is congruous with the belief that in the Person of Christ humanity made a fresh beginning. It coheres with the supernatural element in the life of Christ, indicating a unique inauguration of that unique life. It gives expression to the idea of the response of the human race to God's purpose through the obedience and faith of the Blessed Virgin Mary.

Many of us hold, accordingly, that belief in the Word made flesh is integrally bound up with belief in the Virgin Birth, and that this will increasingly be recognised.

There are, however, some among us who hold that a full belief in the historical Incarnation is more consistent with the supposition that our Lord's birth took place under the normal conditions of human generation. In their minds the notion of a Virgin Birth tends to mar the completeness of the belief that in the Incarnation God revealed Himself at every point in and through human nature.

We are agreed in recognising that belief in our Lord's birth from a Virgin has been in the history of the Church intimately associated with its faith in the Incarnation of the Son of God. Further, we recognise that the work of scholars upon the New Testament has created a new setting of which theologians in their treatment of this article are obliged to take account. We also recognise that both the views outlined above are held by members of the Church, as of the Commission, who fully accept the reality of our Lord's Incarnation, which is the central truth of the Christian faith.

(b) The Resurrection.

The primary evidence for the Resurrection is the existence of the Christian Church. Something is needed to account for the conversion of the dejected followers of a crucified Messiah into the nucleus of the Church Militant. It is clear from the New Testament that this change was due to their conviction that the Lord was risen.

The documents which give us the direct evidence for the fact of the Resurrection are, first the Pauline Epistles, next the Synoptic Gospels, the Acts, and the Fourth Gospel. In St. Paul's Epistles and in the Acts the central place given to the Resurrection by the early Church is unmistakable. All the Gospels culminate, not in the Passion, but in the Resurrection. Indeed, it is worthy of notice that even the record of the Passion is evidence for the Resurrection, inasmuch as this could never have been included as part of the Good News, except by those who believed in the risen Lord. Moreover, it is important to recognise that apart from direct assertions of the event, the New Testament as a whole presupposes the Resurrection as an assured fact. The Commission does not regard the analysis and detailed evaluation of this evidence, which has been fully studied in recent times, as a task which it is called upon to undertake.

The historical evidence, considered simply as such, implies that there is an underlying mystery to be explained. The various narratives in the Gospels (like the Pauline list of appearances in 1 Cor. xv.) are to be understood primarily as presenting in different forms (not necessarily to be harmonised in respect to their details) the apostolic *kerygma** or proclamation of Jesus the Risen Lord; and that which they most directly attest is, in the first instance, the unanimous faith or conviction of the earliest Christians that Jesus was risen and alive from the dead.

When we attempt to go behind the *kerygma*, and ask "What was it exactly that happened?" a variety of answers is possible. Belief that the Lord was risen—the acceptance of the *kerygma* itself—is compatible both with a realisation that we cannot expect to reach clear or full knowledge in detail, and also with a variety of critical views. If a general principle is to be laid down, we may say that the Christian faith is compatible with all such critical reconstructions of the events underlying the narratives as would not have the effect, if accepted, of invalidating the apostolic testimony to Jesus as the Lord who rose from the dead. To speak more positively, we are of opinion that it ought to be affirmed that Jesus was veritably alive and victorious; that He showed Himself, alive from the dead, to the disciples; and that the fact of His rising, however explained (and it involves probably an element beyond our explaining), is to be understood to have been an event as real and concrete as the crucifixion itself (which it reversed) and an act of God, wholly unique in human history. The symbol of this fact in the Gospels is the story of the empty tomb. More than one explanation of this has been suggested; but the majority of the Commission are agreed in holding the traditional explanation—viz., that the tomb was empty because the Lord had risen.

Passing from the historical fact of the Resurrection to its significance, we are agreed on the following affirmations:

(*a*) The Resurrection is the Father's vindication of the Person and work of Jesus of Nazareth, and the victory

---

* The Greek word " Kerygma " is used by St. Paul in 1 Cor. xv. to denote the Gospel message as preached or proclaimed, and the word is used by modern New Testament scholars in this technical sense.

of God over the powers of evil. It is the assertion on the stage of history of the supremacy of the goodness of God, and the pledge of His final victory over sin and death.

(*b*) The Resurrection of the crucified Lord indicates the Christian answer to the problem of suffering. There is no shrinking from, or evasion of, the uttermost tragedy of life, but a conquest of it, in which all followers of Christ may share.

(*c*) The Resurrection confirms man's hope of immortality; and transforms it by the assurance that the future life is a richer and fuller life than that of earth. In the New Testament and in the experience of Christians the Resurrection is the power of the Christian life. We have died to the old life and risen with Christ to newness of life. This new life is the eternal life which is in the Son. It begins here and is made perfect hereafter.

The Resurrection has, moreover, made possible for Christians a new interpretation of the facts of death and mortality. The Cross represents the whole sacrifice of our Lord's life; a sacrifice which through its completion in death characterises for ever His risen and ascended manhood. For the Christian eternal life can only be fully attained through the sacrifice of the self in union with Christ's sacrifice. As means and conditions of such sacrifice the natural facts of human decay and mortality take on a fresh significance, and death becomes not a mere gateway to be passed through, nor the mere casting away of a perishable body, but a loss which is turned into gain, a giving up of life which is made the means whereby that life is received back again, renewed, transfigured, and fulfilled.

(*d*) Further, the teaching of the New Testament about the " Risen Body " expresses the belief that through our Lord's Resurrection the sovereignty of God has been vindicated in the material creation and not outside or apart from it. The belief coheres with the doctrine of Creation which pervades the whole Bible, and supports the Chris-

tian hope, expressed by St. Paul, that the Creator's handi-
work will be brought to its goal in a redemption extend-
ing to the whole creation (*cf.*, *e.g.*, Rom. viii. 19-23).

APPENDED NOTE

Though in the body of the Report the Commission dis-
claims responsibility for a fresh evaluation of the historical
evidence for the Resurrection, it may be useful, both as
indicating the difficulty of such an enterprise and as illustrating the process by which the findings of the Commission have been reached, to set out some of the considerations which have to be taken into account. They cover not
only historical evidence as such, but also a wide range of
theological and metaphysical ideas, ancient and modern.
And the illustration of the Commission's habitual method
here provided should be remembered at other similar points
in the Report.

On the one hand, belief that the dead would rise again
with their bodies at the last day had established itself in
Judaism, though not universally, for some two centuries
before the Crucifixion. It is possible, therefore, that ante-
cedent beliefs as to the resurrection of the dead have played
some part in shaping the tradition of the Resurrection of
Jesus Christ, even as that is recorded in the New Testament itself. This consideration, combined with others of
a more general sort, inclines some of us to the belief that
the connexion made in the New Testament between the
emptiness of a tomb and the appearances of the Risen Lord
belongs rather to the sphere of religious symbolism than to
that of historical fact.

On the other hand, there are reasons which make it difficult simply to dismiss the belief in the Resurrection of the
Lord's body as though it were a temporary and accidental
appendage which attached itself in the minds of His
disciples to the truth of His spiritual survival. Such a view
does scant justice to the significance which the New Testa-

ment gives to the Resurrection of Christ as affecting the whole of creation. And our own estimate of the nature of this significance must inevitably affect our conclusions.

To some of us it appears to be of vital importance that the supremacy of spirit should be vindicated *in* the material creation, and not merely outside or apart from it. In their view it is essential to the full Christian hope that the physical dissolution of life should be reversed by resurrection; and the basing of this hope on Jesus becomes intelligible and justifiable only if it is believed that His physical organism underwent some such transformation as the Gospel narratives suggest. To those who argue thus, the doctrine of a personal but purely spiritual immortality, which is sometimes substituted for the traditional eschatology, appears to involve a false dualism between spirit and matter.

Others of us who would not bind themselves so closely to traditional beliefs would urge, nevertheless, that both in the Apostles' Creed and the Pauline Epistles the resurrection of the dead and the Resurrection of Christ are made correlative the one to the other, and that the beliefs are connected not only by their historical origin, but also in their essential nature. They would maintain that the general freedom long claimed and used in the interpretation of the clause, "the resurrection of the flesh" (*carnis resurrectionem*), cannot leave the interpretation of the other clause, "the third day he rose again from the dead," unaffected. At the same time they would urge that belief in the General Resurrection at the last day inherited by the Church from the later Judaism, though remote and difficult for us as it stands, enshrines a belief with regard to the process of history which has been, and is, of profound importance.* From the standpoint of this faith the history of the individual and of the race cannot be rightly interpreted merely as process; the process looks to a goal and history bears a meaning for eternity. The Resurrection of Christ

* See pp. 208-211.

ought to be placed against the background of those questions and the problems which they involve. For Christians Christ anticipates the goal. The Resurrection lifts His person beyond the temporal circumstances in which He lived and died. His victory over death makes Him what He is for Christian faith—not only a great figure of history, but mediator and revealer in time of an eternal destiny for the race.

Enough has been said to indicate the variety of considerations to be introduced, and the necessity for critical caution to be observed, when the facts underlying the original tradition of Christ's Resurrection are the subject of enquiry. Such complications of the discussion are inevitable. For to Christians the Resurrection of Jesus Christ is the central fact in human history. And, when a fact is so closely linked with such momentous and far-reaching issues in heaven and earth, it is not surprising that opinions should differ when the question is raised how much in the record of it is derived from the sheer occurrence of the fact itself, and how much is due to the primitive interpretation of the fact in the minds which first perceived its transcendent significance and expressed it in forms inevitably belonging to their own manner of thought and speech. Even if we had before us the fullest conceivable statements written down by every one of the eye-witnesses themselves, the difference of opinion mentioned, so far as it refers to the Resurrection appearances, would not necessarily be diminished, and might even be intensified. For no visual experience is devoid of all element of subjective interpretation. And, even if the full and undisputed records of eye-witnesses could be studied, there would still be room for difference of judgment, (a) as to how much was seen with the bodily eye, and how much with spiritual vision; (b) how much was objectively given, and how much was the contribution of subjective interpretation; (c) how much of what is admitted to be subjective interpretation may nevertheless be considered true.

(c) The Ascension and Heavenly Priesthood.

The Commission has not felt called upon to discuss in detail the narratives of the Ascension, or the allusions to it, in the New Testament. Whatever may have been the nature of the event underlying those narratives, and whatever its relation to the Resurrection, its physical features are to be interpreted symbolically since they are closely related to the conception of heaven as a place locally fixed beyond the sky.

In the New Testament as a whole the Ascension has a twofold reference, backwards to the earthly life of Jesus, and forwards to His continuing work as Lord of the Church and to His Coming in Glory.

The theological importance of the Ascension in connection with the earthly ministry of our Lord is that it marks a definite ending of that ministry, demonstrating that His Resurrection was not a return to the conditions of this life, but a completion and transformation of this life through the removal of earthly limitations.

It thus makes plain that the destiny of completed fellowship with God is possible for human nature, and so illuminates the doctrine of human immortality.

Certain conceptions, expressed in striking phrases pictorial in character, are found in the New Testament in relation to the Ascension, such as "sat down at the right hand of God" (Mark xvi. 19), "I go to the Father" (John xiv. 12), "If I go not away the Comforter will not come unto you; but if I go, I will send him unto you" (John xvi. 7), "Christ having come a high priest of the good things to come . . . through his own blood entered in once for all into the holy place" (Heb. ix. 11, 12). These all concur in representing our Lord as inaugurating at the Ascension a new era in the redemptive activity of God.

Thus the metaphor "sitting at the right hand of God," which is included in the Creed, represents the vindication of Christ, and His triumphant exaltation to a share in the sovereignty of God with all the Divine authority and activity which that implies.

Again the phrase "I go to the Father" represents the transcending of the conditions of the earthly ministry implied in the saying, "How am I straitened until it be accomplished" (Luke xii. 50). It was because they were transcended that the disciples could go forth and work everywhere, "the Lord working with them" (Mark xvi. 20), and that the sentence "Lo, I am with you alway, even unto the end of the world" (Matt. xxviii. 20) has been fulfilled, not apocalyptically, but in the living experience of the Church.

That the Ascension necessarily precedes the sending of the Spirit is a belief developed historically in Acts and theologically in the Fourth Gospel. The relation of the Spirit to the Risen Christ is discussed elsewhere.*

The language of the Epistle to the Hebrews in connection with the eternal and timeless high priesthood of our Lord is linked with the Ascension through the conception of the Heavenly Session at the right hand of God (Heb. viii. 1). This again marks the inauguration of a new era in the fulfilment of the Old Testament ideal of sacrifice (Heb. ix. 25-28), and in the ministry of Divine intercession in heaven, which is the fulfilment through Christ's Manhood of the human approach to God in prayer.

III. THE ATONEMENT

The preaching of the Cross is the proclamation of a fact far richer than any theory of the Atonement. In the history of the Church very various theories have been held, and while affirming the fact of reconciliation to God through Christ, the Church as a whole has never formally accepted any particular explanation of that fact. Thus the doctrine of the Atonement has not been defined in the same manner and degree as the doctrine of the Incarna-

* See p. 95.

tion. But there are certain convictions which must control all Christian thinking on the Atonement.

Fundamental to the Christian doctrine of the Atonement is the conviction that it is essentially the work of God, who in Christ reconciles mankind to Himself. In subordination to this primary truth of the Divine initiative Christian theology has also emphasised that which Jesus Christ in His Manhood wrought on behalf of mankind towards God; but the Cross is first of all to be understood as a Divine Victory: God, in the Person of Jesus Christ, triumphs decisively over the forces of sin, death, and the devil.

The doctrine of the Atonement is based on the reality of God's eternal and unchanging love. That love is more than benevolence. It is a holy love, and therefore always actively affirms itself both in condemning sin and also in striving to restore and to remake the sinner.* Thus, on the one hand, God's love upholds the moral order of the universe, which is manifested both in the consequences attendant upon sin, including alienation from God and moral degeneration, and in the conviction of man's conscience that loss or unhappiness is due to him as a penalty for wrong-doing. The traditional phrase, "the wrath of God," should be interpreted in the light of these considerations. On the other hand, God's love, by its own characteristic activity of redeeming sinners, completes and transcends the moral order thus manifested. This is the essence of the contrast between "the law" and "the Gospel."

The Cross is the supreme instrument of this redemptive activity of God. In it there is at once a revelation of the holiness of God and a real breaking of the power of sin. The sinner is enabled to repent,† and he can be freely forgiven. The Divine miracle of forgiveness becomes in its

* See "Justice and Love in God," p. 53.
† It is to be remembered that there is inherent in Christianity an offer not only of "forgiveness to those who repent but of repentance to those who sin."

turn, for the forgiven sinner, the starting-point of a new and victorious spiritual life.

The Cross is not to be separated from the Person of Him who died upon it or from the content of His whole life. It is the consummation of the earthly life of Jesus. It must not be taken in isolation from that life, or from the Resurrection, Ascension, and Pentecost, or from the dispensation of the Spirit and the life of the Church. Nor must it be isolated from His Messianic claim. Historically, Jesus died as the Messiah. His Messiahship in turn must be read in the light of the personal impression of " sinlessness " which He made and of His teaching both about God and man, and about His own relation alike to God and to man; in the light of these His Messiahship is seen to involve not only that His mission is from God but that He is Himself one with God. His Death therefore is of universal significance, and it is true that He died for every one among the sons of men.

The Cross expresses the perfect self-oblation of Christ's human will. In His self-oblation unto death the ideal of all sacrifice was achieved. But it is at the same time true that the thankfulness which this self-oblation has aroused in Christian souls is due to the sense that it is not merely the self-oblation of a human will, but that it is God who in Christ, by an astonishing act of His love, has done that which man could not do for himself.

The Cross is a satisfaction for sin in so far as the moral order of the universe makes it impossible that human souls should be redeemed from sin except at a cost. Of this cost the death on the Cross is the expression. In it the moral order is not abrogated, for the Cross alone fully expresses and reveals the horrible nature and result of sin But, because this is achieved, the moral order can be, and is, transcended. In so far as the sinner responds to the love of God the chain of consequences, in accordance with which sin, left to itself, must inevitably issue in spiritual death, is broken through.

Thus the Cross is a " propitiation " and " expiation "
for the sins of the whole world. Christ, by the submission
of His sinless life to the consequence of sin, created the
conditions in which God can and does take the penitent
sinner into the full fellowship of His Kingdom and treat
Him as His child. The redeeming love of God, through
the life of Jesus Christ sacrificially offered in death upon
the Cross, acted with cleansing power upon a sin-stained
world, and so enables us to be cleansed. This is the meaning of such symbolic language in the New Testament as
the phrase " they washed their robes and made them white
in the blood of the Lamb " (Rev. vii. 14).

Thus the Atonement, though it issues from the eternal
immutability of the Divine love, truly inaugurates " a new
covenant "—that is, a new system of relations between
God and man.

IV. THE DOCTRINES OF THE HOLY SPIRIT AND OF THE TRINITY

(a) The Holy Spirit.

Participation in the Holy Spirit is set forth in the New
Testament as the distinctive mark of Christians, which
separated them off from the surrounding world; in the
Christianity of Apostolic times the experience described
as that of " receiving the Spirit " stands in the forefront
of the Christian life, at once as the secret of its transport-
ing joy and power, and as the source of that " victory "
of " faith " which could " overcome the world." The
Spirit, moreover, was described as being poured out upon
the Church as a community, as the source at once of its
fellowship and of its unity and power.

The events of the first Christian Day of Pentecost are
set forth in the Acts as marking historically the decisive
beginning of the Church's life in this its specific character
as the Spirit-enabled body. The outward symbols of wind
and fire, as recorded in the narrative, have their value as

symbolising the coming of the Spirit. What was essential was the transformed character of the infant Church and its new power to bear witness. The story of St. Peter's proclamation, in the power of the Spirit, of the Christian Gospel on the first Day of Pentecost to a cosmopolitan multitude of pilgrims stands in the forefront of the Book of the Acts as the symbol of the universality of the Christian message, and of the Church's mission to all mankind, of whatever kindred and tribe and tongue. The outpouring of the Spirit represented further to the earliest Christians the fulfilment of Old Testament prophecies of the Messianic age, and was regarded as a foretaste of the future consummation of God's Kingdom.

The word "spirit," like the word "god," has been used with many associations, and has a wide range of meanings within the New Testament itself. The origin of these has been sought by scholars in various sources, partly Jewish and partly Hellenistic. But among these usages the specifically Christian conception of the Divine Spirit is distinctive, and is clearly based upon the thought of the Old Testament, where the phrase "holy spirit" already occurs. It is, moreover, the doctrine of the New Testament that the Holy Spirit spake by the prophets.

In the New Testament the phrase "Holy Spirit" is taken as the name of that Divine Power which was especially operative in the Church. The term "holy" has not a merely ethical significance, but implies also a definite affirmation of the connexion of the Spirit with God, since in the Old Testament "holiness" in the fullest sense is the special mark of God. And though the action of the Spirit in the Church was attested in varying degrees by "charismata" ("gifts"), its special result has always been seen in sanctification, which is not merely goodness but a higher, "pneumatic" ("spiritual"), stage of development, so distinct that St. Paul could only regard it as a new creation. It is by sanctification, as shown in its ethical fruits "love, joy, peace, etc.," that the more striking and emotional of the charismata (*e.g.*, speaking with tongues) were to be tested. Sanctification is, indeed, itself a charisma. It is clear, therefore, that the Christian conception of the Spirit is different from that of a Life Force or of a Soul of the World. The Spirit is the source of the life that is distinctively Christian, and the unifying bond of the Christian fellowship.

The relation of this power of the Spirit to Jesus Himself is variously expressed in the New Testament. Some have even felt that the real thought of the New Testament would be represented by what has been described as a " Binitarian " view—viz., a doctrine of the personal deity of the Father and of the Son, with the Spirit as an influence proceeding from them upon individuals and upon the community. But this does less than justice to the relations between the Spirit and the Son which are implied in the New Testament. For in the New Testament the Holy Spirit inspires Jesus Himself, and again the Holy Spirit is sent by Jesus to continue His work for mankind.

We rightly speak of " Christ in us," for the work of the Holy Spirit in us is to fill us with that life which was in Jesus, and to make us living members of the Body of Christ; and this thought has great devotional and practical value, because it reminds us that no element in the life of the Church or the individual can be regarded as the work of the Holy Spirit unless it is in accordance with the historical revelation of God in the person of Christ.

It is important to emphasise the fact that the Holy Spirit in the New Testament is spoken of primarily as the power known by experience to be at work in the fellowship of Christians—that is, of those who have received the Gospel—rather than as a Divine energy diffused throughout the Creation. Christians may rightly interpret the activity of God elsewhere by their distinctive experience, but it is only in the fellowship of those who have known the love of God in Christ that His activity is found in that fulness of power which lies behind the use of the name " Holy Spirit " among Christians. A parallel is to be recognised between the life of the Spirit-filled Christian and the life of Jesus—Himself empowered by the Spirit— a parallel which is not expressed if we speak only of Christ in us instead of using the traditional language about the Holy Spirit. That language safeguards the conviction that our life of response to Christ is at once our response to Him, and is also not something of our own but is God Himself at work in us. And while the work of Grace may properly be spoken of as the work of Christ in us, there is a real and important distinction to be drawn between the revelation given in the Logos or Word Incarnate and the work of the Holy Spirit in the heart manifested in the Christian's response thereto. It is only from the starting-point of this Christian experience that the doctrine of the Holy Spirit, as distinct from the Logos or Word, can be applied outside that experience. But as we believe this to be the fullest spiritual experience, we accept its testimony as our surest guide to the nature of Deity.

It is through this experience that the Church has been led to speak of the Person of the Holy Spirit and to affirm His Deity and, in consequence, the doctrine of the Trinity. Much of what men have valued in this traditional language is its expression of the assurance that the Holy Spirit, as known at work in the Christian society, is experienced not as an effluence from God but as God Himself. By the help of this experience we are led to the fullest conception we can form of Deity itself. Here no formulation can be adequate, but we know that God must in Himself be such as to be the source of all that Christian experience apprehends concerning Him; and this combines with the conviction that God cannot be a merely unitary personality, because personality, as we know it, always requires for its own completeness personality other than itself. When we come to precise theories of the Divine nature apart from human experience, we are entering on a field where the task of the Church is to condemn any theories which conflict with Christian experience, not to enjoin any one theory upon all Christian people. The Church is concerned to maintain both the reality of Father, Son, and Holy Spirit, as apprehended in the experience of Christians, and the undivided Unity of God.

(b) The Trinity.

The beginning of the doctrine of the Trinity appears within the New Testament itself, notably in the explicit formulas found in St. Matthew xxviii. 19 and 2 Corinthians xiii. 14, and implicitly in a number of other passages.* But though the New Testament clearly implies a belief in the Father, the Son, and the Holy Spirit, each regarded as Divine, the metaphysical implications of this, and the character of the distinctions involved, are nowhere fully worked out.

The belief originated not in speculation but in Christian experience, which was threefold.

First, there was the traditional Jewish belief in and worship of One God, which the Christian Church inherited. The conception of the Creator as also a loving Father of His people was already present, though not central as in the teaching of our Lord, by whom it was immensely enriched and clarified.

Secondly, there was the experience of the Person of our Lord both in His earthly life and as risen from the dead, an experience which could only be expressed by giving Him the titles "Lord" and "Saviour," and which issued spontaneously in worship of Him. And this experience Christians found themselves driven to acknowledge as nothing less than an experience of God, coming to them from without, through the humanity of Jesus of Nazareth.

Thirdly, there was the influx of the Holy Spirit as power upon their lives, and here, again, their experience

* E.g., John xiv. 16-17, 26; xv. 26; 1 Cor. vi. 11; xii. 3; 2 Cor. i. 21-22; Gal. iv. 6; Eph. iv. 4-6.

was of such a character that Christians were driven to claim that it was an experience of God, an experience now of God within them as individuals and in the Christian body as a whole.

But though those three modes of experience were quite distinct they were nevertheless recognised as experiences of the One God and not of three gods. Thus the doctrine of the Trinity arose, at first hardly consciously, as an attempt to preserve the full value of this threefold experience in its distinctive elements and at the same time to assert the sole and unique supremacy of the One God.

It was inevitable that this theology should be formulated by the use of words and conceptions already in existence, such as " god," " word," " spirit," " person," " essence," and " substance." The fact that this was done by the New Testament writers, and more directly by the Fathers, does not impair the distinctively Christian character of their beliefs or their testimony to a distinctively Christian tradition, nor does it affect the close relation between those beliefs and their Christian experience.

The doctrine that thus sprang from experience has proved capable of meeting demands which arise in the sphere of metaphysical thought and has furnished a basis for those philosophic conceptions of the Divine Being which are most adequate to their theme. If God be the supreme good He cannot be less than personal : yet we cannot think of Him simply as a Person, a lonely Sovereign enthroned above the Universe : if He be One, yet His unity must be such as to comprehend and not exclude plurality ; if He be Love, His love must be such as to give scope for self-bestowal within His own Being.

Thus the revelation of God as Father, Son, and Holy Spirit is not to be regarded, on Sabellian lines, as merely relative to our experience, but gives us knowledge of the real Being of God. The purpose of the doctrine of the Trinity is to express and to safeguard the fulness of this revelation.

PART II: THE CHURCH AND SACRAMENTS

I. THE CHURCH AND MINISTRY

THE CHURCH

HAVING dealt according to our terms of reference with the Doctrines of God, of Christ, of Sin and Atonement, we turn to consider the redeemed community and the means of grace—*i.e.*, the divinely instituted means of applying God's saving grace to sinful human nature, of reconciling man to God in the fellowship which Christ has inaugurated, and of accomplishing the divine purpose for mankind. First in this connexion we turn to the Church.

PREFATORY NOTE

Many people to-day find difficulty in seeing any necessity for a Church at all. They regard religion as a purely personal and individual activity, and recognise the utility of associations of like-minded people in order that they may effectively announce their convictions for whoso will to heed and perhaps accept. But they see no need for a Christian community which is bound up with the Gospel entrusted to it in such sense that to accept the Gospel in its fulness must involve membership in that community, so that the Church is part of its own creed. *217405*

It is not our function to write a volume of apologetics, but it is relevant to submit the following consideration:

That God should fulfil His purpose in and by means of the Church is in accord with the laws or principles which, by Divine appointment, hold sway in the ordering of human life generally. The nature of man is inherently social, and the way of progress has always been found to lie in and through the development of some form of community life. The essentially social nature of Man and of the sin of Man calls for a social redemption, constituting a fellowship of those who have laid hold of the redemption wrought and offered by God through Christ.

Thus the constitution of human nature generally is such as to call for a community as the channel of the divine activity in redemption, while that activity itself is distinct from the channel through which it operates; for it is a vital element in Christian faith that God Himself and not man, nor any tendency of human nature in general, takes the initiative in redemption as in creation.

There is no doubt that in the Bible and in Christian tradition the action of God through a community is emphasised, and we start accordingly from this point of view.

A. THE CHURCH IN SCRIPTURE

The Church in the New Testament is the body of those who are to be the heirs of the coming kingdom, and in whom "the powers of the Age to come" are already at work. It is God's creation for Himself of a "people for His own possession." It is the new, redeemed People of God—the "Israel" of God after the Spirit. This is constituted by the acts of God of which the Gospel is the proclamation, and the whole life and activity of the Christian Church derive their distinctive character from the Gospel.

To some schools of thought it has seemed more important to emphasise the freshness of the new start through the new covenant, without denying the continuity of the Christian Church with Israel; to others it has seemed more important to emphasise the continuity with Israel without denying the freshness of the start. The truth appears to be that both are of vital importance, and there should be no question of sacrificing the one to the other: the need is to relate them rightly.

It has therefore to be recognised that the Church has

connexions backwards as well as forwards. It is the fulfilment of Israel, and as such its beginnings are lost in the
period where history fades into the mythology of origins.
Its members are described as having been "chosen" in
Christ "before the foundation of the world" (Eph. i. 4).
"Abraham, Isaac, and Jacob," as types of faithful Israel-
ites, are conceived as belonging to it, despite the fact that
they lived on earth before Christ came, for they were the
"heirs" with us "of the same promise" (Heb. xi. 9;
cf. xi. 39, 40). At the same time, the principle expressed
in St. Augustine's phrase, *multi qui foris videntur intus
sunt, et multi qui intus videntur foris sunt* (Aug., *De
Bapt.*, v. 38), must be held to apply to pre-Christian times
—"Many shall come from the east and the west, and shall
sit down with Abraham, and Isaac, and Jacob in the kingdom of heaven" (Matt. viii. 11; Luke xiii. 29).

It is to be presumed that the term ἐκκλησία in the New
Testament is not derived from the ordinary Greek use, of
which the associations were not directly relevant, but
follows the established use of the word in the Septuagint,
where it is the equivalent of the Hebrew *Kahal*, meaning
the solemn assembly of Israel, the people of God.

It is noteworthy that phrases and terms which in the Old
Testament denote or describe Israel in its ideal aspect as
the people of God are in the New Testament carried over
and applied to the Church as the new, redeemed Israel in
which God's ideal for His people is held to be actualised.
Thus the Church is not only the "Israel of God" (Gal. vi.
16); it is also (see 1 Pet. ii. 9-10) the "elect race" (cf.
Deut. x. 15; Isa. xliii. 20), the "royal priesthood" (Exod.
xix. 6), the "holy nation" (*ibid.*; cf. also Deut. vii. 6;
Isa. lxii. 12), the "people for God's own possession"
(Exod. xix. 5; Deut. vii. 6; Isa. xliii. 21; Mal. iii. 17),
and the "people of God" that has now "obtained mercy"
(Hos. i. 6, 9, 10, ii. 23). The "twelve apostles of the
Lamb" correspond as "foundations" with the twelve
Patriarchs (Rev. xxi. 14; cf. Eph. ii. 20; Matt. xix. 28;

Luke xxii. 30). The "new covenant" supersedes and re-
places, but corresponds with, the old (1 Cor. xi. 25 and
synoptic parallels; *cf.* Exod. xxiv. 8). Even the figure of
the "true vine" (= Christ), wherein the faithful must
inhere, and whereof they are "branches" (John xv. 1 *sqq.*),
is to be understood probably as "involving as part of its
background" an implicit allusion to the reconstitution in
Christ of the "vine" (= Israel) which God had anciently
"brought out of Egypt" (Ps. lxxx. 8 *sqq.*; *cf.* Isa. v.
1-7; Mark xii. 1 *sqq.* and parallels).

Yet it is the affirmation of the New Testament that
the ancient Israel—"Israel after the flesh"—has forfeited
its claim to the promises. When the Messiah, in and
through whom alone the vocation of Israel as the people
of God could be realised, stands alone before the high
priest, deserted even by the chosen disciples, His rejection
is a turning-point, decisive both for the Messiah Himself
and for Israel who rejected Him. He is the sole representative at that moment of God's holy people; He bears in His
own Person the whole burden of Israel's appointed destiny.
His activity thus constituted plainly a new beginning,
transforming as well as fulfilling the old order. The
ἐκκλησία of God was among the things that in Him "have
become new" (2 Cor. v. 17).*

The Church, in its Christian form, as the new redeemed Israel, is the Church of the Spirit. It is, as such,
universal; it transcends the boundaries of race, language,
and colour ("Ye all are one man in Christ Jesus"—Gal.
iii. 28; *cf.* Col. iii. 11); there is from henceforth but "one
body" and "one spirit" (Eph. iv. 4). The New Testament phrase "fellowship of the spirit" (κοινωνία τοῦ
πνεύματος) denotes not "brotherliness" merely—even
though "love of the brethren" is in the New Testament
the pledge and proof of the love of God (*cf.* 1 John iv.

---

* Even so, St. Paul in another context is careful to emphasise
the idea of a real continuity with the ancient "olive-tree" of the
Synagogue (Rom. xi. 13-24).

20, 21)—but joint participation in the Spirit poured forth from Christ and from the Father.

Although in the primary sense of the term "Church" there can only be one Church, nevertheless we read in the New Testament of ἐκκλησίαι or "Churches." As thus used in the plural, the term denotes local groups or "assemblies" of Christians, each of which, in its own locality, or in the place where it assembles, is held to be *the* Church; it is a local manifestation (distinguishable, *quâ* local, from others) of the one indivisible Church or ἐκκλησία of God. (There were, of course, in the New Testament period no competing or rival "denominations" within Christendom.)

The life of the Church is not merely of this "world" or "age." The Church, as the society of those who are to inherit the coming Kingdom of God, has its roots in eternity; its "citizenship" (in St. Paul's phrase) is "in heaven" (Phil. iii. 20). So likewise the "gates of Hades" (or Death) do not "prevail" over it; physical death constitutes no separation in the spiritual fellowship of the redeemed, which transcends death and the grave.

Salvation is offered to men through the redemptive activity of God. It can be received by the individual only through the free response of his own will. But the salvation offered is, according to the teaching of the New Testament, not merely individual; it is, indeed, in one and the same act, the reconciliation of the individual with God, and his enfranchisement in the Communion of Saints, which is the fellowship of the redeemed, united to one another in the communion of the Holy Spirit. It is as a member of the Body, as a "fellow-heir" and a "joint-partaker" in the common "inheritance" of the saints," that the individual, through faith in Christ, hopes for salvation—a salvation which is essentially social and corporate.* The

* The word "salvation" is here used, not in the sense of God's first gift of forgiveness or man's first appropriation of it, but rather as denoting the fulness of redemption.

saying *extra ecclesiam nulla salus* expresses, therefore, a vital truth; though it must not, of course, be understood to affirm without qualifications the indispensability, with a view to " salvation," of outward and visible membership in any particular society of Christians on earth, or indeed (of necessity) in the Church as visibly organised in this world at all.

The Church is described in Scripture as the " bride " of Christ, which He is to present to Himself " glorious, without spot or wrinkle or any such thing " (Eph. v. 27)— a description of the Church as destined one day to be perfected (Rev. xxi. 9 *sqq.*); as the " body " of Christ, of which the faithful are " members " (1 Cor. xii. 12-27), and of which Christ is the " head " (Eph. i. 22, iv. 15; Col. i. 18); as the sphere within which, it is implied, the Spirit specially operates (Eph. iv. 4); and as being destined to grow up in Christ into unity, so as to constitute in Him one " full-grown man," the *pleroma* or " fulness " of the Christ who is at last to be " all and in all " (Eph iv. 13, i. 23; Col. iii. 11).

It is noteworthy that in these latter passages the goal of perfected unity is placed in the future, though the purpose of God to achieve it is regarded as sure.

B. The Christian Church in Idea and in History

The life of the Church as visible and militant here in earth is expressed and manifested in the visible life of Christendom, the beginnings of which, as an historical phenomenon, go back to and spring from the redemptive work of the Lord Jesus Christ in His life upon earth. The New Testament traces back the beginning of the organised life of the Church in this sense to the little company of disciples of Jesus, assembled together under the leadership of the Apostles who had been " made " and " sent out " by Him, upon whom the Spirit descended at Pentecost, who became the nucleus of an ever-expanding missionary brotherhood (admission to which was by Baptism, on the basis of repentance and faith in Jesus as the appointed Messiah and Redeemer), and of whom we read that they " continued steadfastly in the apostles' teaching, and in the fellowship, and in the breaking of bread, and in the prayers " (Acts ii. 42).

But the Christian Church, from the point of view of those who believe in it, is something more than a phenomenon of history. It has its roots, as has already been said, in God's ancient Israel, which in a true sense finds its fulfilment and consummation in the new Society which emerges historically with Jesus Christ and His Apostles; but a merely historical survey, whether of the Bible, or of the history of the Church as an institution, will not itself yield (though it may suggest) all that believers mean when they declare: "I *believe* in . . . the Holy Catholic Church." The Church, in other words, is for Christians an object not only of sight, but of spiritual discernment or insight. It emerges in history, but it is essentially a Fellowship, constituted by a relation between God and Man, which in the last resort must be discerned and apprehended by faith.

An historical person—Jesus of Nazareth—and a whole process of historical events (the story of Israel, the events underlying the Gospel history, and their sequel in Christendom) are indeed essential to the idea of the Church; but the events of the sacred history, and the story of Jesus Himself, can have this significance only in so far as they are recognised as in some sense organs of revelation and means of Fellowship between God and Man. The meaning of the Church discloses itself when we ask general questions as to the relation between God and Mankind, and answer them by the affirmation that Jesus Christ is the revelation of the ultimate truth about God which it concerns Man to know. "He that hath seen me hath seen the Father." "No man cometh to the Father but by me." Fellowship in the Church of Christ is Fellowship with the Father, which we have in Jesus Christ as the Son. But from the standpoint of faith, which looks forward to the consummation of all things, the Church is mankind redeemed in Christ.

This fellowship between Man and God can be otherwise described by saying that the Church is the whole company of those who share in the regenerate life. When the Church is so conceived, its unity is comparable to that of a race or people, which, while it may be divided as regards the outward organisations which condition its life, yet has a real and concrete unity underlying these divisions. Further, even if there is division in political organisation, the unity of a race or people may find external expression in a common outlook and common practices. So the unity, which is inherent in the nature of the Church, is not destroyed by outward divisions, and is grounded, according to both Pauline and Johannine doctrine, in the unity of God Himself.

Nevertheless Christians, as creatures of time and history, are not exempt from the necessity of giving definite shape to this life which they share in common; and they do so in forms which are at once correlated to their own past history and to present needs. Examples of such forms which have actually been developed are the formulation of the faith, the articulation of the ministry, and the liturgical structure of worship. Some such forms are essential for the perpetuation of the Christian Society in the process of history, though at the same time no one particular system of such forms is to be taken as being of necessity constitutive of the fundamental idea of the Church. That idea, as has been already stated above, hinges essentially upon the unity of mankind as redeemed in Christ, and as in Him finding fellowship with the Father, and thereby also with one another.

The Church has traditionally been affirmed to be characterised by the "notes" of Unity, Holiness, Catholicity, and Apostolicity.

(*a*) *Unity.*—The Church is one, for it is the Body of Christ. This unity is not confined to the present world; all those who are in Christ are members of His Body, whether they are in this world or beyond it. What has been said above is immediately relevant to this note of Unity.

It is clear that this fundamental unity ought to be expressed in the visible unity of the Church on earth. Such full outward expression would involve unity in the declaration of a common faith, in proclamation of the Gospel and in the offering of worship, and all members of Christ on earth would be in visible communion with one another; differences in the interpretation of the faith and in forms of worship are inevitable, but such differences would be recognised as differences within the one Body; they would not interfere with the bond of peace, of which sacramental unity is the outward sign.

It is clear that the actual state of Christendom is very far from realising this unity. Further, it frequently happens that the life of Christian bodies appears to be more vigorous when they exist side by side in separation from one another, and less vigorous when one particular body has undisputed possession of a wide field. This diminished vigour may be due in part to the tacit assumption that unity demands such a measure of uniformity in faith and worship as, in effect, leaves no room for healthy criticism, and to the spirit of complacency which the absence of criticism tends to foster. The defects, however, which spring from a too rigid uniformity do not inherently belong to visible unity as such. And we believe that, whenever the Church is loyal to its mission, it will retain or seek to recover outward unity both in order and in the expression of its faith. We hold, therefore, that the Church of England is entirely right in attempting to combine retention of the historical creeds and Ministry of the Church with recognition, within that framework, of various types of Christian teaching and devotion.

(*b*) *Holiness.*—The Creed affirms that the Church is "holy." In this it repeats the language of the New Testament, where all Christians are called "saints"; this means on the one hand that they belong to the Holy God, are members of His holy people, and have received His Holy Spirit, and on the other that they are under obligation to exhibit holiness in actual sanctification of life. Between a Church charged with such a vocation and the world in which it works there must inevitably be tension; in face of this the first duty of the Church is to maintain the faith and life entrusted to it, and this may involve withdrawal from the world in varying manners and degrees. But such withdrawal must never be an abandonment of the world to its own tendencies, but a means of bearing witness to the Gospel before the world.

It is plain that at no time did all Christians, corporately or individually, so fully respond to their position as to exhibit entire sanctification. In New Testament times this contrast between expectation and achievement was already apparent and an occasion of perplexity. What was the position in the "holy" people of God of members who were guilty of grave offences? Could Christians, who after Baptism had fallen into open and grievous sin, be received back into fellowship? Hence arose in later times secessions from a church that included bad Christians, and also attempts to form a "pure" church consisting of none but the actually and completely holy. But our use of the term in the Creed does not involve the claim that the Church is in this sense actually holy. Rather it is holy as being a body set apart for God and owing its existence to His will, and therefore called to exhibit that life of holiness which God demands, by an ever-deepening response to His Holy Spirit. Thus holiness denotes not present attainment but the character of the Church in the divine purpose. The Church exists to be both the home of Christians, a school of moral growth and discipline, and a means of grace. In spite of the manifold sins and scandals which disfigure Church history, it is not right either to infer that there is no real visible church, or to break it up in the vain attempt to found a " pure " church consisting only of members whose lives are perfectly controlled by the Holy Spirit.

(c) *Catholicity.*—The title " Catholic " as applied to the Christian Church is first found early in the second century in the Epistles of Ignatius (*ad Smyrn.* 8). There it denotes " the general or universal Church, as opposed to a particular body of Christians."[*] At a later date it acquired the technical meaning of " the Great Church," regarded as the main guardian of the Christian tradition, as opposed to heretical sects which broke off from the main body. At the same time, the use of the term from early days connoted the belief that " the Great Church " was potentially universal and all-inclusive, as entrusted with a mission to all mankind. Since the date of the Great Schism, 1054, the Roman Catholic Church and the Eastern Orthodox Church have each claimed to be the one Catholic Church, at least in the sense of being the sole authoritative guardian of the apostolic tradition. In the Church of England, on the other hand, it has been a widely held doctrine that no single communion can justly claim any such exclusive title, but that the term " Catholic " is properly used of all those Churches which maintain the faith of the Creeds and the Ecumenical Councils, the practice of the Sacraments, and the episcopate in historical succession from the Apostles. Other Christians, including many Anglicans, have ceased to think that any body or bodies of believers ought to be called " Catholic " in distinction from others, except purely as a matter of terminological convenience; but almost all of these would insist on the value of the idea of the Catholicity of the Church as emphasising the potential universality which is implied by its divinely appointed mission to the world. Thus there is general agreement that the note of Catholicity presents the positive relation of the Church to the world, viz., its

* Lightfoot, *ad loc.*

potential inclusiveness resting on a divine mission, just as the note of Holiness presents the negative relation of the Church to the world, viz., its separateness as consecrated to God.

More, however, than this is required if the meaning of the term "Catholic" is to be fully drawn out. At one time there actually and visibly existed in Christendom a "Great Church" of which all that is meant by this term could be broadly affirmed. But after the Great Schism this manifestly was no longer so, and indeed at an even earlier date there had been great and continuous divisions in the Eastern Church. The difficulty thus created in the use of the term "Catholic" has been further aggravated by later divisions, notably those of the Reformation period. Nevertheless, that difficulty should not be allowed to lead to the abandonment of the ideal of Catholicity.

The inclusive unity for which the term "Catholic" stands implies that the Church is supra-national, and links in fellowship the citizens of every rank in every nation, though in its mission to each it may rightly admit a certain recognition of distinctive national characteristics. Further, the appeal to the Catholic Church or to Catholic tradition appears to us to involve in modern circumstances a refusal to become wholly immersed in the tradition of any one Christian communion, and a determination to recognise the experience and teaching of Christendom as a whole as possessing more fully than any partial system the authority of the Catholic Church. It is the mark of a sectarian mind to refuse to acknowledge what is of permanent truth and value in the tradition of other communions; the "Catholic" should never be "sectarian," however large the "sect" to which he belongs.

The term "Catholic" also implies the conviction that according to the Divine Will the true Church on earth was from the beginning, and was meant to continue doctrinally and sacramentally, as well as spiritually, one. The recovery of this unity can only be found in a synthesis which does full justice to the truth represented in every tradi-tion.

(*d*) *Apostolicity*.—The Church has been called apostolic primarily in that it preserves the essential tradition of the apostolic preaching and teaching, and maintains, as a safe-guard of that tradition, a duly appointed order of ministers, who derive their commission in historical succession from the original apostolate. The Church may also be called apostolic as being charged with the mission to bear witness to Christ and to declare His Gospel before the world. By its apostolicity, therefore, the Church of to-day is linked to the Church of primitive times through an essential identity of doctrine, a continuity of order, and a fellowship in mis-sionary duty.

The divisions among Christians, as a result of which Christendom is split up into a number of competing and rival " denominations " and " communions," are not the least grievous among the scandals that have been men-tioned. There is a long history behind them; and in some cases, at least, there are serious divergences of principle involved, such as must needs make the way to reconciliation neither easy nor obvious. It is, moreover, to be remem-bered that the life of the Christian Body is enriched by varieties of emphasis and interpretation, and that historic-ally these have been developed in their familiar forms in the several communions which have resulted from the divisions in the Church. Yet it often happens that in developing one valuable interpretation of the Gospel, a particular com-munion becomes unduly restricted to this interpretation, while others may fail to receive the benefit as a result of their separation from that communion. Further, there is a natural tendency to form sectional loyalties, which make men unappreciative of new ideas arising outside their own communion, and prompt them to defend, out of regard for their founders and heroes of the past, traditions for which the justifying circumstances have disappeared. Thus any gain due to division is offset by loss to the whole Body and to its parts. The gain can be secured without loss only through a real combination of unity with liberty.

The term " schism " has historically been used with some fluctuation of meaning. It should, however, be recognised that " schism " is, in fact, a division within the Christian Body. That Body is not to be thought of as consisting of a single true Church, or group of Churches, with a number of " schismatic " bodies gathered about it, but as a whole which is in a state of division or " schism." The various " denominations " may and do differ in respect of the degree in which they approximate either to orthodoxy of doctrine or to fulness of organised life; but, just in so far as their very existence as separate organisations constitutes a real division within Christendom, it becomes true to affirm that if any are in schism, all are in schism, so long as the breaches remain unhealed, and are affected by its consequences, at least in the sense that each in its own degree suffers the loss or defect involved in schism; and this irrespective of the question on which side rests the major responsibility for the schism.

C. INSTITUTIONS OF THE CHURCH

The Church exists to worship God made known in Christ, and bears His commission in this world to bear witness to Him, to proclaim His Gospel, to bring all mankind within the membership, range, and fellowship of the redeemed Society, and to gain for the principles involved in the Gospel application to the conditions of human life from time to time. In so far as conditions vary from age to age and from place to place, the Church's methods must vary. For the maintenance, however, of the Church's own essential nature as the fellowship of those who have received the Gospel and are called to bear witness to it before those who have not received it, the Church has four institutional safeguards of its own continuity in the activity of that fellowship and of that witness. These are the Scriptures, the Creeds, the Sacraments, and the Ministry.

The Church is constituted by the acts of God, and under the guidance of the Holy Spirit has accepted the Scriptures as bearing inspired witness to those acts; the Scriptures therefore take priority over all other standards of faith and doctrine; and among the Scriptures those of the New Testament again take priority as containing the record of the fulfilment, and therefore the clue to the true theological significance, of those of the Old Testament, and as setting forth the Good News of the redemption and reconstitution of the People of God in the Person and redemptive work of Jesus the Christ.

The Scriptures of the Old Testament the Church took over and claimed as its own by inheritance from Judaism. The Canon of the New Testament was formed gradually by a process of discrimination among Christian writings of the Apostolic and Sub-apostolic ages which were read as authoritative in the Church. The Church itself decided in the course of the first few centuries what writings should be accounted canonical. But the Gospel contained in Scripture is in no sense the work of the Church, though of necessity it rested with the Church to decide what writings authentically contain it. The Gospel itself is the proclamation concerning what God is and what He has done for mankind, as disclosed in the Birth, Life, Activity, Teaching, Death, Resurrection, and Ascension of Jesus Christ, and in the consequent gift of the Holy Spirit.

The Creeds are formulations of the faith of the Church. In the Scriptures of the New Testament we already see the beginnings of the tendency to formulate Christian confessions of faith (cf., e.g., Rom. x. 9). The authority of a Creed rests upon its acceptance by the body of believers as a true expression of scriptural doctrine, and not merely upon its formulation or acceptance by a Council.*

The Sacraments are characteristic acts of the Church

* See p. 37.

as the fellowship of believers. Their nature and significance are discussed elsewhere.

The Ministry is a continuing institution in the fellowship of believers from the time when the Lord " appointed Twelve, that they might be with him, and that he might send them forth to make the proclamation and to have authority to cast out devils " (Mark iii. 14).

THE MINISTRY

A. ITS PRINCIPLE

The fundamental Christian Ministry is the Ministry of Christ. There is no Christian Priesthood or Ministry apart from His. His priestly and ministerial function is to reconcile the world to God in and through Himself, by His Incarnation and by His " one sacrifice once offered," delivering men from the power of sin and death.

The Church as the Body of Christ, sharing His life, has a ministerial function derived from that of Christ. In this function every member has his place and share according to his different capabilities and calling. The work of the Church is to bring all the various activities and relationships of men under the control of the Holy Spirit, and in this work each member has his part. The particular function of the official Ministry can only be rightly understood as seen against the background of this universal ministry.*

The Church on the Day of Pentecost is set before us in the book of the Acts of the Apostles as a body of believers having within it, as its recognised focus of unity and organ of authority, the Apostolate, which owed its origin to the action of the Lord Himself. There was not first an Apostolate which gathered a body of believers about itself; nor was there a completely structureless collection of believers

* In the text, ministry is printed with a small initial when used in the wider sense, with a capital when it means the specialised Ministry.

which gave authority to the Apostles to speak and act on its behalf. To suppose that the organisation of the Church must have begun in one or other of these ways is to misconceive the situation. From the first there was the fellowship of believers finding its unity in the Twelve.* Thus the New Testament bears witness to the principle of a distinctive Ministry, as an original element, but not the sole constitutive element, in the life of the Church. This fact is of great importance in any consideration of the relation which should subsist between the ministerial Body of Christ and the Ministry which is its organ for the performance of certain distinctive and characteristic acts.

The Ministry, then, is to be regarded as an original and essential element in the Church. We must remember that in a historical process of growth the appearance of formality is often increased in retrospect, and we must beware of reading back into the earliest period the systematic organisation of later times. St. Paul was called to the Apostolate by a special revelation; James, the brother of the Lord, who presided over the Church in Jerusalem, was not one of the Twelve; the position of Barnabas does not fit easily into a clear-cut scheme. But a distinction corresponding to that drawn later between Clergy and Laity— κλῆρος and λαός—is there from the outset. In the same way, whether or not the succession of the Ministry as known from (at latest) the end of the second century can be traced through all its stages to the Apostles, yet the Ministry exists in succession to the original Apostolate. The Ministry does not exist apart from the Body, nor the Body apart from the Ministry. But Christ, in drawing men to Himself, unites them in a fellowship of which the Apostolate, which He appointed, and the Ministry, which is its successor, are the ministerial organs. The commission to exercise Ministry is bestowed through those who

* The story of the election of Matthias is evidence of a concern to maintain the Apostolic number, and therefore also for the Apostolate as an element within the Church.

already hold it, but it comes from the Risen, Reigning, and Present Lord Himself.

The same Risen Christ may call men to be prophets, evangelists, or teachers, and in Pauline lists these appear, together with Apostles, as His gifts to the Church. Gradually the situation was defined under the pressure of experience interpreted by the guidance of the Holy Spirit. But while the upshot was the securely established Ministry of succession, there always remains the power of God to give to the Church prophets, evangelists, and teachers apart from the succession no less than within it; and room should be freely found within the ordered life of the Church for the exercise of their gifts, while they, on their part, must be careful to fulfil their own vocation with due recognition of the function of the regular Ministry. Only if we recognise these wider and more episodic activities of the Spirit in the Church can we rightly conceive the principles which determine the nature of the regular Ministry and its place in the Church's life.

The Spirit of Christ is at work throughout the body of believers subduing all things to Himself. But this does not mean that any member may perform any function indifferently, any more than every function of the human body can be performed indifferently by any limb. Each has its own function, and the one life of the body is expressed through the due performance by each of its own function. The official and ritual functions of the Church exist in order to express and mediate the life of Christ in His Body, alike in worship offered to the Father and in ministry to the needs of men; and for these functions an official Ministry is required, holding commission to act in the name of the whole Church. This necessity for the regular Ministry is not diminished by the fact that many laymen are effectual prophets and evangelists through whom the saving power of the life of Christ is expressed and mediated, sometimes with striking and enduring results. The distinctive functions of the Ministry, which, besides the regular preaching of the Gospel, include the continuous leadership of the people in worship, systematic teaching and pastoral care, would still be necessary even though " all the Lord's people were prophets." More-over, the effective witness of Christian prophets and evangelists, either within the Ministry or without it, is given from within the Church, and is an expression of the continuous life of the Church which the regular Ministry of Word and Sacraments sustains from generation to generation.

B. Its Form

It has been a common practice to search the New Testament for precedents and principles of Church Order, with the understanding that if these were found they would be at once decisive. Appeal to the New Testament has been made by defenders of every form of Order—Papal, Episcopal, Presbyterian, and Congregationalist—for sanction of what they upheld. There is not sufficient agreement among scholars to give hope of unity through such an appeal; and there are those who hold that more than one form of Order can be illustrated from the New Testament. Appeal to the New Testament therefore fails to produce agreement.

Another familiar view has been that the primitive form is not decisive, but that the continuous historical development which led to universal acceptance of a certain Order is decisive. But the term " universal," as used in the context of our actual problem, raises insuperable difficulties, for there is no Order now accepted by all who claim the name of Christian, and universal acceptance can only be predicated by excluding from the body of the Church all those who do not accept.

We believe that there has come a change in our outlook which must be fully acknowledged. We no longer regard precedents, as such, as decisive for all time.* Their

* This view has been increasingly emphasised of late, but it is not entirely a modern discovery, and we may claim to stand in line

authority depends upon the principles which they embody, and upon the conformity of those principles to the Mind of Christ. Indeed the principles of Church Order in the most general sense are grounded in the Being of God, who " is not a God of confusion but of peace." Further, the Church, as the fellowship of Christians, is the people and flock of which Christ is " Shepherd and Bishop." Its order and structure are necessarily such as to provide the

---

with the classical defender of Anglican polity. Arguing against the Puritan contention that " Nothing ought to be established in the Church, but that which is commanded in the word of God," Hooker will not allow the Puritan claim that the Genevan discipline does in fact reproduce the order of the New Testament. " Our persuasion is," he writes, " that no age ever had knowledge of it, but only ours; that they which defend it devised it; that neither Christ nor His Apostles at any time taught it, but the contrary." The " government that is by Bishops " he holds to be ' that which best agreeth with the Sacred Scripture." Therefore ne urges that " if we did seek to maintain that which most advantageth our own cause, the very best way for us, and the strongest against them were to hold even as they do, that in Scripture there must needs be found some particular form of Church polity which God hath instituted, and which for that very cause belongeth to all churches and to all times." But this line he will not adopt, for " with any such partial eye to respect our-selves, and by cunning to make those things seem the truest which are the fittest to serve our purpose, is a thing which we neither like, nor mean to follow." His own view is that a distinction must be drawn between " points of doctrine " and " matters of regiment." " To make new articles of faith and doctrine, no man thinketh it lawful; new laws of government, what Commonwealth or Church is there which maketh not either at one time or another?" After a careful defence of the distinction between immutability and divine institution he concludes : " Neither God's being author of Laws for government of His Church, nor his com-mitting them unto Scripture, is any reason sufficient wherefore all Churches should for ever be bound to keep them without change." And again : " [Matters of ecclesiastical polity] are not so strictly nor everlastingly commanded in Scripture, but that unto the com-plete form of Church polity much may be requisite which the Scripture teacheth not, and much which it hath taught become unrequisite, some time because we need not use it, some time also because we cannot." (*Laws of Ecclesiastical Polity*, Bk. III, cc. x., xi.)

means through which He may exercise His oversight and pastoral care. In this sense provision for pastoral oversight—*Episcope*—is an essential element in the life of the Church. Moreover it belongs to the full witness of the Church that it should be manifestly one, not only throughout the world at any one time, but also through successive generations; for its task is continuously to proclaim and apply the salvation once for all wrought by Christ.

C. THE MINISTRY AS ORGAN OF UNITY AND CONTINUITY

It is of practical religious importance that the worship in which the individual believer takes part is the worship of the whole Church, and it is essential to the idea of the Ministry which leads that worship that it is an organ of the whole Church, not of a single group or congregation. Further, since it is a function of the Ministry thus to be a symbol and effective instrument of the unity of the Church, it is appropriate that it should be constituted by a rite of ordination having an agreed, universal, and traditional character. The ideal of the Church's Ministry requires that it be " acknowledged by every part of the Church as possessing . . . the authority of the whole body."*

Such considerations make it clear why the Church has in fact preserved and set store by the continuity of the Ministry as, along with the Scriptures, Creeds, and Sacraments, a guarantee of its continuous identity. They also make it clear why, in our judgment, the acceptance of any Order of Ministry cannot be based on considerations of evangelistic effectiveness alone, apart from any regard for continuity and unity.

The life of the Church is continuous from generation to generation; continuity of ministerial commission embodies in the sphere of Order the principle of Apostolicity in the sense of continuous mission from Christ and the Father

* See "An Appeal to All Christian People," in *Report of the Lambeth Conference*, 1920.

(John xx. 21). The commission continuously given expresses the unceasing exercise of the pastoral oversight of the Good Shepherd in His care for the "lambs" and "sheep" of His flock (John xxi. 15-17). We have already pointed out that the Apostles governed the early Christian community as having a commission from the Lord, and that their pastoral authority was not derived from election by the flock, but was inherent in the office to which they were called by Christ. The ministers of the Church in all later generations have possessed a pastoral authority as themselves holding commission from the Lord in succession to the Apostles, and the status of ministers in this succession has been guaranteed from one generation to another by a continuously transmitted commission : consequently to preserve continuity in this respect is at all times of great importance. In the specific sphere of Order, it is the pledge of the Ministry's commission from Christ Himself; moreover, it expresses the unity of the Church to-day with the Church of all ages.

On the other hand, important as such continuity is, it is possible to pay too high a price for it. There are possible circumstances, such as gross and long-continued abuse of authority by its rightful holders, where fundamental loyalty to the Lord may involve rebellion against the existing ministry, and even the establishment of a new ministry, as the lesser of two evils, though still a grave evil. Because of the spiritual character of the Church not only the normal duty of loyalty, but also the duty in the last resort of revolution is more imperative in Church than in State. On the other hand, the view advanced implies that such a revolution is only justifiable when there is no reasonable possibility of preserving continuity without sacrifice of what is still more important, and that any breach of continuity should be repaired, alike for its own sake and in the interest of unity, as soon as is compatible with due regard to the whole historical and practical position.

Thus it will be seen that we cannot accept a conception of ordination which is exclusively hierarchical, as though the ministerial succession alone constituted the essence of the Church apart from any continuing body of the faithful, or, on the other hand, a conception which would make the ministry representative only of the congregation, or of the whole body of the laity, or, again, a conception which represents it as having its justification only in administrative convenience. The Ministry is to be regarded as having its entire existence and significance within the life of the Body as a whole. The fact that the Ministry does not derive its commission from a Church which initially had no Ministry, but derives it, within the Church, from Christ Himself, the Head of the Church, His Body, does not involve the consequence that it can perform its function apart from the Body. Continuity of ministerial succession, though it is the pledge of unity and continuity in the sphere of Order, is not the only pledge of the unity and continuity of the Church's life.

D. THE EPISCOPATE

Historically the combined principles of oversight and continuity have been associated with the institution known as the Episcopate. The Historic Episcopate has a position as an organ of continuity which belongs, in fact, to no other order of Ministry in that it early became the one recognised organ for transmitting the ministerial commission and that for more than a thousand years it alone held the field.* That this is so is part of the bequest of history, an element in the given totality of the Christian tradition. Thus the actual historical process of the development of the ministry is of high importance as a symbol and guarantee of continuity with the Church's origin.

The institution of Episcopacy—that is, of oversight

* This is the point mainly emphasised in connexion with the Historic Episcopate in the Report of the Committee on Christian Unity presented to the Lambeth Conference of 1930. (See *Report of the Lambeth Conference.* 1930, pp. 114-116.)

exercised under a continuously given commission—has taken a variety of forms, and it cannot be maintained that any one particular form of it is necessary. So, for example, the monarchical diocesan episcopate might conceivably be changed to a collegiate episcopate if this seemed likely to render better service; we shall give reasons shortly for supposing that this would not be so. But in any case, whatever the form that Episcopacy may take, the transition should be effected by the bestowal of commission through those who have received commission to bestow it. We do not doubt that God has accepted and used other Ministries which through breach of continuity in the past are deficient in outward authorisation; but we are convinced that the Anglican Communion has been right to regard the historic Episcopate as in a special sense the organ of unity and continuity.

The argument for Episcopacy derives its strength from the convergence of many different considerations. We may state these in summary form; but the very nature of the office depends upon the union of all these elements:

1. The Episcopate symbolises and secures in an abiding form the apostolic mission and authority within the Church; historically the Episcopate became the organ of this mission and authority.

2. In early times the continuous successions of Bishops in tenure of the various Sees were valued because they secured the purity of apostolic teaching as against (for example) the danger of the introduction of novel and erroneous teaching by means of writings or secret traditions falsely ascribed to apostolic authors. No doubt the need for this safeguard became less urgent when authoritative formulations of doctrine were drawn up and the Canon of Scripture was finally fixed. But it has remained a function of the Episcopate to guard the Church against erroneous teaching.

3. The Bishop in his official capacity represents the whole Church in and to his diocese, and his diocese in and

to the Councils of the Church. He is thus a living representative of the unity and universality of the Church.

4. The Bishop in his diocese represents the Good Shepherd; the idea of pastoral care is inherent in his office. Both clergy and laity look to him as Chief Pastor, and he represents in a special degree the paternal quality of pastoral care.

5. Inasmuch as the unity of the Church is in part secured by an orderly method of making new ministers and the Bishop is the proper organ of unity and universality, he is the appropriate agent for carrying on through ordination the authority of the apostolic mission of the Church.

It is, as has been said, the coalescence of all of these elements in a single person that gives to the Episcopate its peculiar importance. Such coalescence could not effectively take place in a committee or assembly. And the full development of these several elements will prevent the undue development of any. Thus the Bishop cannot be a true representative of his diocese in the Councils of the Church at large if he administers it in an autocratic spirit, but only if he is in close and sympathetic relations with both clergy and laity.

In the Church, the household of God, the Bishop should represent in his own appointed area the principle of Fatherhood. An assemblage of persons cannot be a "father in God"; and the lack of this element is an impoverishment of the Church's spiritual life. The Bishop should always exercise Oversight as a father, not "as lording it over the flock"; and the individual man who holds the office of a Bishop should never forget that he is himself a sheep of Christ's flock who needs as much as any the benefit of pastoral care.

E. THE GRADES OF THE MINISTRY

The actual duties and status of Bishops, Priests, and Deacons have varied greatly within the continuity of a long historical development, but in principle all are traceable to the Church of the New Testament. It is not to be supposed that development in this respect has necessarily ceased, or that the threefold ministry may not require further adaptation to the needs of the Church in a perpetually changing world.

The Bishop is the chief minister of the Church in his diocese, and through him the commission to exercise various forms of Ministry is given, because his office comprises them all. He has the cure of souls throughout his diocese, and is in a special sense the representative in his diocese of the Universal Church. He is the proper minister not only of Ordination, but also of Confirmation, and there are reserved to him certain important disciplinary powers.

The Priest (i.e., Presbyter)* is qualified by his ordination to " preach the Word of God and to minister the Holy Sacraments in the congregation," to lead the people in worship, and, if licensed or instituted thereto by the Bishop, to exercise the cure of souls. Thus he exercises part of the episcopal office, and it is significant that in the Anglican Ordinals, as in the general practice of the Western Church, which is itself based on very early usage, presbyters are associated with the Bishop in the laying on of hands at the ordination of presbyters.

The diaconate originally represented the ministry of the Church to men's bodily needs, but not as though these were separable from their spiritual state. Though the original function is still emphasised in the Anglican Ordinal, the Deacon to-day exercises his office almost entirely in spiritual activities. Thus he may read the Gospel at the Eucharist; he may be licensed to preach; and he is directly required to assist in the administration of the Holy Communion and, in the absence of the priest, to baptise infants. Holding a ministerial commission, he also appropriately assists the priest in pastoral work.

* See pp. 156 f.

NOTE A

INDELIBILITY

It is part of the traditional doctrine of Ordination to the Ministry that it, like Baptism and Confirmation, confers what in traditional language is called an "indelible character."* This means in practice that Ordination to any grade of the Ministry is a rite which cannot be repeated, a man who has been ordained has once and for all received the commission, whether he exercise it or not.

NOTE B

THE PAPACY

It is impossible to issue a statement concerning the Christian ministry without reference to an institution which has played so great a part in the history of Christendom as the Papacy. In the Roman Catholic Church it is matter of dogmatic faith that the Roman Pontiff, speaking *ex cathedra* on questions of faith and morals, is infallible, and that the true Church is that which is in communion with the Papal See. But the Eastern Churches have never admitted this claim in its developed form; indeed, it has been, from the time of the Great Schism, a main cause of the separation between East and West. It is well known that in the sixteenth century the Church of England repudiated the Papal supremacy.

To discuss the Papal claims and the rejection of them by the Church of England would require such an elaborate historical exposition as would be beyond the scope of this report. We are united in holding that the Church of England was right to take the stand which it took in the sixteenth century and is still bound to resist the claims of the contemporary Papacy. The account which we have already given of the nature of spiritual and doctrinal

* Of course, the word "character" is here used in its Greek sense, as the "impress" of a seal, and has no ethical significance.

authority supplies in large measure the ground of our conviction on this point. With regard to the Church of the future, some of us look forward to a reunion of Christendom having its centre in a Primacy such as might be found in a Papacy which had renounced certain of its present claims; some, on the other hand, look forward to union by a more federal type of constitution which would have no need for such a Primacy.

II. SACRAMENTS

From the Church and the Ministry we pass naturally to the Sacraments. We proceed first to discuss Sacraments in general and the notion of Validity in connexion with them; after this we consider the two great Sacraments of the Gospel—Baptism and the Supper of the Lord; finally we consider with varying degrees of fulness the five rites " commonly called Sacraments."

(A) INTRODUCTORY

(a) THE GENERAL DOCTRINE OF SACRAMENTS

Sacraments, in addition to what is to be said concerning them distinctively, are a special illustration of institutional religion, of which, indeed, they constitute the fullest development. Institutional religion brings into exercise various elements of human nature which would otherwise be without religious expression, and might thus lack consecration:

(i) Inasmuch as the Sacraments belong to the Church, they afford in special measure an instance of that corporate action without which the corporate life of the Church as of any other society must atrophy.

(ii.) Again, inasmuch as man consists of body and soul, it is fitting that he should offer his worship and receive divine grace through outward actions expressive of spiritual activity.

(iii.) Further, it is to be noticed that the actual use of sacraments may strengthen the right disposition for their profitable reception in conformity with the familiar fact of experience that the expression of any emotion, conviction or intention, and especially its corporate expression, tends to strengthen that emotion, conviction or intention.

All of these considerations have application beyond the sphere of sacraments; but they find illustration in that sphere also.

In the Sacraments, therefore, Christ, availing Himself of the principles of our nature, offers to men through the Church the redeeming power of His life in ways appropriate to their various needs.

NOTE.—It is important to be clear in what sense the word "sacrament" is being used on each occasion. The ordinary scholastic use is to employ the word as meaning the outward and visible sign. On the other hand, there has been in theology, and still more in popular and devotional language, a considerable tendency to use the word "sacrament" at once of the sign and of whatever is effected (or conveyed) by the sign—*e.g.*, by the "Sacrament of Baptism" is often meant not merely the outward sign (affusion with, or immersion in, water with the use of a baptismal formula), but also incorporation into Christ by means of this sign. We have found it impossible in practice to avoid using the word in both senses. But in the following series of propositions where the former sense is intended (the outward sign) the word will be printed "sacrament," where the latter sense is intended it will be printed "Sacrament."

1. It is of the essence of the Christian doctrine of Sacraments that in each Sacrament God Himself is active, bestowing grace by means of external signs.

2. All sacramental rites are grounded in this principle

and derive their virtue from the activity in them of Christ who, through the Holy Spirit, thus continues the work begun in the days of His flesh.

3. That work is always redemptive, and the sacraments are means whereby the benefits of Christ's passion are applied to the needs of a sinful world.

4. Christ now acts in the world through His Body the Church. The Sacraments belong to the Church, being part of its corporate life, and having their meaning within that corporate life.

5. The way, therefore, to attempt to reach an understanding of the Sacraments is to consider their place in the corporate life of the Christian society, and to proceed from this to their value for the individual. To invert this process, and to ask first (e.g.) what is the difference between a baptised infant and an unbaptised, is to confuse the problem in advance. The Sacraments are social and corporate rites of the Church in which by means of divinely appointed signs spiritual life flows from God.

6. The external signs are not arbitrary or irrational, but symbolise the promised gift which by means of the sacrament is pledged to and bestowed upon those who receive it with faith.

7. The bestowal of grace by means of sacraments has in Christian theology been held to rest upon divine appointment, which thus supplies the basis of assurance to the worshipper. Divine appointment may have been effected in various ways, and need not be restricted to explicit institution by our Lord Himself; it may also be found in the action of the Apostolic Church taken under His authority and guided by His Spirit.

8. There is here at once a sharp distinction of Sacraments from magic. In magic the use of the formula is held to enable the wizard to control powers other than human. Belief in the efficacy of Sacraments is rooted in faith in the revealed will of God to bestow gifts of grace through certain appointed signs.

9. Everyone who makes use of any Sacrament as such does so on the basis of a conviction that it has some recognised form or matter or both. Though, for example, there are differences among Christians about what is required for a Eucharist—that is, for assurance that the rite being performed really is a Eucharist—all are agreed that such requirements exist. In order that there may be a Sacrament at all, some action must be performed which is recognised to be the proper action of that Sacrament. If a congregation comes to receive Holy Communion, and the priest only prays with them, or preaches to them, they do not receive the sacrament, though they may by an act of spiritual communion receive the grace of it. These considerations form the basis of the traditional conception of "validity" as applied to Sacraments.

10. A deep need of the spiritual life is met by the appointment of rites to which the gift of divine grace is attached. One purpose of Sacraments is to give us assurance of receiving the divine grace even when our conscious minds or feelings are distracted or numb. We do what God commands in the faith that He will give what He has promised—a faith which may be utterly independent of any momentary feeling of assurance or of exaltation or of receptiveness. The psychological value of Sacraments is derived from the fact that they are not psychological processes.

11. But for this reason they are liable to an unspiritual interpretation. The belief that through them grace is given in greater measure than consciousness apprehends may be misinterpreted to imply that the due performance of the rite is alone of importance, the worshipper's spiritual disposition being regarded as indifferent. This is no less erroneous than to suppose that the sacrament is nothing more than a spur to the receptiveness of the conscious mind.

12. Different groups of Christians are influenced in their sacramental theology both by their positive beliefs and experience and by their fears of the different possible

aberrations. Thus those of the more " Catholic" tradition fear especially a limitation of the grace of Sacraments to what is consciously apprehended as thus received ; while those of the more " Evangelical" tradition fear especially the supposition that an outward rite, without penitence and faith in the heart of the worshipper, can confer grace.

13. The history of Christendom shows that there is real ground for both of these types of anxiety. Nevertheless the Evangelical is convinced that the gift bestowed is not limited by his powers of conscious apprehension, and Catholic theology always insists that a right disposition is necessary if the soul is to benefit from the use of sacraments, such " right disposition" including both penitence and faith.

14. The sacraments are rightly called " effectual signs." As signs they represent the gifts of grace offered through them ; as effectual they are instrumental means whereby God confers those gifts on worshippers who receive them with faith.

15. Sacramental rites illustrate the familiar principle already noticed, that the action appropriate to an emotion or intention may stimulate that emotion or intention. But such a statement is not a complete account of the spiritual value of Sacraments. As regards the specific manner in which the sacraments as such convey grace we are divided. Some of us hold that by the sacraments grace is directly conferred ; some hold that the sacraments convey opportunities of grace, which it remains for the recipient to appropriate. Others, who would not find it natural to employ this kind of language, would prefer to say that Sacraments, like spoken prayers, both express and confirm a state of mind and will which fits us profitably to receive the gift of God.

(*b*) VALIDITY

The necessity and meaning of the concept of validity depends upon the facts that the sacraments are *specially appointed* signs, and that they involve representative action on behalf both of Christ Himself and of the Church which is His Body. The meaning of the word *valid* is best defined by the statement that a valid sacrament exists wherever the specially appointed conditions constituting the sacrament are duly and intentionally fulfilled. The meaning of *validity* is thus distinguishable from that of the closely related terms *efficacy* and *regularity*.

A sacrament is said to be *efficacious* in so far as it actually effects the purpose for which it was instituted.* In order that a sacrament may fully effect that purpose, it must result in grace to the recipient. But the reception of grace does not depend solely upon the fulfilment of the appointed conditions of the sacrament, but also upon the spiritual fitness of the recipient, which is not a matter of special appointment, but arises from the general nature of spiritual reality and its laws. It follows, therefore, that the unfitness of the recipient hinders a valid sacrament from becoming efficacious in his case. On the other hand, since "God is not bound by His sacraments," a rite, which is not a valid sacrament, may result in a reception of grace which is not distinguishable from that of which the sacrament is appointed to be the means; and in that case the rite in question may be said to have the efficacy of the sacrament in so far as the spiritual effect in the recipient is concerned.†

A sacrament is called *regular* if it is performed in accordance with general rules laid down by competent

---

* A sacrament therefore cannot be *efficacious* to condemnation. Wherever condemnation is the result of reception, the efficient cause of the condemnation is in the recipient himself and not in the action of the sacrament as such.

† It does not follow that the effect must be caused in the same way in both cases. A strict upholder of scholastic distinctions might argue that, whereas the valid sacrament causes grace *ex opere operato*, in the other case grace is received only *ex opere operantis*—the latter phrase being understood to refer to the human persons concerned, not only to the ministrant. See the extract from Billot at the end of this section.

authority for the due administration of the sacraments.
Irregularity may be either justifiable or unjustifiable. It
is recognised that in certain circumstances it is the duty of
a layman or woman to baptise, and baptism so administered is then an example of justifiable irregularity. If on
the other hand the general rules governing the administration of a sacrament are set aside without sufficient reason,
the sacrament thus performed is unjustifiably irregular,
but it is still valid, if the appointed conditions constituting
the sacrament itself are fulfilled. It must be noted that the
main tradition of the Church has condemned the celebration of the Eucharist by anyone except a priest on the
ground not of irregularity but of invalidity; the validity
of the minister's "priesthood" would thus become in
effect (according to the definition of validity given above)
one of the appointed conditions actually constituting the
sacrament of the Eucharist. Some of us are unable to
adhere to tradition so strictly in this matter as to affirm
that the Eucharist cannot in any circumstances be celebrated by a lay person acting with due intention and
using sufficient form and matter. But even those of us
who would affirm that the sacrament so celebrated ought
to be reckoned as valid, though irregular, would agree
that it is wrong for a lay person to attempt to celebrate the
Eucharist except in the most abnormal circumstances.

The appointed conditions constitutive of a sacrament,
which are the basis of a judgment of validity, fall under
three general heads: (a) appointment by Christ, (b) proper
form and matter, (c) qualification of the minister.

(a) The necessity of appointment by Christ Himself
must be understood in a broad sense, so as not to exclude
the right and duty of the Church, acting under the
guidance of the Holy Spirit, to interpret the will of Christ
concerning the sacraments in matters which His words
and acts before His Ascension have left undetermined, or
wherever sufficient evidence to decide what His words and
acts were is lacking.

(*b*) The essential form and matter of Baptism and of the Eucharist have been handed down to us with but little variation from the earliest times, and we have no hesitation in accepting in regard to them the almost universal tradition of the Church as to the form and matter required for validity. In this respect these two sacraments hold a unique position. The form and matter of other rites which have been called sacraments have varied considerably at different times and places in the history of the Church, and in their case no precise definition can be given of what is universally essential.

(*c*) The question of the minister's qualification raises two important issues:

(i.) According to the post-Augustinian tradition of the Western Church it is held that the Sacrament of Baptism is of such necessity for salvation that in its case alone no qualification whatever in the minister, save that of intention, is absolutely requisite. Thus in cases of necessity even an unbaptised and unbelieving person can validly baptise. The reason generally given for the traditional doctrine seems to us to come dangerously near to suggesting a magical view of Baptism, as though in the absence of the outward sign the soul cannot be saved. Moreover, the recognition of baptisms administered by persons who are not members of the Church tends to obscure the vital principle that the sacraments involve representative action on behalf of the Church as well as of Christ Himself; and this principle would seem to be of special force in the case of the sacrament whereby a new member is incorporated into Christ's Body. Nevertheless, the Church of England has followed Western tradition in accepting as valid baptisms performed by unbaptised persons. We do not desire to challenge this practice, and most of us hold it to be free from theological objection, since one who administers baptism with the intention to do what the Church does should be regarded as an agent of the Church for that purpose, even though he is not a member of it; some of us, however, hold that the practice is open to objection, on the ground that it may appear to impugn the doctrine that the sacraments are sacraments of the Church.

(ii.) The same tradition of the Western Church also teaches that whenever a special qualification in the minister of a sacrament is required with a view to its validity, this depends solely upon an " indelible character " received in ordination, and that therefore the qualification remains in the minister as long as he lives, even if he becomes apostate or is in any other way separated from the Church. An exception is made in the case of the power to pronounce valid absolution. But it is held that the ordinations of an excommunicate or isolated Bishop, cut off from association with any Christian body, are nevertheless valid if performed with sufficient form, matter and intention. We do not question that a man once validly ordained retains his order during his life and must never be ordained again. But we hold, nevertheless, that the power to administer valid sacraments depends upon a commission, received in ordination, to act in the name of Christ in the Church;* and we cannot affirm that this commission is unaffected by the severance of the minister from the Church's body as represented at least by some congregation of baptised and faithful Christians. It is in the light of this principle that we interpret the refusal of the Anglican Bishops to accept as valid ordinations performed by isolated Bishops who have acted apart from the authorisation of any Christian body.† On the larger question concerning the validity (in the sense defined) of sacraments performed by ministers who have not received their commission in the historical succession of the episcopate, there is divergence of opinion among us.

* If it be held that a Eucharist celebrated by a layman is valid, the ground for this opinion would be that a commission to celebrate this sacrament (as well as Baptism) in certain abnormal cases is implicitly contained in the lay person's status as a member of Christ's Body.

† *Cf.* Report of the Lambeth Conference, 1920, Resolution 28.

For the validity of a Sacrament it is necessary not only that things should be done and said which conform to the specially appointed conditions constitutive of the sacrament, but also that these things should be done and said *intentionally*. The intention necessary to validity consists in the minister's intention " to do what the Church does," and this does not of itself involve any correct belief as to what in fact it is that the Church does or intends to do. Moreover, the minister's intention is sufficiently declared by his outward acts in administering or celebrating what publicly appears and purports to be the sacrament of the Church. Where such a publicly apparent intention exists, we are unanimous in holding that the sacrament cannot be invalidated by any merely private intention on the minister's part not to perform the sacrament.

NOTE

The Doctrine of Intention.—The Doctrine of Intention maintained above is that technically known as the doctrine of " Exterior Intention "; it is substantially the same as that put forward by Catharinus in the sixteenth century. It has never been formally condemned by the Church of Rome, although, since the eighteenth century, it has received very little support from its theologians. At the present day nearly all Roman Catholic authorities hold to the doctrine of " Interior Intention " (rejected above), and it is argued (*e.g.*, by Billot, *De Eccl. Sacr.*, I., p. 198) that the condemnation by Pope Alexander VIII. (1690) of a certain proposition about intention in Baptism logically requires the rejection of the opinion of Catharinus. Among Anglican theologians, Hooker expresses himself thus: " Inasmuch as Sacraments are actions religious and mystical, which nature they have not unless they proceed from a serious meaning, and what every man's private mind is, as we cannot know, so neither are we bound to examine, therefore, always in these cases the known intent of the Church generally doth suffice, and where the contrary is not manifest, we may presume that he which outwardly doth the work, hath inwardly the purpose of the Church of God" (*Eccl. Pol.*, V., lviii. 3). "The Church of God hath hitherto always constantly maintained . . . that if Baptism seriously be administered in the same element and with the same form of words which Christ's institution teacheth, there is no other defect in the world that can make it frustrate, or deprive it of the nature of a true Sacrament" (*ibid.*, lxii. 12).

(B) THE TWO GREAT SACRAMENTS OF THE GOSPEL

I. BAPTISM

In Baptism the outward sign is washing with water (by immersion or affusion) with the use of a formula which indicates the purpose of the action and includes, at least normally,* explicit use of the Triune Name of God.

Baptism signifies and effects spiritual cleansing, "death unto sin† and new birth unto righteousness," through incorporation into the Body of Christ, the Church. This is the fellowship of the redeemed in whom the power of the Holy Spirit as given through the revelation of God in Christ is at work, in distinction from "the world." It therefore carries with it the promise of purification from what is evil in "the world," or in our own nature as a part and product of "the world."

* It appears that in primitive times Baptism was administered in the Name of the Lord Jesus (cf., *e.g.*, Acts ii. 38, x. 48), though the use of the Trinitarian formula must very quickly have become general (*cf.* Matt. xxviii. 19).

† The older ritual of complete immersion more effectively symbolised the Pauline doctrine of " burial with Christ " in Baptism than the later use of affusion which coheres rather with the other Pauline doctrine of " washing."

The Church which is Christ's Body is not the company only of those who at any given time confess His Name on earth. It includes the Church beyond the grave. It is into this eternal fellowship that Baptism gives admission. Baptism, standing at the beginning of the Christian life, on the one hand signifies a state of salvation which is fully reached only through the whole process of life, and on the other effects forthwith the necessary first stage of that life.

There is in the New Testament a constant paradox in the expression of the status of Christians; they are described as washed, sanctified, victorious, seated with Christ in heavenly places, but are also bidden to walk worthily of their vocation, and there is full recognition that the evil powers of " the world " or of " the old Adam " are still active within them. Each side of the paradox is the expression of reality, and neither must be sacrificed to the other.

The significance of Baptism may be further elucidated by the consideration of certain difficulties. In the case of infant Baptism a special question arises as to the applicability of the statement that Baptism cleanses from sin. Clearly it cannot cleanse from actual sin, since actual sin has not been committed. On the other hand, so far as " Original Sin " implies a tendency to sin, resulting from membership in the natural community and from the influences which this involves, Baptism meets these influences by incorporating into the redeemed community and by admitting to the realm of Christian grace. In consequence Baptism, even infant Baptism, is a means of deliverance from the domination of influences which predispose to sin, and in that sense it is a means of deliverance from " Original Sin."

A further difficulty arises from the Church's practice of baptising infants, in that the infant has no consciousness of what is taking place. But an infant is a personality in germ—as a brute animal is not—and the practice witnesses, as nothing else can, to the universality of the Gospel of the Love of God, including all persons, Jew or Gentile, black or white, child or grown-up, legitimate or illegitimate. The witness to this fundamental truth compensates for the loss of the greater impressiveness of adult Baptism.

Again, the fact that a man's reception into the Church was prior to his consciousness powerfully represents the priority of God in the spiritual life. " Ye did not choose me, but I chose you " is a saying that applies not only to the ministry but to all the people of Christ.

What is conferred in Baptism is membership in Christ's Body with the corresponding potentiality of worthy membership; but whether or not the person baptised becomes actually a worthy member depends (*a*) on whether the godparents and other members of the Church do their duty, and (*b*) on whether the person baptised takes up and discharges the responsibilities which membership involves.

This consideration applies to a difficulty concerning the necessity of Baptism which is sometimes presented in this form : If there are two persons, one baptised yet left without Christian training, and one trained as a loyal disciple yet not baptised, and if it be held that the latter is more fitly described as a true Christian, how is it still to be maintained that Baptism is the necessary means of incorporation into the Body of Christ?

The following points may be suggested :

(*a*) We have already said that the true approach to the understanding of Sacraments is to consider first their place in the spiritual life of the Church, not first their value for any individual.

(*b*) In both cases described there is defect. To the individual complete absence of Christian teaching is the more serious; but to the society in its continuing life the defect of rite may be, if not equally, yet gravely serious; and if the Church lost by neglect its sacramental character, its value for individuals would be calamitously diminished.

(c) In the life of the unbaptised " saint " there is a defect. The unbaptised person can hardly remain ignorant of Baptism, and either seeks it, or, by omitting to do so, treats as a matter of indifference an ordinance of the New Testament which the Church from the first has regarded as vital.

(d) If the Church is to survive in its sacramental character it must maintain a sacrament of initiation into its membership. This is one reason why such a rite has been ordained. Nevertheless, it is always to be recognised that (in the Augustinian phrase) many who seem to be within are without, and many who seem to be without are within. (*De Bapt.*, v. 38.)*

II. THE LORD'S SUPPER, OR HOLY COMMUNION

It may seem to be a strange fact in the history of the Church that the Sacrament of the Lord's Supper should have become not only the centre of acute controversy, but the actual sphere within which the divisions between Christians take effect; yet it is easy to see how this should come to pass, since in one of its aspects it is the supreme expression of Christian fellowship, and where that fellowship is actually broken the maintenance of a formal sacrament of fellowship must needs be a mockery. The Commission is, however, united in deploring the tragic consequences of this breach of communion between Christians, and its discussion of the underlying significance of this Sacrament would be disproportionate and academic if it did not recognise the urgency of taking every step through which the full communion of Christian people may rightly be restored.

* This thought found later expression in the phrase : Some who are of the soul of the Church are yet not of its body, and some who are of its body are yet not of its soul.

The two names given in the Book of Common Prayer to this Sacrament are "the Lord's Supper" and "Holy Communion." Of these, the first, derived from 1 Cor. xi. 20, looks back directly to the institution of a memorial by Jesus Himself at the Last Supper, and the second, derived from 1 Cor. x. 16, 17, suggests both the partaking of Christ, and the fellowship of Christians with one another in Him. A third ancient and appropriate title, "the Eucharist," emphasising the formal offering of thanksgiving, may be scriptural (1 Cor. xiv. 16; 1 Tim. ii. 1), and was in any case in common use by the beginning of the second century. Another scriptural title, "the Breaking of Bread" (Acts ii. 42; xx. 7), has not come into common use among Christians generally. The familiar mediæval title, the Mass, is of uncertain origin, and had originally no doctrinal significance, but was used as a brief and convenient title. It was discarded in England at the time of the Reformation through its association with certain doctrines and practices.* It has been revived in some circles in the Church of England in the nineteenth century, commonly, though not always, in association with the doctrine of the Eucharistic Sacrifice. The propriety of its revival is a matter upon which there is still a wide and strongly felt difference of opinion in the Church of England.

That which is common to all these titles is that they are liturgical; in fact, in the Eastern Church the familiar title for this service is The Liturgy. These various titles refer not to the act of the individual, but to the social and organic worship of the Christian Church; that worship has many aspects, and it is a matter of history that the liturgical fulfilment in the Church of Christ's recorded command, "Do this in remembrance of Me," has gathered all these aspects into itself. Though the reference to the worship of the whole Church is not always clearly recognised,

---

* This association was not felt to exist throughout Protestant Christendom; in the Lutheran Churches of Scandinavia the term "Mass" has been retained and is still in use.

it is inevitably present in the liturgies or forms of worship of every Christian communion which observes the rite at all.

In what follows the term "Eucharist" will be used, as being non-controversial, and less likely than other titles to confuse the issue.

Before discussing the Eucharist directly it is desirable to deal more generally with two subjects which have been occasions of misunderstanding and of controversy. These are the conceptions of Sacrifice and of Priesthood.

(A) SACRIFICE

The term "sacrifice," being essentially a term of worship, may properly be called liturgical, and is applied, in the history of religion, to certain acts which, though greatly diverse in detail and in interpretation, have a definite character as acts of ritual. These acts, where they are found, have always a peculiarly solemn and sacred character. They are carefully prescribed in a form which makes them communal, even though their application, as in some cases with the sin-offering, may be individual. They are directed towards God, and their effect in creating a common mind in the worshippers is secondary to that direction. The chief agent in the sacrifice is normally not the worshipper but a priest or liturgical person, whose status is communal. The action of the sacrifice normally comprises two principal elements or "moments," one the gift, death, or consumption of the thing offered, representing its complete donation to the Higher Power, who is the object of worship; the other certain ritual acts, frequently connected with the blood, investing the death with its sacred and supernatural significance. And the second of these elements is at least as important as the first. It is noteworthy, for example, that in the Jewish sacrificial system, while the killing of the victim was done by a subordinate official, or by the offerer himself, the ritual acts which followed were performed by the priest.

It is noticeable that all over the world outside Christianity sacrifice has been prevalent, and has then tended to disappear. Mohammedanism and Buddhism in their purer forms have dispensed with it. A living theology of sacrifice survives in Christianity and we believe that Christianity has here preserved for mankind something which is of permanent value, resting as it does upon some of the deepest intuitions of the human spirit. For sacrifice is a uniquely vivid expression of profoundly important truths: (1) the absolute claim of God upon man, all that he is and all that he has; (2) the inability of man to meet that claim in his own person, and his need for an adequate and acceptable offering; (3) the necessity upon man's part to express his worship in an outward act or rite; (4) the unity between man and God, and so between man and man, which is expressed in the fellowship meal which is frequently part of the sacrifice. But the full significance of these truths is determined for Christians by the revelation of God as holy Love, and the Christian doctrine of sacrifice thus gains at once a completeness and an ethical character unknown elsewhere.

It is to the Old Testament that we must turn if we are to appreciate the emotional and intellectual background against which the Last Supper and the Cross are set, and which provides the key to their interpretation in the writings of the New Testament. Clearly this background is made up of various elements, and it would be misleading to give any one of these an isolated prominence, even though both in New Testament times and now different individuals are naturally drawn to give special weight to one or another. The various elements in fact all unite to give the whole background.

Each of these elements appears in early days of Hebrew history, and continues into the New Testament period. These various streams of development start with primitive and crude conceptions, which yet provide a system of metaphors and phrases that endure to the end. As time goes on these primitive conceptions are purified and ethicised, under the influence of prophet and priest. When we come to ask what is the significance of any of these streams for New Testament interpretation, we must not be misled by the metaphors which have survived from early days, but must judge the content of the phrases by their later use.

The Old Testament conception of sacrifice may be analysed under five heads:

(a) Gift

Recent scholars lay emphasis on sacrifice rather as a gift to the deity than as communion with the deity. Thus Gray argues that this conception of a gift is implied in the original names used for sacrifice; " whenever in later times the Jew sacrificed he was consciously intending his sacrifice to be a gift to God."[*]

The purpose of the gift might be twofold. It might be an expression of gratitude. In this sense the Deuteronomic Code dwells on the offering to God of first-fruits, etc., as a grateful recognition that the whole harvest comes from Him. Alternatively, the purpose might be to win the favour of God, and so the elements of propitiation and expiation enter in.

The ethicising process in this conception of the gift-sacrifice is again conspicuous. In early times the fruits of the earth, or the smoke of sacrifice, are offered for the direct enjoyment of God in a physical sense. This provides a metaphor which persists in the Holiness Code, and even in the New Testament (Lev. xxvi. 31, " I will not smell the savour of your sweet odours "; Phil. iv. 18, " An odour of a sweet smell, a sacrifice acceptable, well-pleasing to God "). There are even traces in the Old Testament of human sacrifice to God, though it is nowhere approved and is condemned at a noticeably early stage (Genesis xxii.; Exodus xiii.). Such sacrifice, and the sacrifice of

* G. B. Gray, *Sacrifice in the Old Testament*, p. 20.

first-fruits, is commuted for a money payment (Exod.
xxxiv. 20, etc.).   Where this takes place the anthropomorphic picture of God is dying out.   God is conceived
not as taking the gift for Himself, but as receiving it and
using it for His priests or for the upkeep of His temple.

Under the inspiration of the prophets the conception is
developed ethically into the form that what God really requires is the gift of a good will and a good heart (*cf.*
Micah vi. 8, " What doth the Lord require of thee, but to
do justly and to love mercy and to walk humbly with thy
God ?"; Psalm li. 17, " The sacrifices of God are a broken
spirit "; *cf.* Ecclus. xxxv. 1-3).   This ethical conception
appears also in Philo at a date contemporary with the New
Testament (*De Leg. Spec.* I. iv. 277, " With God it is not
the number of things slain in sacrifice that is of value, but
the entire purity of the soul of him that sacrificeth ").   Thus
the conception of gift-sacrifice finds its fulfilment in the
dedication of the will to God in Christ Himself, and in
His true followers (*cf.* Mark xiv. 36, " Not what I will,
but what thou wilt "; Heb. x. 7, " Then, said I, Lo,
I am come . . . to do thy will, O God ").   Its culminating
expression is in the Passion of Christ, to which He dedicated Himself at the Last Supper.

(b) *The Fellowship Meal*

The fellowship meal is clearly one element in the primitive
conception of sacrifice; this statement would be accepted
by all modern scholars, even though they would not lay so
much emphasis upon it as is done by Robertson Smith.*

In its earliest crude form there are two sides.   The deity
is given food or drink, *e.g.*, through burning or through
pouring on the ground (*cf.* Judges ix. 13), and the remnant
is consumed by the worshippers, who thus may be said to
share a meal with their God.   Sometimes the meal may be
regarded as the consuming of a sacred animal, which con-

* See his *Religion of the Semites*, where the evidence is fully set
forth.

tains the strength of the god and which so imparts that
strength to the worshippers. It is, however, by no means
certain that this last in any way affects the conception of
sacrifice as we find it in the Old Testament, or that there
is in the Old Testament any real trace of totemism.

But the idea that man shares a banquet at the table of
his God survived the stage at which it was supposed that
the God Himself shares in it (see Psalm l. 13). Thus, for
example, the sacrificial meal endures to the end in the Passover. The phrase for this ceremony remains, " to eat the
Passover." But the early conceptions are left behind.
Their place is taken by the element of memorial. The meal
becomes an occasion when the worshippers remember His
work in delivering them from Egypt, and look and ask for
similar favour in the future (for an early stage in this
development *cf.* Deut. xxvi. 1-11).

Such a meal is obviously invested with the religious
sense of fellowship with God and hence also of the mutual
fellowship of believers in God; the Passover meal has
always had this significance strongly marked as the focus
of Jewish brotherhood. There can be no doubt that part
of the significance of the Last Supper is derived from the
fact that it was a meal of fellowship and that this was intensified by its Paschal associations. There is equally no
doubt that Jesus gave this significance a new and particular reference to His own person, and that He related it
to the coming events of the Passion. From the very beginning the disciples practised " the Breaking of the Bread "
as a corporate act of fellowship (Acts ii. 42). The statement that " he was made known in the breaking of the
bread " (Luke xxiv. 35) is thought by some scholars to
imply that our Lord had had some special manner of
breaking bread with His disciples. Possibly the distri-
buting of fragments at the miracles of feeding had some
such ritual character. Certainly it came, in the Fourth
Gospel, to be linked with the spiritual interpretation of the
Eucharist.

(c) Propitiation and Expiation

The fact of sin, and of a conscience laden by sin in the would-be worshipper, leads him to feel the need of an offering that shall have the character of propitiation. In such sacrifice man conceives himself as meeting and receiving the forgiveness of God. It was this development which led to the progressive sense of separation of the worshipper from God in the ritual of the burnt-offering, the sin-offering, and the guilt-offering. It is noteworthy that in all these sacrifices the death of an animate victim is required; and the ritual acts associated with the death are not only expressive of the worshipper's desire to offer something to God, but also constitute an acknowledgment of the nature of sin and its significance. Here the element of the fellowship meal has vanished. Not only is the gift wholly appropriated to God, but man's continuing guilt makes necessary the repetition of sacrifices, which nevertheless at the last fail to satisfy his need (Heb. x. 1-4).

An early and crude instance of winning the favour of God by sacrifice is found in 1 Sam. xxvi. 19, " If it be the Lord that hath stirred thee up against me, let him accept an offering." It is important to notice that, while the term " propitiation " is used throughout the Bible, yet in the Old Testament the fact that God provides the means of propitiation makes plain the belief that there is in God goodwill towards the sinner, and in the New Testament the whole redemptive process is initiated and carried through by the divine love. The notion of propitiation as the placating by man of an angry God is definitely unchristian.*

In the various narratives of the institution of the Eucharist our Lord's words combine the idea of propitia-

---

* The fundamental verb ἱλάσκεσθαι, though frequent in the LXX version of the Old Testament, is very rarely used with God as its object, and is not so used in the New Testament passages where it occurs. See also p. 90, The Atonement.

tion ("unto remission of sins," Matt. xxvi. 28) with
the idea of the covenant ("my blood of the covenant,"
Mark xiv. 24, and parallel passages; *cf.* 1 Cor. xi. 25),
a combination adumbrated by Jeremiah, who rooted the
"New Covenant" in the forgiveness of sins (Jer. xxxi.
34). And this complex of ideas is expressed in the rite,
which is thus an open acknowledgment ("Ye proclaim,"
1 Cor. xi. 26) of Christ's death as the ground of the new
relationship between God and man in which the Christian
community stands.

The operation of the forgiveness of God means subjec-
tively a cleansing of the soul from guilt before God. In
the Old Testament worshipper, priest, and victim were
all required to be ritually clean (*cf.* Exod. xix. 10; Lev.
xvi. 4; iii. 1, etc.). In Ezekiel, who inherited from earlier
prophets the emphasis on moral righteousness as the essential requirement of God, we find already the sense of the
inadequacy of the customary ritual cleansing, and stress is
accordingly laid on a further ritual atonement as a preparation of the worshipper (this is the meaning in Ezek.
xlv. 15, where the verb "atone" governs the people in
the accusative case; *cf.* Ezek. xxxvi. 25, 26). The ritual
of the Day of Atonement, which was established at a
date later than Ezekiel, has this expiatory reference (Lev.
xvi. 30, "For on this day shall atonement be made for
you, to cleanse you; from all your sins shall ye be clean
before the Lord"). This cleansing of the sinner is linked
in the New Testament with the forgiveness of God through
the Cross, *e.g.*, in Rev. i. 5, "loosed" (in some texts
"washed") "us from our sins by his blood."

(d) Covenant

The conception of the covenant-sacrifice is very ancient;
cf. Baal-Berith, the "Lord of the covenant," at Shechem
Judges viii. 33; ix. 4, 46). It appears in Hebrew tradition
in Gen. xv. 9, and underlies the whole interpretation of

the revelation at Sinai (*cf.* Exod. xxiv. 5, for the sealing of the primitive Torah with burnt-offering). Though there is no mention of such a sealing with sacrifice in connexion with the New Covenant of Jer xxxi. 31, yet the phrase " This is my blood of the Covenant " clearly links the idea of redemption with the conception of a covenant-sacrifice in which our Lord Himself was to be the victim; and in Hebrews x. 15-17, Jeremiah's prophecy of the New Covenant is explicitly quoted.

The above analysis has already made clear the general character of the complex whole of thought and of phraseology which makes up the concept of Sacrifice which the first disciples applied to the Cross of Christ. The connexions with the Passover are emphasised in the Fourth Gospel, and are implicit elsewhere in the New Testament (*cf.* especially 1 Cor. v. 7, " Our passover also hath been sacrificed, even Christ "; 1 Pet. i. 19, etc.). The Lord's words at the Last Supper quite definitely relate the death which He was about to undergo with the ritual sacrifices of the Old Testament, and though that death was a judicial murder, carried out by Jews and Romans, He invested it at the Last Supper with a sacrificial character, representing the love and mercy of God. It was thus that the celebration of the Eucharist became the commemoration of that " one oblation of Himself once offered," in which every aspect of Jewish sacrifice was fulfilled, so that no repetition was either necessary or possible.

Even though it be thought that it was through what the Lord said and did at the Last Supper that the disciples were enabled to interpret the Crucifixion as a sacrifice, it is also true that the Crucifixion altered the conception of sacrifice, because this one perfect sacrifice is an offering of self, so that for the Christian thereafter the word " sacrifice " must always mean primarily the offering of the self to

God, and this must be to him the inner meaning of any ritual sacrifice.

Christianity grew up within Judaism, but soon found the Jewish sacrificial cultus to be unessential. It recognised, as is explained in *Hebrews*, that the death of Jesus was in fact the one final sacrifice, accomplishing all that which could never be accomplished by the old sacrifices. Thus the Cross became the full and complete expression of all that men had sought to express in their worship of God, and that worship finds its full meaning when interpreted in relation to the work of Christ, at once High Priest and Victim, Himself passing within the veil, Himself as a priest sealing the Covenant of Forgiveness in His own blood.

It should be noted that while the full implications of the sacrificial system of the Old Testament were applied to the Cross, the term "sacrifice" was also applied to the God-ward acts of the Christian believer in a sense which is relatively detached from ritual association and which in fact carries on the ethical tradition of Judaism. Jesus Himself, who accepted and took part in the Jewish system of worship, quotes and emphasises the saying of Hosea vi. 6, " I desire mercy and not sacrifice." New Testament writers occasionally use the term " sacrifice " in a metaphorical sense, *e.g.*, Rom. xii. 1, " To present your bodies a living sacrifice "; Phil. ii. 17, " If I am offered upon the sacrifice and service of your faith "; Phil. iv. 18, " Having received from Epaphroditus the things that came from you . . . a sacrifice acceptable, well-pleasing to God "; Heb. xiii. 15, " A sacrifice of praise." It is significant that the writer of the Epistle to the Hebrews, who emphasises the sacrificial character of Calvary, interprets that sacrifice in terms of ethical obedience (Heb. x. 5-10).

The recognition of a certain analogy between the Eucharist and the sacrifices of Judaism and of the pagan world was almost inevitable, and had indeed begun in New Testament times. The majority of scholars do not

regard the phrase " we have an altar " in Heb. xiii. 10 as
containing any direct reference to the Eucharist; but the
parallels in 1 Cor. x. 14-22 show how close at hand this
analogy lay. The whole commemoration of the Lord's
Supper, with its close association with the Cross itself, had
much of that atmosphere of dramatic mystery which sur-
rounds sacrifice in the cults in which it is a living reality.
It contained an actual offering of bread and wine. Its institution expressly pointed to the death of the Lord, the
full and perfect sacrifice.

In the Didache (c. 14) we find the term " sacrifice " applied
to the breaking of the bread and thanksgiving, though
this is not explicitly connected with the Cross. Ignatius
(*Ad Philad.* iv) associated the term " altar " with the
" eucharist," now itself a formal title for this commemoration. Justin Martyr in his *Apology* (i. 65-67) makes
hardly any use of sacrificial phraseology in his full account
of the Eucharist, but a passage in *Dial. cum Tryphone* (cc.
116, 117), where the argument is with Judaism, shows how
inevitable such language was : " Now God receives sacrifices from no one, except through His priests. Therefore
God, anticipating all the sacrifices which we do through
His name, and which Jesus the Christ enjoined us to do—
i.e., in the Eucharist of the bread and of the cup, and
which are done by Christians in all places throughout the
world—bears witness that they are well-pleasing to Him.
. . . Now that prayers and thanksgivings (or eucharists),
when offered by worthy men, are the only perfect and
well-pleasing sacrifices to God, I also admit."

The oblation by the people of the elements of bread and
wine, which were to be hallowed and received in communion, was a prominent part of the eucharistic service
of early times, and sacrificial language was used in connexion therewith. The bread and wine were " offered "
to God in acknowledgment of His lordship over the
creation. " It is fitting," writes Irenæus, " that we make
an offering to God, and in all things be found grateful

to God the Creator, with a pure mind, and faith unfeigned, in sure hope and fervent love, offering to Him the first-fruits (*i.e.*, the bread and wine of the Eucharist) of the creatures, since they are His. And this pure oblation the Church alone offers to the Creator, offering to Him of His creation with thanksgiving" (*Adv. Haeres.* IV, xxxi. 3 (Harvey); *cf. ibid.*, xxix. 5, xxxi. 5). In later days, as the sacrifice of the Eucharist came to be thought of primarily as an offering of the sacrifice of Calvary, this thought tended to recede: the offering of the bread and wine by the body of the faithful fell for the most part into disuse and the oblation of the elements came to be regarded rather as an anticipation of the true sacrifice which, on this view, only took place at the prayer of Consecration.

By the latter part of the fourth century sacrificial terms, "altar," "priest," "sacrifice," "offering," are fully established in connection with the Eucharist, and this usage continued without question down to the time of the Reformation.

It remains therefore to consider how far the term "sacrifice" bore, throughout this whole period, the more precise ritual meaning derived from the Old Testament, and how far it had assumed a more general sense.

In general it is true that the metaphors and phrases of early types of thought and cult, Hebrew and pagan, survive without clear analysis of their meaning. Thus Origen, working out Old Testament types, makes a free blend of propitiatory, expiatory, and ethical language: *Hom. in Num.* xxiv. 1, ". . . the necessity of sin demands a propitiation, and since propitiation cannot be made except through a victim, it was necessary that a victim should be provided. . . . [There follows a passage contrasting Christ with other victims.] For the rest put away sins by entreaty, He by power . . . the mind being purified through the offering of spiritual sacrifices." Sometimes we find an almost purely expiatory sense: *Comm. in Rom.* iii. 8; *Hom. in Lev.* ix. 10; *Con. Cels.* i. 1. The broadest of the definitions given is that of Augustine: "A true sacrifice is any work done that we may cleave to God in holy fellowship; a work, that is to say, that has reference to the good end of our attainment to true blessedness" (*De Civ. Dei*, x. 6). Aquinas quotes this definition, but in his thought, which dominates the Western Church down to the Council of Trent, sacrifice is conceived primarily as propitiatory, and is defined as "anything done as an honour properly due to God, for the purpose of placating Him" (*Summa Theol.*, Pars. III., Q. 48). This definition is applied by Aquinas directly to the Cross (*ibid.*, Q. 49), and the sacrificial language of the Eucharist is interpreted in precisely the same way. For the Roman Catholic Church the formal and authoritative expression of the doctrine of the Eucharistic sacrifice was given by the Council of Trent (*Sess.* xxii. 2): "Forasmuch as, in this divine sacrifice which is celebrated in the mass, that same Christ is contained and offered in an unbloody manner, who once offered Himself in a bloody manner on the altar of the Cross; the holy synod teaches that this sacrifice is truly propitiatory, and that by means thereof we obtain mercy, and find grace in seasonable aid. . . . For the Lord, appeased by the offering thereof, and granting the grace and gift of repentance, forgives even heinous crimes and sins."

In Roman Catholic writers of the period after the Counter-Reformation sacrifice is partly determined by the above definition, and is thus regarded as propitiatory, and partly by the Anselmic conception of satisfaction, as an offering made with direct reference to the honour of God. This was worked out in the eighteenth century at the Sorbonne, until in some writers the assimilation of sacrifice and satisfaction is complete, and sacrifice is declared to be the highest of all acts of satisfaction (Plowden, *Traité du Sacrifice de Jésus Christ*, 1778). A widely current modern Roman Catholic definition runs as follows: "Sacrifice is the spontaneous expression of the homage

due from the creature to the Creator. . . . Sin impressed
on it, as on all human acts of devotion, an additional
character of reparation.''

The Continental Reformers accept in its most rigid form
the propitiatory conception of sacrifice, with the interpretation of the character of God which it implies. So Christ is
said to be '' a Victim not only for original guilt but for
all actual sins of men '' (*Augsburg Conf.*, 3; *cf.* Thirty-
Nine Articles, *Art.* xxxi.). So Melanchthon defines propitiatory sacrifice as '' a work which merits for others remission of guilt and of eternal punishment, or a work reconciling God, and placating God's wrath on behalf of
others and making satisfaction for guilt and for eternal
punishment'' (*Corpus Doctrinæ Christianæ*, Leipzig, 1550,
p. 571).

The English Reformers make explicit the distinction
between the different aspects of sacrifice. In principle the
definition of Aquinas is accepted, but it is pointed out that
since the character of reparation is only imposed upon
sacrifice by sin, we can only speak properly of propitiatory
sacrifice in connexion with the one '' full, perfect, and
sufficient sacrifice, oblation, and satisfaction '' made upon
the Cross. Thus Cranmer attacks the application of the
conception of the propitiatory sacrifice of the Cross to the
Eucharist: '' In very deed there is but one such sacrifice,
whereby our sins be pardoned and God's mercy and favour
obtained, which is the death of the Son of God, our Lord
Jesus Christ; nor was ever any other sacrifice propitiatory
at any time, nor never shall be. . . . Another kind of
sacrifice there is which doth not reconcile us to God, but
is made of them that be reconciled by Christ, to testify
our duties unto God, and to show ourselves thankful unto
Him. And therefore they be called sacrifices of laud,
praise, and thanksgiving '' (*On the Lord's Supper*, Parker
Soc. ed., p. 346; *cf.* pp. 360 f.). With this we may compare the reference to sacrifices of praise of the earlier
liturgy and the '' sacrifice of praise and thanksgiving '' of

the Anglican Liturgy and similar language appears in the writings of Roman Catholic theologians.*

So far as the Church of England is concerned these various streams of development unite in the "Arminian High-churchmen" of the seventeenth century, who had links with Scotist and even with Socinian theology in the emphasis laid upon the High-Priesthood of Christ. Through their influence sacrificial language came once more to be applied to the Eucharist in a manner much less restricted than that laid down by Cranmer.

We may also note a tendency among the learned divines of the seventeenth century to recover the language of sacrifice in reference to the Eucharist by a return to the teaching of the early fathers such as Irenæus, who, as we have seen above, spoke of "offering" the bread and wine to God the Creator as the first-fruits of creation. The bread and wine thus offered are made the material of a commemorative sacrifice. (So, among others, Joseph Mede, Dr. Grabe, the learned editor of Irenæus, and Bishop Bull.) This type of teaching was not uncontested in the seventeenth century (e.g., by Cudworth, the Cambridge Platonist), and in the eighteenth Waterland, while stoutly maintaining that the Eucharist is a proper sacrifice, will allow only of spiritual, not material, oblations to God under the Christian system. In more recent expositions of the sacrificial aspects of the Eucharist the conception of the offering to God of the material elements does not appear to have held a conspicuous place.

It remains to note here the actual position as to the meaning of the term "sacrifice" to-day.

The word "sacrifice" has become current in popular speech with a widely extended significance. This extension is justified in principle because it is grounded in the re-interpretation of sacrifice effected by the Cross. It is this which gives to the word for our minds the ethical meaning of self-sacrifice, a meaning which, though not

* E.g., Massiot, Traité du Sacerdoce et du Sacrifice de Jésus Christ, 1708; Plowden, Traité du Sacrifice de Jésus Christ, 1778.

wholly unknown to the ancients, was for them entirely
secondary. But the extension is often carried beyond what
is legitimate. In any theological context it must be insisted
that the word always includes the thought of an offering to
God. The nature of God, as revealed in Christ, involves
that an offering made to God is also, at least by implication,
an offering on behalf of men for His sake. For example, a
costly action done from the motive of love, in the Christian sense of that word, has in itself the true quality of
sacrifice, whether so conceived by the agent or not and
even though there is no conscious Godward reference; but
this is so because God is Love, so that in such an action
there is a positive relationship to God even though this be
outside the field of attention. But the popular use of the
word as indicating mere loss, as when goods are offered
for sale " at a sacrifice," is altogether illegitimate. The
word means essentially an offering to God and is historically associated with a ritual offering to God.

The essential elements in the ritual or liturgical concept
of sacrifice are shown by the history of the term to be the
following:

(1) Sacrifice is an act in which man worships God,
and the form of the act is an expression of the homage due
from the creature to the Creator.

(2) It is a formal and ritual act, so that even when used
by an individual to express his private worship its character is social or corporate.

(3) The character of the sacrifice varies with the varying
relationships in which those who offer it may stand towards God and towards one another. Thus sacrifice may
be regarded simply as a gift, or as a pledge and means
of fellowship, or as the formal sealing of a covenant, or,
where the sense of sin is present, it may have a propitiatory or expiatory character.

The conception of sacrifice has undergone a progressive
interpretation upon ethical and spiritual lines. This re-
interpretation has not destroyed the ritual or liturgical

aspects of sacrifice, or its significance as homage to God. But while it is true that Christianity recognises and expresses the deep-seated tendencies of human nature which have given rise to the institution of sacrifice, it is also true that the Christian conception of God is not determined by these tendencies, and that while the character and meaning of the Cross have been illuminated by the application to it of the concept of sacrifice, it is conversely the case that it is the Cross which determines the true significance to be attached to the idea of sacrifice itself.

(B) PRIESTHOOD

In every sacrificial system it has been a necessary part of the ritual that it should be performed by representatives of the community. In many types of religion Priesthoods with sacrificial functions are for this purpose such representatives of the community, or fellowship, or Church, as a worshipping body. The priest is a liturgical or ritual person, acting in that character, not only on behalf of the individuals who may at the moment be worshipping, but of the whole community within which they so worship.

In Christianity the conviction was early reached that this priestly function was wholly and finally fulfilled by the work of Christ upon the Cross. The Epistle to the Hebrews speaks of all other mediatorial sacrifice and priesthood as ineffective in the past, and as abrogated in Him in the present and for the future. For the conception of a priesthood "after the order of Melchizedek," applied in that Epistle to Jesus, is not there applied to any other than Him, nor is anything said of a participation in it by any other.

The self-offering of Christ, having been accomplished once for all, the whole Church, as His Body, thereafter continues to be the sphere within which His mediatorial office is exercised. The whole organic structure of the Church, in its unity and in its diversity of function, has as its essential character the mediation of the divine grace through access to the mercy-seat, and the cleansing of the human soul through the " full, perfect, and sufficient sacrifice," once offered.

The fundamental priesthood of the Church is thus the priesthood of the whole Body. This is the meaning of the doctrine of the priesthood of the laity, a doctrine which does not mean that laymen are individually priests, but that the laity are, as such, members of that Body which is in its entirety priestly.*

The " representative " conception of priesthood is an expression of this truth, and means that the priest acts as the commissioned representative not either of the hierarchy or of the laity, but of the whole Body of Christ.

The fundamental character of the Christian priesthood, as one of the three historical Orders, has been discussed in the section on the Ministry (see pp. 119 ff.). It is there shown that the organic unity of the Church came to be expressed primarily through the Episcopate, and that the presbyterate gradually took over certain aspects of the episcopal office, and so developed into the priesthood as it is now known.

In our discussion of the Ministry (see p. 124) we have set out the respective parts played by the episcopate and the presbyterate in the exercise of the representative function described above. Because the episcopate came to be in a special sense representative of the organic unity of the Church, it was natural that (as will be mentioned later) the term *sacerdos*, when it began to be used among Christians, was applied especially to the Bishop. But so far as the presbyterate shares the functions of the episcopate, the *sacerdotium* is regarded as belonging equally to the presbyterate. Thus certain ritual or liturgical functions have been definitely assigned to the Presbyter no less than to the Bishop, as characteristic of his office. A lay person may, and on occasion should, proclaim the word of

* See above, p. 114.

God's forgiveness, but it is only the priest who is authorised to pronounce the word of absolution in the Church. And though the thankful commemoration of the Lord's Death in Holy Communion is the common act of all Christians, its formal expression has been definitely committed to the priest, so that in the general Christian tradition the celebration of the Eucharist has become the most characteristic of his functions.

It is not easy to draw out with any exactness the resemblances and differences between the priesthoods of the Christian Church and those of either the Jewish dispensation or of pagan sacrificial systems. The difficulty arises very largely through the immense range of meaning which has been covered historically by the term "sacrifice," and the question as to whether the priesthood of the Anglican or of any other communion is properly a sacrificing priesthood depends entirely upon the significance which is given to the term.

Sacerdotal terms were not at first applied freely to the Christian Ministry. In the Latin tradition, though the word *sacerdos* occurs earlier, as in Tertullian's saying: "*Nonne et nos laici sacerdotes sumus?*" the terms *sacerdos* and *sacerdotium* were first regularly used of the Ministry by Cyprian in the third century, and were by him applied to the Bishop. In the Greek tradition it is not until the fourth century that the term *hiereus* and its cognates appear as applied to the celebrant of the Eucharist, though before that time they were in common use as applied to Christ and to the Christian community as a whole. Thus in the earliest period the Christian "presbyter" was distinguished from the Jewish or pagan "priest" by the use of a different name. But in the Middle Ages, when the Christian presbyter had stepped into the place in the social system previously held by the heathen priest, and when moreover his office as celebrant of the Eucharist had come to be generally regarded as sacrificial, the words *hiereus* and *sacerdos* were translated in English and other modern

European languages by derivatives of *presbyter*.* When, at the Reformation, it was desired by many to dissociate the office of the presbyter who celebrated the Eucharist from the sacrificial interpretation of his function, this led to some confusion both of language and of thought. But it is clear that from the very first days of Christianity the "breaking of the bread" had a ritual character, and that it was linked, through the commemoration of the Last Supper and the recital of the words of Jesus, with that which was done by Him as the one High-Priest upon the Cross. There was thus a priestly character implicit in the celebration of the Eucharist from the beginning, though it was only very gradually that this led to a formally sacerdotal interpretation of the functions of the celebrant.

Thus while there is a real parallel between the Christian and other priesthoods, this parallel must not be pressed too far. The Christian priest is a ritual or liturgical person, acting, whether for the individual worshipper or in the local community, as the appointed representative of the whole Church. But the significance of his acts is derived from the Christian revelation of God in Christ, and from that work of Christ upon the Cross which his words and acts commemorate, and not from the current conceptions of the priestly function in sacrifice, even at the highest level of evolution which it had reached.

(C) THE EUCHARISTIC RITE

The Eucharist has been the central act of worship in the Christian Church. It gathers up and holds together the various aspects of the Gospel, as well as the many elements of worship—corporate and individual, objective and subjective. It has its being and significance within, and in relation to, the life of the Church as a whole. It is therefore to be thought of first as an act of the Church, or, more strictly, as the act of Christ through the Church.

* *E.g.*, Priest, prêtre, Priester, prete.

But the Church, though far more than the assembly of worshippers at any one time, nevertheless consists of its members. Accordingly, while the worship is that of the whole Church, yet if no individuals are actually offering it, no worship is being offered. But as the individuals offer this worship, they are taking their share in the worship of the universal Church, and it is with Angels and Archangels and the whole Company of Heaven that they laud and magnify the glorious Name of God.

The form of this act of corporate and individual worship is determined by the record of the Last Supper.* It is worth while therefore to consider certain broad differences in the attitude of different Christians to that record. The view that the Eucharist as we now have it has no basis in any actual words or deeds of Jesus at the Last Supper, but originated in a visionary experience of St. Paul, the Commission is unanimous in rejecting. There are those for whom the vital matter is their belief that our Lord at the Last Supper instituted a rite for the permanent observance of the Church; they would lay stress on the idea of obedience to our Lord's commands, and for the vast majority of them it is important to regard the words " This do in remembrance of Me " as an actual saying of Christ, or as the true interpretation of His intention.

---

* This is certainly true of the main stream of liturgical tradition, and the association of the record of the Last Supper with the Christian rite is explicit in one of the earliest of the New Testament writings, St. Paul's first Epistle to the Corinthians. It is however to be noted that there are indications both in the New Testament and in early liturgical usage that the rite was not always exclusively associated with the Last Supper, and that it had one of its roots in a customary " breaking of bread " practised by Jesus and His disciples during His earthly life, and perpetuated in the Church after His death and Resurrection. It will be recalled that the Fourth Gospel attaches our Lord's Eucharistic teaching to the feeding of the multitude in Galilee. But the last of the " breakings of bread " in the earthly life of Jesus, that on the night in which He was betrayed, held a prominent place in the Gospel tradition and naturally played an all-important part in the shaping of the Christian rite.

There are others, however, who on grounds of historical criticism do not think it possible to affirm with confidence what was in our Lord's mind with regard to the future at the actual time of the Last Supper, or who even think it improbable that He was at that time explicitly instituting a rite for future observance: many of these would nevertheless trace much of the value of the Eucharist to the fact that it is rooted in what our Lord said and did on that occasion—*i.e.*, in the words and deeds whereby He interpreted in advance His approaching Passion and Death as a sacrifice for the sins of the world. For them it is a vital thought that in the Eucharist we seek to be spiritually united with our Lord, through the power of His Spirit, in His self-offering, by repetition of the very words and deeds in which He revealed the sacrificial character of His Death. They would lay stress upon the idea of the Spirit as guiding the Church into all truth, and as therein revealing more fully after Pentecost the significance of what our Lord did at the Last Supper.

In the New Testament period many ideas were current in connexion with sacrifice (see the section on *Sacrifice*). This fact bears upon the interpretation of the words used by our Lord at the Last Supper. Thoughts of the Passover were in the minds of all present. His words were suggestive of Covenant-Sacrifice; the Covenant of Sinai was closely connected with the deliverance from Egypt, the New Covenant of Jeremiah with the deliverance from sin. Christ was preparing His disciples to interpret His approaching death as the fulfilment of Old Testament prophecy, and was dedicating Himself for that act which was the culmination of His life of sacrificial obedience (*cf.* the use made of Psalm xl. in the Epistle to the Hebrews, and St. Bernard's *Non mors placuit sed voluntas sponte morientis*).

The Eucharist is a corporate act of the Church towards God, wherein it is united with its Lord, victorious and triumphant, Himself both Priest and Victim in the Sacrifice of the Cross. This connexion has been expressed in at least four ways: (1) Through stress upon the union of ourselves with Christ in the act of communion, and in that union the offering of the "sacrifice of praise and thanksgiving" and of "ourselves, our souls and bodies"—a view generally held in the Church of England, many members of which would find here alone the sacrificial element in the rite; (2) through emphasis on the fact that in the Eucharist we repeat the words and acts of Christ at the Last Supper—words and acts whereby it is held that He invested His approaching Death with the character of a sacrifice; (3) through the insistence that the rite is a representation before the Father of the actual sacrifice of the Cross; (4) through the doctrine of the Heavenly Altar, at which we join in the perpetual offering by Christ of Himself, and share the Life of Christ crucified and risen. The extent to which any of these interpretations would find acceptance in the Church of England is very various. They are not necessarily exclusive of one another. There are those who would combine all the views stated, while some of them would be repudiated in certain quarters. We consider that all of them should be regarded as legitimate in the Church of England, and we are agreed in general terms in holding that the Eucharist may rightly be termed a sacrifice—which we have defined as "an act in which man worships God, the form of the act being an expression of the homage due from the creature to the Creator." But if the Eucharist is thus spoken of as a sacrifice, it must be understood as a sacrifice in which (to speak as exactly as the subject allows) we do not offer Christ but where Christ unites us with Himself in the self-offering of the life that was "obedient unto death, yea the death of the Cross."

Our union with Christ in the Eucharist is most fully expressed and mediated in "communion." The term *Koinonia*, of which this is the equivalent, has from the first (1 Cor. x. 16) been used to connect the partaking of the consecrated elements of bread and wine with the partaking of the "body" and "blood" of Christ, and so with the receiving of Christ Himself, and with our participation one with another in His Life. Communion is an element in the rite which has always and everywhere been regarded as essential, despite wide divergences in different traditions as to the desirability of frequent reception, or of the presence at the Eucharist of those who do not communicate but attend for the purpose of worship.

The history of Eucharistic doctrine has been marked by two stages which are significant in this connexion. For about eight hundred years the attempt to understand and to express precisely how the Gift is given, and to provide an account of the Gift in its various relations, was quite subordinate to a thankful recognition of the reality of the Gift itself. The almost complete absence of Eucharistic controversy during the patristic period is familiar to students of doctrine, and is a noteworthy fact; in this respect the history of the doctrine of the Eucharist differs notably from that of the doctrine of the Incarnation. The spiritual enjoyment of the heavenly food of the Lord's Body and Blood in the life of the Church was the dominating fact; questions of speculative theology remained in the background.

There then followed a stage of definition and controversy, beginning in the ninth century, and marked by attempts at precision. Eucharistic theology was gradually built up in connexion with, and to some extent in dependence upon, a generally accepted intellectual point of view, with one main philosophical tradition dominant. In the Middle Ages the element of communion was overshadowed for the ordinary worshipper, but the central importance of communion, even when this was represented only by the communion of the celebrant, has always been recognised by theologians.

From the time of the Reformation onwards there have been varying traditions of Eucharistic doctrine within the

Church of England. All the main types of Anglican tradition, however, agree in regarding communion as a central
and essential element in the Eucharist. The very fact that
controversy is not raised upon this point has tended to
diminish the stress laid upon it in doctrinal statement, and
clear thinking about its nature and implications is often
neglected, simply because it is not a subject of dispute.
Eucharistic communion is communion with Christ, crucified
for us and risen from death that we might be united with
Him in fulness of life.   This communion is mediated
through a rite which He Himself instituted,* the observance
of which is an obligation upon all members of the Church.
Thus communion with Christ becomes also the communion
of the Christian with his fellow-Christians.

The actual symbolism of the rite is based upon that of
the corporate meal, "the strengthening and refreshing of
our souls by the Body and Blood of Christ, as our bodies
are by the bread and wine."   As has been pointed out
above, this symbolism has a long history and has
been significant both of communion with God and of
fellowship among men.   In general this traditional symbolism remains natural and appropriate, but in some
respects it has become widely unfamiliar. Even the elements of bread and wine themselves are not in all parts of
the world the everyday food and drink of ordinary people.
Further, the phrases "eating the flesh" and "drinking
the blood" appear unnatural and even repulsive to many;
but this is nothing new, for the Jews in St. John vi. are represented as feeling it acutely. For these reasons there is
a real difficulty in commending the Christian use to many
outside the tradition.   But the difficulty disappears, as is
common in the case of symbolism, for those who themselves come within the tradition in question and learn its
rich heritage of historical associations and of devotion.
The continuity of the rite in its essential character has
given it an unique position as both the symbol of unity

* See p. 160.

among Christians and the means whereby that unity is maintained.

The essence of communion, in this Christian sense, is that it is at every point fully personal. It includes (*a*) an activity of God in Christ towards His faithful people, (*b*) the appropriation of Christ by the faithful, (*c*) their surrender of themselves in an outgoing towards God in worship, (*d*) the unity of the faithful one with another as fellow-members of Christ, and (*e*) individual union with Christ, both God and Man, in whom the self-giving of God and the self-surrender of man meet.

The Eucharistic symbolism and language appropriately express the essential character of the rite as thus conceived. It is of importance that the rite is historical and determinate, so that it is not dependent for its symbolism or its efficacy upon the transient emotions or circumstances of the worshippers.

No Christian doubts that in some sense Christ is present in the Holy Communion. But the use of the words " present " and " presence " gives rise to many questions, and has led to deep divisions of thought and of devotional practice among Christians. We believe that there is in the different traditions a greater measure of agreement than their habitual phraseology suggests.

God, we believe, is always and everywhere accessible, in the sense that in His love He is always eager to welcome men to fellowship with Himself. But we are hindered from availing ourselves of that welcome, partly perhaps by the limitations of our nature, partly by the vitiation of that nature through sin. God has taken action to remedy this, supremely through the Incarnation and the Atonement. Moreover, Jesus Christ Himself (either by explicit command at the Last Supper, or by His Holy Spirit afterwards interpreting the event)* has appointed a means whereby, through ritual association with the acts of the Lord at the supreme moment of His own spiritual sacrifice (" in the

* See p. 161.

same night that He was betrayed "), we may be united to Himself.   Thus, wherever the Eucharist is offered, Christ is the agent uniting us with Himself; and the elements become, through their consecration, effectual signs whereby as our sacrifice He is given to be our food.

In one sense no doubt it is true that the communion between Christ and His faithful people is always and everywhere being realised.   If we direct our thoughts to a still wider sphere, we may say with equal truth that it is only by God's continuously sustaining and directing power that any of His creatures realises its own nature and per-fection in obeying His will.   But the abiding relationship depends in either case upon the activity of the living God.   And from one occasion to another that activity must vary in respect of the particular gift which it bestows or the particular purpose towards which it is directed.   Indeed redemption itself, as understood by Christians, consists essentially in specific action on the part of God.

Since, therefore, God is the living God, able and willing to take specific action, there is no conflict between the belief that He is always and everywhere present (*i.e.*, accessible and active towards His creatures) and the belief that He has made special provision to meet the needs of sinful mankind through (*a*) the Incarnation and the Atonement, (*b*) the life of the Church and our incorporation into it, and (*c*) the Eucharist as the central act of the Church's worship and as Christ's act of perpetual self-communica-tion to His people.   Having regard, therefore, to the special purpose with which Christ is both active and accessible in the Eucharist, we may appropriately speak of a special presence of Christ both as giving Himself and as thus given.

Again in regard to the term " Body " it is to be noticed that this is used in Scripture alike with reference to the Lord's fleshly Body and to His sacramental Body and to His mystical Body (the Church).   This usage is justified by the fact that these are alternative means of our Lord's

self-expression and self-communication. We have no right
to infer from the fact that the Bible uses the term " Body "
in these three ways any one particular theory as to the
relationship between the fleshly, the sacramental, and the
mystical Body.

The plea that these words—"This is My Body "—
cannot now bear a meaning different from that which they
bore when our Lord uttered them is only partially valid.
We should agree that they cannot bear a meaning inconsistent with that of their first utterance, but their meaning
is now profoundly affected and enriched by the completion
of their historical setting. For us Calvary, the Resurrection and the Ascension have supervened, and through the
coming of the Holy Spirit the Church has now a richer
understanding of all that the words convey.

Eucharistic doctrine inevitably starts from Scriptural
phrases, and develops in close association with devotion and worship. Neither the language of Scripture nor
the language appropriate to worship is, as a rule, such as
to afford a basis for argumentation drawn from details
of its wording or from isolated phrases. Thus in regard
to our Lord's saying, " This is My Body," we cannot
accept any argument which bases itself primarily upon the
exegesis of the word " is."

Differences concerning Eucharistic doctrine have been
accentuated by different uses of language, and especially
of the phrase " Real Presence." This was originally
used with specialised reference to the Presence of the
Body and Blood of Christ under the forms of bread and
wine. But the phrase has been constantly used in Anglican
theology (as, for example, by the Caroline divines) with
a wider reference, and it would be quite impossible now
to confine its use to the specialised reference. Nor should
we think this desirable; for in practice if the Real Presence
is denied wherever Presence in the narrower sense is not
intended, many will be led to suppose that Christ is not
believed to be present at all in any special manner unless

His Presence is thus specially associated with the elements. Much misunderstanding has in fact arisen from the ambiguity of the phrase "Real Presence." And it is therefore the more important to make it clear that what causes division of theological opinion in the Church of England is not any question concerning the real and spiritual presence of the living Christ at every Eucharist (for this is acknowledged by all), but only the questions whether and in what way that presence is to be specially associated with the consecrated bread and wine. With regard to the answer to these latter questions three main schools of traditional thought are to be distinguished. But the classification involved is logically rather than historically exact, the actual teaching given by particular theologians being sometimes inconsistent, and often ambiguous or perhaps intentionally indefinite.

(1) The first school is that which teaches that the bread and wine in some sense really or actually *become* through consecration the Lord's Body and Blood. Those who maintain this doctrine usually speak of the Lord's Body and Blood as being present "under the forms of bread and wine,"* and therefore also of Christ Himself as being really present "in the sacrament" (*i.e.*, the outward sign). They would at the same time affirm that the manner of this presence is altogether spiritual, being apprehended only by faith and in no way perceptible to any bodily sense. The doctrine thus described is that of "the Real Presence" in the narrower meaning of the phrase. It has been given greater precision in varying forms. Historically the most important of these forms have been (i.) Transubstantiation,† which received universal authority in the Western Church at the Fourth Lateran Council and has remained a dogma of the Roman Catholic Church, and (ii.) Consubstantiation,‡ which is the classical doctrine of

---

* For the sacramental significance of the terms Body and Blood and of the prepositions "in" and "under," see Appendix, p. 224.
† See below, p. 172.   ‡ See below, p. 173.

Lutheranism. Of these Transubstantiation is explicitly rejected by the Thirty-Nine Articles; but the doctrine of "the Real Presence," even in that narrower meaning with which we are now concerned, is not exclusively committed to either Transubstantiation or Consubstantiation: the theologians of the Oxford Movement, who were mainly responsible for the revival of the doctrine of the Real Presence in the Church of England, rejected the Roman Catholic dogma of Transubstantiation, and did not, on the other hand, adopt Luther's alternative theory. The doctrine which they revived is now, without any precise definition, widely taught by one school of thought in our Church. Among Anglican theologians of the present day a considerable number believe that this doctrine is sound in essence. Some of them are content with the use of traditional language to express it; but others, especially in recent years, have felt the need for some restatement of it designed to remove traditional objections; and various suggestions for such restatement have been made, a brief account of which is to be found in a separate memorandum.*

(2) Most clearly opposed to the doctrine of the "Real Presence" is that commonly known as Receptionism. Receptionism derives its name from its teaching that, though the Body and Blood of the Lord are really received by the faithful in the Lord's Supper, yet their presence is real in the hearts of the recipients only, and not in the elements prior to reception. According to this doctrine the consecrated bread and wine are said to be the Lord's Body and Blood only in a figure. The special presence of Christ, therefore, is to be associated not with the elements but with the reception of them. Moreover, many Receptionists would strongly affirm that Christ Himself is really and spiritually present at every Eucharist as the unseen host at His own Table. Nor would they deny that, as thus present, Christ offers Himself as their

* See below, p. 172.

spiritual food to all communicants alike, although they would maintain that those who approach the Lord's Table unworthily and without faith do not so receive Him.

(3) A doctrine intermediate between the two already mentioned is that called Virtualism. The Virtualist is not content to affirm that the consecrated elements are only a figure of spiritual realities. Like the believer in the " Real Presence " he maintains that a spiritual change in the elements themselves is effected through consecration. But, in affirming that the bread and wine become the Body and Blood of Christ in a spiritual manner, he understands his statement to mean that the bread and wine become the Body and Blood, not *in substance* (as though the elements could be identified with the natural Body and Blood which were on the Cross), but *in spiritual power and virtue and effect.** Generally speaking, the holders of this doctrine desire to affirm that through consecration the bread and wine are endowed with spiritual properties which justify the description of them as the sacramental Body and Blood, or as being sacramentally the Body and Blood, while they shrink from language which would seem to them to imply that the consecrated elements are the same as the flesh which was crucified and rose again from the grave. Virtualism, however, is not always stated in the same way. Sometimes the language of Virtualists suggests Receptionism, whereas more often it attributes a kind of sacredness to the sacramental signs which is only intelligible on the assumption that the Lord's presence is specially associated with them.

It remains to be said that perhaps the strongest and most characteristic tradition of Anglicanism is to affirm such a real presence of Christ in the Eucharist as enables the faithful communicant both to receive His life as a spiritual gift and to acknowledge Him as the giver, while at the same time the affirmation is combined with a determination to avoid as far as possible all precise, scholastic

* See below, pp. 178 ff

definitions as to the manner of the giving.* It seems unfair to force into an artificial classification as though they were adherents of a particular " middle " theory those who are thus reluctant to commit themselves to definition. Many Anglicans would point to the fact that their Church does not require them to hold any particular theory as to the manner of the Eucharistic Presence, and would say that for their part they find it quite unnecessary to do so.

The more exact significance of the terms " Body " and " Blood " is discussed elsewhere.† At this point we emphasise once more the agreement of all these schools of thought in holding that in the Eucharist Christ is active and accessible in a special manner as Giver and as Gift, and accordingly that the Eucharist affords a natural and appropriate occasion for the Church's thankful adoration of Him as the Lamb slain from the foundation of the world.

MEMORANDA

The two following memoranda represent two main lines of approach to Eucharistic doctrine. It will be noticed that the view sometimes called Virtualism appears in both, having indeed some affinities with each. The memoranda are not offered as expressing views held by the whole Commission, nor as covering all varieties of interpretation, but the Commission is glad to present them with its Report as expressing types of theology admissible in the Church of England, and as illustrating a clear convergence, both doctrinal and devotional, of those who come to the understanding of this mystery from two standpoints which are both traditional in the Church of England.

* *Cf.* Elizabeth's rhyme (T. Fuller, *The Holy State* [1642], p. 315) :
> 'Twas God the word that spake it,
> He took the bread and brake it ;
> And what the word did make it,
> That I believe and take it.

† See p. 224.

(A) The Doctrine of the Real Presence

The phrase "real presence" (*realis præsentia*) is of mediæval origin; and it is in this period that the doctrine of the Real Presence in the narrower sense came to be defined in opposition to other views. In patristic times, while a broadly realistic doctrine of Christ's presence in the consecrated elements seems to have been generally held, there was little or no controversy on the subject, and passages from the Fathers may be quoted which, if taken by themselves, suggest what modern theologians would call a symbolic interpretation of the relation of the sacramental sign to the reality signified. There was little attempt to frame a systematic theory, and therefore patristic teaching falls outside this memorandum.

Both in the Middle Ages and in the period immediately succeeding them discussions of the Real Presence were largely influenced by the general belief that our Lord had ascended with His human body into a local heaven in which that body now exists in spatial dimensions. Accordingly, one of the main objections which defenders of the doctrine were called upon to meet was the obvious argument that it is contrary to the nature of a body to be in two places at once—viz., both in heaven and on the altar. The weight given to this objection by the Reformers is clearly indicated in the so-called Black Rubric of our Prayer-Book. The Thomist theory of Transubstantiation had been designed in part to supply an extremely subtle answer. Scholastic philosophy was accustomed to distinguish the *substance* of any physical object from its *accidents*, the *substance* being that which makes the object to be what it really and essentially is, the *accidents* including all the sensible properties or qualities by which the object is recognised. Thus, in any piece of bread the substance of bread is that which makes it to be what it really is—viz., bread—and that substance remains identically the same in all pieces. On the other hand,

the accidents or sensible properties of a piece of bread—
size, shape, colour, taste, softness, etc.—may vary in-
definitely in different pieces, although, apart from *all*
accidents, we should not be able to recognise the object
as bread at all. It follows, therefore, that the substance
of bread, considered strictly as such, is not characterised
by any particular accident of any piece of bread. It
cannot therefore be perceived by the senses, nor can it
occupy space, since it is without spatial dimensions. Now
on the theory of Transubstantiation it is supposed that at
consecration the substance of the bread is wholly converted
into the substance of Christ's Body, but that all the accidents (which in this case are the species or sensible appearances) of the bread really remain exactly as they were
before, while the accidents and species of the Body remain
in the only *place* where the Body is—viz., in heaven.
Thus the logical contradiction of supposing the Body to
be in two places at once is logically avoided, while it is
still maintained that what is on the altar is really and
substantially the Body of Christ.

The Lutheran theory of Consubstantiation, which supposed the substance of bread and the substance of the
Lord's Body to be both together in the consecrated
element, overcame the contradiction in a different way,
by postulating the ubiquity of our Lord's ascended
Body.

The Roman Catholic doctrine of Transubstantiation
was condemned in the Thirty-Nine Articles upon three
grounds, of which the strongest is that the doctrine
"overthrows the nature of a sacrament." This criticism
requires a brief explanation to make its force apparent.
A careful examination of the theory of Transubstantiation,
as stated by St. Thomas Aquinas and defined by the
Council of Trent, vindicates it from any charge of super-
stitious grossness or materialism. St. Thomas is careful to insist that the Lord's Body and Blood are present
in the sacrament only invisibly and after a spiritual

manner, so that they are not at all perceptible by the bodily senses, but by faith alone. But the criticism of the Article is not thus invalidated. Its meaning may be stated thus: Granted that the essence of a sacrament is the use of material things as effectual signs of spiritual grace, the proper nature of a sacrament is destroyed if the reality of the material thing as such is removed by its sacramental use. The substance of a material object can only be known through the accidents perceptible to the senses; and, if the accidents remain the same while the substance is altogether changed, it must follow (granted that such an occurrence is conceivable at all) that the evidence of the accidents becomes false evidence. Or, to put what is essentially the same point differently, if the bread and wine cease after consecration to be really bread and wine, they cease really to be sacramental signs; for on this supposition what has happened is that the accidents or species of bread and wine have become a disguise or veil for a substantial reality quite different from their own. And indeed it is evident from the language of Roman Catholic devotion that the consecrated species are commonly thought of as a veil which hides, rather than as a sign which declares, spiritual realities. There is therefore solid ground for the Anglican rejection of the doctrine of Transubstantiation as formulated by St. Thomas and at the Council of Trent.

It can hardly be denied that the thought and research, which philosophy and science from the time of Descartes onwards have directed to the relations of spirit and matter and of space and time, have caused a shifting of many landmarks in the old controversies. On the one hand, the idea of a local heaven, in which our Lord's body can be thought of as occupying space, has been by tacit and general consent abandoned. The words "Body and Blood of the Lord" are themselves recognised to be symbols which denote essentially, not a corporeal and extended object, but rather the abiding life of the sacred humanity once offered in humiliation on the Cross and glorified for ever in the Ascension. On the other hand, few philosophers to-day continue to think of the substance of any physical object as a fixed core of being which remains the same behind all the changes which affect its accidents or sensible appearances. Granted that the term substance is still to be used for that which makes a thing to be what it essentially and really is, some would identify the substance with the totality of its appearances, others with its value, others with the whole complex of opportunities of experience which it affords, while others again hold that the substance of a material thing can only be expressed in mathematical formulæ.

Inevitably such new lines of thought and systems of definition lead to fresh statements of sacramental doctrine. And in particular some Anglican theologians to-day are putting forward tentative restatements of the doctrine of the Real Presence which have the effect of destroying the boundary-line between the older doctrine of the " Real Presence " and that of Virtualism. If, for instance, substance is identified with value, it is obvious that the doctrines of Real Presence and of Virtualism become indistinguishable from one another; and the substance of the consecrated elements may be said to be for Christian faith the substance of Christ's Body and Blood, without any suggestion that they lose their physical substance or value as bread and wine. This type of doctrine may be illustrated by pointing out that a pound-note is not just an elaborately printed piece of paper, but has the value in currency of a pound-sterling, which fact justifies us in commonly speaking of it as " a pound." Or, again, if a thing consists in the opportunities of experience which it affords, we may argue that the bread and wine are changed by consecration, inasmuch as they now afford as means of communion new opportunities of spiritual experience in addition to those which they originally afforded as physical objects. They may truly be said to be spiritually the Body and Blood of Christ, in so far as they afford opportunities of a spiritual partaking of His sacrificed life. It is arguable that both the ways just mentioned of justifying the doctrine of the Real Presence approach more nearly to a restatement of Consubstantiation than of Transubstantiation, in so far as they do not teach that the substance of the bread and wine is wholly converted into another, but rather that a new substance is added to it. Nevertheless some of those who defend these interpretations would not reject the term Transubstantiation in every sense which the word could reasonably bear. They would argue that there is a real change of substance through consecration.

Finally, there are some who would prefer to restate the doctrine of the Real Presence in a way which seems to them simpler, though it is perhaps less easy to relate to traditional language on the one hand or to modern philosophical theories on the other. They would not affirm that the bread and wine are in themselves at all changed by consecration, either by receiving a new substance or by acquiring any new properties which can be rightly said to be theirs. Yet they believe that in the Eucharist the bread and wine are themselves taken up into a new spiritual relation to the living Christ. Consecration sets them apart to be the very organ of Christ's gracious self-revelation and action towards His faithful people; and they actually become that organ in so far as, in and through these material objects and what is done with them, the life of Christ, once offered through the breaking of His Body and the shedding of His Blood, is now really given to be the spiritual food of Christians. The bread and wine then become the Body and Blood simply through Christ's use of them to be the very means of His self-communication. To this use they are dedicated by consecration, and in it they have that real and spiritual relation to Christ Himself which belongs to the proper meaning of the terms Christ's Body and Christ's Blood.*

These ways of reinterpreting the doctrine have been mentioned only as examples of the results of recent theological thought upon the subject; nor is it intended to suggest that they are necessarily exclusive of one another. Probably the most serious point of difference among those who hold them is concerned with the deductions to be drawn as to the presence of Christ in the reserved Sacrament, and as to the justification for extra-liturgical devotion in its various forms. Some of those who incline to the third of the interpretations mentioned see in it no warrant whatever for teaching that the Eucharistic presence of Christ remains with the consecrated elements after they have been reserved, until in their use for communion they are again taken up into that Eucharistic action in which they become the Body and Blood of Christ. Others, on the other hand, to whom also this general line of interpretation is congenial, would maintain that the reserved Sacrament ought never to be, and properly never can be, dissociated from its Eucharistic use, and that therefore there is no valid objection of theology to be brought against those who would make it at all times a focus for their worship of Christ, who in it gives Himself to be their spiritual food. A similar justification in theological principle for some forms of extra-liturgical devotion would be accepted by most of those who would prefer one of the first two interpretations mentioned above.

With the merits of this vexed and difficult question the present memorandum is not concerned. Its main purpose is merely to indicate the possibility that a great traditional doctrine of Eucharistic theology, which has been maintained at the cost of so much controversy in the past, may

* Such a restatement would lay a special emphasis on the truth of St. Thomas Aquinas's teaching when he wrote, " Per hoc, quod dicimus ipsum (Christum) esse sub hoc sacramento, significatur quædam habitudo ejus ad hoc sacramentum."

yet be found capable of a statement and interpretation which at least need not offend the conscience even of those Christians who for their own part still prefer to give a different theological expression to the common assurance of our faith that the bread which we break is the communion of the Body of Christ.

(B) RECEPTIONISM

"Receptionism" and "Virtualism" are terms of modern coinage* to indicate variant forms of a type of Eucharistic doctrine which, while denying the Real Presence of Christ's actual Body and Blood in or under the elements of bread and wine, teaches that with and by means of the reception of the elements in communion believers are truly made partakers of the heavenly gifts whereof the elements are efficacious signs. In almost all doctrinal statements of this type there is a negative as well as a positive element. The oft-quoted sentence of Hooker is in this respect characteristic: "The real presence of Christ's most blessed body and blood is not therefore to be sought for in the Sacrament, but in the worthy receiver of the Sacrament."† Lutheran theologians—Martensen is an example‡—have sometimes urged against doctrine of this type that it has been unduly influenced by antagonism to the doctrine of Transubstantiation, and that it fails to maintain the balance of affirmation, which they find better preserved in the difficult Lutheran doctrine of Consubstantiation, according to which the substances of the Body and of the Blood of Christ are present in the use of the communion

* Both terms are found in a book on Eucharistic Doctrine by the late Mr. Gerard Francis Cobb of Trinity College, Cambridge, entitled *The Kiss of Peace* (1st ed. 1867), and there is reason to think that this was their first appearance in English theological literature. Earlier writers often classified the teachings in question as " Doctrine of a spiritual presence."

† *Eccles. Pol.*, Bk. V., ch. lxvii. 6 *init.*

‡ *Christian Dogmatics*, § 263.

alongside and together with the substances of bread and wine.

The negative strain is undoubtedly present in " Receptionist " doctrine. It finds its context and, as many would hold, its justification in the necessity which lay upon its advocates of fashioning an order of worship in harmony with the Reformation conception of the visible Church as " a congregation of faithful men " ruled by the Word of God. The Church as the Reformers found it depended in its entirety upon the hierarchical system which, as the authorised custodian and exponent of the Christian revelation, claimed in its own sphere the obedience of the laity. This general dependence upon the official ministry was reflected in the established worship of the Church centring upon the Mass. In the Mass it was held that the Body and Blood of Christ were verily present under the forms of bread and wine in virtue of the consecration, and that for this the ministry of the priesthood was necessary. Receptionist doctrine of the Eucharist was one aspect of a general movement affecting the whole theology of Church and Sacraments. It was not indeed the only form of Reformation doctrine of the Eucharist, for the Lutherans differed seriously from the Reformed; but they both agreed in finding the presence of Christ in the use of the elements in communion, and not outside that use. The Receptionist type of doctrine so far distinguished the sign and the thing signified that it was only willing to allow an instrumental value to the elements. Others, to whom the term " Virtualist " has been applied, affirmed more explicitly that the elements were themselves endowed with the virtues of Christ's Body and Blood. There were indeed many varieties of emphasis. Nor must it be overlooked that in the Church of England, especially in the seventeenth century, there were many who almost made a principle of eschewing doctrinal definition, and who fell back in general terms upon scriptural and patristic language. But, with all varieties of emphasis, those who may be spoken of as

" Receptionists," as well as those who may be spoken of
as " Virtualists," were agreed that the Real Presence of
Christ's very Body and Blood was not, as it had been previously taught, upon the altar, and they were agreed that
when the faithful raised their hearts to heaven, and received the elements in accordance with Christ's word of
promise, they were truly made partakers of the heavenly
gifts.

Theologians of the Reformation quite rightly urged that
in making the communion of the people a necessary element of the rite they were recovering the ancient practice
of the Catholic Church.   In the early centuries nobody had
thought of a Eucharistic celebration which did not lead up
to the communion of the people.   Such a proceeding would
have appeared pointless.   But the Church's practice
changed—not of set purpose, but slowly, under the pressure of new conditions; and as communions became rarer,
while attendance at the rite without participation became
normal, emphasis gradually shifted—more slowly in the
West than in the East*—to " a moment of consecration."
At that moment, and not before, a Holy Presence was
vouchsafed upon the altar.   The people, of course, continued
to communicate at intervals, but the rite came to be regarded as satisfactorily complete whether or not a communion of the people followed.   This was a new thing in
Christian worship, and it contributed to a profound modification of the officiant's function.   The fierce polemics of
the sixteenth century over Transubstantiation must be set
against this background.   With Transubstantiation in

* " It is instructive to cast a glance at the numerous expositions
of the Roman Mass of the ninth and tenth centuries, of which
several are in print, and compare them with Narsai's.   Any such
idea as the ' moment of consecration ' is not so much as thought of
in them " (Edmund Bishop, Appendix to R. H. Connolly's edition
of the *Homilies of Narsai. Texts and Studies*, vol. viii., p. 128, n. 2).
Mr. Bishop observes that certitude as to the " moment of consecration " was first acquired by common people in the West in the
twelfth or at the earliest in the eleventh century.   *Ib.*, p. 128.

view Receptionism was negative, but this negation was in
the interest of recovering a balance that had been lost.
The ancient communion of the Church was to replace the
priestly sacrifice of the Mass. Receptionism provided a
doctrinal weapon to effect this change. Both sides
appealed to the past. The writings of the Fathers were
ransacked for proofs that they did, or that they did not,
teach Transubstantiation. It need scarcely be said that
the polemical treatment of history which ensued was profoundly unsatisfactory, though eventually it led to a better
understanding of the past. Theologians of the Reformation successfully countered the Roman contention that the
Church had always taught the Real Presence of the actual
Body and Blood of Christ in the sacrament of the altar:
we may recall Archbishop Parker's apt appeal to Aelfric's
Paschal Homily, which shows a representative Anglo-
Saxon teacher, early in the eleventh century, siding with
Ratramnus against the Transubstantiationism of Radbertus.
Receptionism itself, in the stricter sense, had a foothold in
St. Augustine's teaching on the sacrament. On the other
hand, Reforming theologians were often disposed to do
less than justice to the prevailing realism of the early
Church in its attitude towards the sacramental elements.
Most writers on both sides allowed insufficiently for the
all-important fact that in the early centuries there was little
if any controversial sensitiveness on the question. For our
present purpose we may be content to remark the determination of the Reformers to make the Church's Eucharist
again what it had been before—a Service of Communion.
Receptionism was mainly a means to this end.

Many of those who to-day are content to think and feel
in this matter along the lines of Cranmer, Hooker, Waterland, and Westcott, have no wish to assert the negative
side of their doctrine for its own sake. They hold the Real
Presence of Jesus Christ in the Eucharistic rite. It should
also be pointed out that certain objections sometimes advanced against Receptionist doctrine rest upon misunder-

standing of the view as actually held by its adherents. Thus one objection sometimes urged against the Receptionist view is that it is individualistic; but in fact Receptionists, as we have seen, have laid especial emphasis on the communion of the congregation, and have valued the Receptionist view because it lays stress on this. Again, it has been objected that by emphasis upon the worthiness of the recipient a false direction is given to thought, as when men absent themselves because they are not good enough to receive. But this also is a misrepresentation of the view as actually held and valued, for to approach worthily is to approach in penitence, faith, and charity. Once more, it is sometimes thought that Receptionism is inherently subjective; but in fact the Receptionist insists that there is an objective gift offered for his reception.

In the preceding memorandum one reinterpretation of the doctrine which is historically the antithesis of Receptionism—the doctrine of the Real Presence of the Body and Blood of Christ under the forms of bread and wine— is offered in these terms: "[It is not affirmed] that the bread and wine are in themselves at all changed by consecration either by receiving a new substance or by acquiring any new properties which can rightly be said to be theirs. Yet [it is believed] that in the Eucharist the bread and wine are themselves taken up into a new spiritual relation to the living Christ. Consecration sets them apart to be the very organ of Christ's gracious self-revelation and action towards His faithful people; and they actually become that organ in so far as, in and through these material objects and what is done with them, the life of Christ, once offered through the breaking of His Body and the shedding of His Blood, is now really given to be the spiritual food of Christians." Many of those who value the Receptionist strain in our doctrine can understand and feel at home with a doctrine of the Real Presence as thus stated. It lays the emphasis where they wish to lay it—"the life of Christ really given to be the spiritual food of Christians.'' With that emphasis the preceding words which deal more directly with the elements can be recognised as saying what is true. The problems of those Churchmen of whom we here speak are created less by doctrine than by practice. In so far as a tendency manifests itself to separate ritual consecration from the communion for which it prepares, or to remove the elements consecrated outside the service at which consecration takes place, the Receptionist cannot but feel a danger not merely to his doctrine, but to the main interest which that doctrine is meant to serve. For him consecration, communion, oblation make one whole, and the value and effect of this tradition in doctrine is to safeguard the unity and integrity of the rite.

NOTE

Reservation and Devotions

The members of the Commission are agreed that the use of the reserved sacrament is a '' valid '' means of giving sacramental communion; they are agreed also that the extent to which and the circumstances in which this method should be employed may properly be determined by any particular Church. The decision on these questions involves, however, a variety of practical considerations (e.g., what will best tend to edification, will best secure the Communion of the Sick, and will best promote a right attitude and sound beliefs as to the Eucharist), and we hold it to be outside the province of the Commission, here as elsewhere, to express an opinion on administrative or pastoral questions.

The same is true, as it appears to us, in regard to devotions connected with the reserved sacrament. The question whether they ought to be allowed by any particular Church in the Anglican Communion, or whether the rules or formularies of the Church of England ought to be changed so as to countenance such devotions, is again a question involving considerations with some of which we are not concerned. But we are concerned with the question of the truth or falsehood of the theology on which the practices in question are based. We are all agreed that the special Presence (that is, activity and accessibility) of Christ in the Eucharist is given in the context of that rite and for the purpose which that rite subserves. Some of us hold that accordingly any observance of the Presence or reverence to the sanctified Holy Gifts should be confined within the period of the service of Holy Communion, and other times when the reserved sacrament is being used in administration. This is the general practice of the Orthodox Church, as it was throughout the Church in early centuries. Others hold that inasmuch as the consecrated species are reserved for the purpose of Holy Communion, they are of their own nature always within the context of the Eucharistic rite, and thus at all times afford a legitimate focus for the adoration of our Lord, who through them offers Himself to be the sacrificial food of the faithful.

Although our concern is with questions of theology proper, and not with those of pastoral administration, we would wish to call attention to a point which appears to us to be important whenever matters of pastoral administration are closely affected by theology. When a decision has to be taken whether some devotional practice should or should not be allowed, it is not enough only to consider whether or not it is logically possible to base it upon a theology which is free from objection; it is necessary also to consider what will in fact be its effect by way of fostering the spiritual life of the faithful, or by way of giving occasion to conceptions which are objectionable, and also how it will operate in maintaining, restoring, or disturbing the due " proportion of the faith " and the unity of the Church. Thus, even if it be judged that the practice of Devotions does not itself logically involve any wrong theological doctrine, it is still possible that in given circumstances a permission of the practice might on the whole be harmful.

And, on the other hand, even if it be judged that the practice does logically involve a doctrine which in principle is erroneous, it might still be inexpedient to attempt to put an end to it by any direct or absolute prohibition.

The theological question, with which we as a Commission are directly concerned, may be formulated thus. The Christian believes that in the Eucharist Christ, who is everywhere present, is present (that is, active and accessible) in a special manner, and for a special purpose—namely, to be the sacrificial food of the faithful. If then devout Christians find (as multitudes have found) that, when the consecrated elements are reserved, they are helped to adore their Lord by offering their adoration in the presence of those outward things by means of which He offers Himself to be the food of the faithful, is there any theological principle involved which renders the encouragement or even the permission of such a practice inadmissible?

To that question we are unable to give a decisive answer, because we are not agreed upon the application of the determining consideration. That consideration is that the special sacramental Presence of the Lord is to be sought only within the context of those sacramental acts with which the original promise of it was associated. Upon the truth and importance of that principle we are fully agreed; we are not agreed whether or not its application provides a sufficient theological justification for the practice of " Devotions."

The mode of Christ's special activity and accessibility in the Eucharist has been interpreted in various ways, some of which we have considered above. Some, perhaps all, of the main types of interpretation are liable to become occasions of error, and to some forms of such error we have drawn attention. The forms of error or perversions in doctrine which " Devotions " are sometimes liable to encourage are chiefly two: (*a*) A doctrine of the Presence which removes it from the context of Christ's offering of Himself to be the sacrificial food of the faithful in that rite in which His Church according to His ordinance commemorates His passion; (*b*) a doctrine of the Presence of Christ in or by means of the Reserved Sacrament such as leads those who seek it to depreciate, or to become generally insensitive to, His Presence elsewhere. As to the reality of these dangers we are also fully agreed.

Some of us, however, hold that " Devotions " either logically involve what we have called perversions of the true doctrine, or that, even if no necessary logical connexion can be traced, they inevitably encourage those perversions. Others, who hold that the practice of " Devotions " is consistent with what we all agree to be the essential principles of true doctrine, consider that it can be sufficiently safeguarded against these wrong tendencies, and help to foster true adoration of our Lord. In spite of our divergent opinions on this critical point, we venture to think that the agreement we have reached on questions of more general principle is of considerable importance.

(C) " THOSE FIVE COMMONLY CALLED SACRAMENTS "

It seemed to us appropriate to add here some discussion or notes on " those five commonly called Sacraments."

1. *Confirmation*

Confirmation is the name given by the Western Church since the fifth century to the act closely associated with Baptism, in which prayer for the descent of the Holy Spirit is accompanied by the laying-on of hands, and also in the greater part of Christendom, both East and West, by the anointing with oil and the sign of the Cross. In the early days of the Church the imposition of the Bishop's hands together with prayer for the Spirit normally followed immediately upon the baptismal immersion. The evidence of the New Testament enables us to trace this custom to Apostolic times. Baptism in close connection with the laying-on of hands is explicitly mentioned in

Acts xix. 3-6, Heb. vi. 2. In Acts viii. the imposition of the Apostles' hands on those who have been baptised is apparently required to convey the gift of the Holy Spirit. On the other hand, the language of Acts ii. 38 and 1 Cor. vi. 11 might suggest that Baptism by itself conferred the Holy Spirit. In the early Church Baptism and Confirmation virtually formed a single rite. Origen in the third century could write: "Through the laying-on of hands the Holy Spirit was given in Baptism." Whether unction was actually used in Apostolic, as in later, times is extremely doubtful. The phrases of 2 Cor. i. 21-22, 1 John ii. 20 and 27 are probably metaphorical.

The minister in Confirmation is traditionally the Bishop. The decrees of Councils imply attempts to establish confirmation by presbyters, which were denounced and forbidden. But instances where by express commission from the Bishop presbyters have confirmed can be quoted. And today the Eastern Church preserves the ancient custom by which infants are confirmed at Baptism, but the minister is a presbyter who employs oil blessed by the Bishop for the purpose. In the Roman Church also in extraordinary cases the Sacrament may be administered by a priest if he has special authority for the purpose from the Pope. In such cases the chrism used must have been consecrated by a Bishop. In the West Confirmation has come normally to be separated from Baptism, as in the narrative of Acts viii., a case which stands by itself in the New Testament. An anticipation of this custom can be seen in instances where converts from schismatical bodies were no longer rebaptised, but were confirmed. But the real cause was the difficulty of securing the presence of a Bishop at Baptism when dioceses increased in area and infant Baptism prevailed. Even so in theory Baptism was always followed by Confirmation at the earliest possible moment. On the eve of the Reformation, though movements to postpone Confirmation to mature years had long arisen, infant Confirmation was still regarded as normal in theory, but in practice, in many parts of the Latin Church, was usually delayed owing to the difficulty of recourse to the Bishop. By the latter half of the sixteenth century, both in the Anglican and Roman communions, it had become the rule for candidates to attain years of discretion, to the extent of being able to answer the questions of a Catechism.

The form of Confirmation is prayer for the Holy Spirit. In our English Prayer Book this is preceded by the candidates confirming or renewing their baptismal promises. This, however, is not an essential element in the rite.

The matter is, in the Anglican rite, the laying-on of hands—a deliberate return to the New Testament. In the Roman rite it is the act of unction, but this is commonly held to constitute an imposition of hands.

The precise relation between the gift bestowed in Baptism and the gift bestowed in Confirmation cannot be defined. Attempts to explain it are as old as Tertullian and Augustine. A clear-cut answer is impossible, since originally the two were closely conjoined. All theologians agree that in Confirmation the Holy Spirit is given to strengthen the Christian. Some Anglicans have pressed the language of Acts viii. 16-17 and xix. 6 to mean that in the laying-on of hands the Holy Spirit is bestowed for the first time; whereas in Baptism He acts, as it were, *ab extra*. Such spatial symbolism is precarious. The Holy Spirit is active throughout the Body of Christ and therefore in each of its members; and it is by Baptism that we are made members of Christ. But the gifts of the Holy Spirit traditionally associated with Confirmation are those with which in Isa. xi. the Messiah is said to be endowed. The familiar prayer which precedes the laying-on of hands in the rite directly refers to these; the evident implication is that in Confirmation the person, already incorporated into Christ in Baptism, is made a partaker in the gifts proper to the Messianic community and its mission to the world. Thus there is a real gift of grace bestowed in Confirmation.

The rule of the Prayer Book—"there shall none be admitted to the Holy Communion until such time as he be confirmed, or be ready and desirous to be confirmed" —is an ancient rule of discipline which is traceable in England as far back as Archbishop Peckham's "Constitutions" (A.D. 1281). It is evidently appropriate that the rite wherein the gift of the Holy Spirit is bestowed in its fulness should normally precede admission to participation in the rite which expresses the completeness of Church-membership and of its obligations.

2. *Confession and Absolution*

The Christian life has been defined by an Apostolic writer as "fellowship with the Father and with his Son Jesus Christ" (1 John i. 3). But this is only made possible for men by a severance from sin. Thus we read that "the blood of Jesus Christ his Son cleanseth us from all sin" (*ibid.*, verse 7). Indeed, the quality of the Christian life appears to be itself determined by that forgiveness of sin which is its pre-condition. When the Apostles set out to evangelise the world, they proclaimed a Gospel which offered in Jesus Christ remission of sins. The baptismal rite marked the decisive change when men "put on Jesus Christ" and therewith received forgiveness for sins of their past life. This change was the indispensable preliminary to the life of a Christian disciple.

Our subject here is the more restricted topic of the forgiveness of sins committed by Christians within the Christian society, but in dealing with this particular aspect of the problem it is essential to bear in mind the wider issues, for in fact the question of confession and absolution is at any time and in every place closely bound up with the general relations which obtain between the Church and society and with the general circumstances of Christian initiation. For Christian theology of all types and in all ages the dictum of Tertullian holds good: *Fiunt, non nascuntur Christiani* (men are made Christians, they are not born Christians).   But this principle carries different associations in different circumstances.   In the early Christian centuries, even when infant Baptism was widely practised, adult Baptism remained normative; and the fundamental doctrine held that in the baptismal washing all previous sins committed in the condition of pagan ignorance were remitted.   When such conditions prevail, whether in the Church of early centuries or in the mission field today, grave sin committed by Christians bears the stigma of deliberate apostasy following upon deliberate conversion.   The question presents itself whether it is possible for the Church to remit grave sin committed in such circumstances, and, if it is possible, on what conditions. The penitential system of the early Church rested upon considerations of this kind.   It was not concerned with the ordinary failings and shortcomings of everyday life, which for the most part were left to private prayer and confession to God, but chiefly with scandalous offences such as homicide, adultery, apostasy, which involved plain transgression of the moral standards of the Christian society. In the early days the status of penitent was a merciful privilege granted to such offenders in order to give them another chance.

When the world became nominally Christian the public penitential system broke down.   The Church was no longer a comparatively small society concerned to defend itself and its members against the enticements of a pagan environment.   All citizens were Christians and all actual sin was post-baptismal sin.   This momentous change goes far to explain the collapse of the public disciplinary system, and the gradual extension of a system of private or auricular confession to the priest which gained ground in the early Middle Ages and in the thirteenth century was made obligatory throughout the Latin Church.   In the scholastic theology it was treated as a sacrament of the Church, and as necessary to salvation in the case of those who have fallen into "mortal sin."   Confession and

Absolution under such a system might mean a searching discipline applicable to the whole range of everyday life, though in practice it could easily become formal. At the same time "penance" was individualised. In practice the matter lay between the individual and the priest as the representative of God and His Church, the Church as a society being no further implicated in the penance and the remission of sin.

In the Middle Ages the Church of England, being part of the Western Church, shared in the institution of obligatory private confession. But since the sixteenth century the Church of England has abrogated the obligation. The universal duty of sincere confession of sin and shortcoming in public worship as well as in private prayer is enjoined upon the individual, and the Church through the mouth of its minister pronounces absolution to the penitent. But whereas in the scholastic theology it is taught that even perfect contrition does not win God's forgiveness unless it is coupled with at least the wish for absolution given in the Sacrament of Penance, the authoritative teaching of the Church of England neither enjoins nor advises the regular and universal practice of auricular confession. Nevertheless, the Church of England does not minimise the need of confession and absolution. Sin is always an act which injures the whole Body of Christ. Confession in the congregation or to an authorised and appointed representative of the whole Church involves a recognition of the wrong done to the whole body. Sin is not simply a matter of the individual's private relation to God, it concerns his relation to all his fellow-Christians.

The conditions of Church life in England today make difficult and undesirable such exercise of ecclesiastical discipline as existed in early days. Nevertheless, the Church possesses and must retain the means of exercising discipline in the administration of the Sacraments as occasion may arise.

So far as the pastoral function of the Church is con-

cerned, the experience of our own time and of past ages
testifies to a widespread need for confession not only to
God but also to man. The practice of auricular confession
over the greater part of Christendom today shows at least
that a deep-seated instinct of human nature is thereby
satisfied. However conscious we may be of the abuses
which such a system may engender, we should not fail to
perceive the need which it meets. The mutual confession
of sins which an Apostolic writer enjoined upon his readers
(James v. 16) may unquestionably be an effectual means of
grace, but the normal functioning of the Christian Church
requires in addition some more regular provision for the
strengthening and absolution of the troubled penitent.
Our own Church has expressly advised that all those who
cannot quiet their consciences, and those sick persons who
are troubled with any weighty matter, should have private
recourse to the help and counsel of a " learned and discreet
minister of God's Word," and it authorises its priesthood
to pronounce not only to the congregation but also, when
it is desired, to the individual penitent, the authoritative
word of Absolution.

The present position in the Anglican communion is that
there is a widespread and increasing desire on the part of
individuals to avail themselves of this direct and private
ministry.   There has, however, been no change in the
formal teaching of the Church of England.   While the
regular practice of auricular confession has now become
more frequent, and is by no means confined to one school
of thought within the Church of England, it is important
to recognise that it is a ministry of the Word which is
open to all but obligatory upon none.

The ministry of reconciliation in all its aspects must
be understood in its place in the life of the Christian
fellowship as the Body of Christ.   The priest on the
authority of the Gospel proclaims God's forgiveness to the
penitent, and the penitent should be able to accept this
with full assurance. But the penitent is a member of the

Church through which the Gospel is mediated to him. Consequently the appropriation of the divine forgiveness by the penitent may in fact be hindered unless in the congregation the spirit of forgiveness is actually at work. The Christian Church possesses this inherent quality as a fellowship of reconciliation in virtue of its institution by Christ and its relation to Christ as its Head. Sin demands reconciliation because it is a breach of the unity of the fellowship and a barrier set up by man's disobedience between man and God. It is also an evidence and a cause of conflict within the sinner himself, which may need expert treatment in addition to reconciliation.

Sins vary in degree of sinfulness, and the appropriate treatment varies accordingly. Many would recommend that a man who has committed a grave sin should resort to auricular confession; but in the Church of England this must be regarded as a matter of pastoral counsel, not of ecclesiastical requirement. There is undoubtedly a moral need that the penitent should express his penitence for grave sin in some specially grave manner; and where the sin has been notorious there is need for some act of reconciliation which can be publicly notified to the congregation, if occasion so require.

The treatment of sin within the fellowship of the Church has corporate, personal and sacramental aspects.

(1) The corporate aspect has been already discussed upon its formal side. But this treatment in its practical working is also corporate in that there should be no barriers of pride or false shame as between Christians, and the penitence of the sinner should be met by a forgiveness which is ready, unaffected and unreserved. On the side of the sinner restitution must be made where such restitution is possible and wise, since restitution is not only a guarantee of sincerity but also a real attempt to restore the broken unity of the fellowship.

(2) It is personal in so far as the sinner is enabled to " open his grief " to some other person, priest or layman,

himself a sinner, so that the deepest strains and tendencies of personality are released through the loving and sympathetic contact of another personality. This direct and intimate handling of sin is far-reaching in its psychological effects, and is an integral part of the task of the Christian Church.

It is very necessary to distinguish between sin, which may have no strictly abnormal elements, and conditions in which offences against the fellowship and against God result wholly or in part from abnormal physical or mental states. In these cases treatment should be given by a specialist who may or may not be a minister of the Church, or, at the least, expert opinion should be available.

(3) The sacramental aspect of the Christian treatment of sin appears when the ministry of reconciliation which is entrusted to the whole Christian fellowship is exercised by its ordained ministers. No doubt a secret and purely individual confession of sin is met by the forgiveness which God in His love bestows on all who repent. But sin is always an outrage of personal relationship with God and with neighbours, and reconciliation is reconciliation to the fellowship. Consequently confession of sin should be made in the fellowship and the word of pardon and reconciliation should be uttered by one who holds commission to speak in its name.

In the actual practice of a penitential system three elements are to be distinguished: the pastoral bestowal of the "benefit of absolution," the judicial function shown in its extreme form in a decision to refuse absolution, and the pastoral activity of giving spiritual counsel. Of these the last is separable from the other two. There are some who practise auricular confession in order to obtain such counsel; and it is certainly natural that the priest who has just heard a confession from a penitent should give counsel to that penitent for the future conduct of his life. But this guidance can be sought and given apart from any specific confession and from any kind of absolution.

The "benefit of absolution" is not primarily the quieting of the conscience of the penitent, but pardon—that is to say, an express and authoritative declaration of forgiveness, given in the Name of Christ and carrying with it the fulness of reconciliation to God and in Him to the fellowship.

The Church makes provision for such confession and absolution, both in its public services and by private or auricular confession. For both alike the basis is to be found in the fact that "Almighty God . . . hath given power and commandment to his Ministers to declare and pronounce to his people, being penitent, the Absolution and Remission of their sins." The words which follow these are to be understood, as the syntax of the passage requires, in the sense of such a declaration then and there made by the minister who utters them. The people have confessed their sins, both as individuals and as a congregation; and the duly commissioned minister has uttered the assurance of God's forgiveness to them, if they be truly penitent; so that the conditions for the bestowal and appropriation of pardon are fulfilled. Consequently this is not merely a general statement of God's will to forgive those who repent; to any who have not previously appropriated by faith the divine forgiveness of their sins, and who with faith receive it, it is the actual occasion and vehicle of that forgiveness; to all it is the word of pardon, the authoritative declaration of divine forgiveness whereby they are assured and certified of restoration to fulness of fellowship with God and His Church.

The same principles apply to the service of Holy Communion. But here the context is set by the words of the Invitation (" Ye that do truly," etc.); those addressed are intending communicants; and the words of Absolution, being addressed to them in the second person, emphasise the application to them of the pardon pronounced.

In these public services there is no question of a *judicium* exercised by the minister. Where, however, a penitent individually approaches the minister for private confession and absolution, some such *judicium* must be exercised. But this necessity arises from the circumstances; under a system in which resort to auricular confession is not obligatory it assumes the form of a discipline which the penitent voluntarily imposes upon himself. It is not imposed upon him externally by the Church.

Thus there is no distinction in principle between the general confession and absolution in the public services of the Church, and the direct and individual confession and absolution for which provision is made in the Office for the Visitation of the Sick or to which reference is made in the Exhortation attached to the Order of Holy Communion. In all cases the basis of action is the Gospel itself, the proclamation of the Divine Love seeking and saving the lost and uniting them in the fellowship of the redeemed. In all cases the divine forgiveness is declared. In all cases the purpose is the bestowal of the benefit of absolution, though in one set of circumstances a special judicial element is introduced by the nature of those circumstances.

Combined with confession and absolution so understood we often find on the side of the penitent a desire for the "release" which often accompanies "making a clean breast," and on the side of the minister the giving of spiritual counsel. It is in this way that there arises a connection between the practical aspect of confession and absolution and the scientific treatment of abnormal states by psycho-therapy. The practice of psycho-therapy has emphasised the need for deep and sincere self-examination and for willingness to disclose the secret troubles of the soul, which has always been emphasised by the Church.* There is urgent need for closer co-operation between this

---

* We are not here speaking of such psycho-analysis as brings the contents of the subconscious mind into consciousness. Confession, and any pastoral treatment based upon it, can only concern what is within consciousness.

development of medical practice and the pastoral ministry of the Church, though this co-operation can only be thorough if it is based on Christian principles on both sides. This subject lies outside our proper province, but we may mention two points :

(1) There is no doubt that the " release " described often results from confession, to whomsoever made, and it can be a great blessing to the troubled soul; but such " release " is not necessarily identical with, or accompanied by, restoration to fellowship with God, though such restoration when truly appropriated is always accompanied by " release." Indeed, a method of psycho-therapy which ignores God may sometimes lead to an apparent solution of internal conflict which yet from a religious standpoint may be a disaster. The mental release which the patient often receives from medical treatment is fundamentally different from the peace of God which can only be ours as the result of repentance and forgiveness. There can be nothing worse for the soul than to become contented while alienated from God.

(2) The giving of spiritual counsel is a great responsibility not lightly to be undertaken. Those who are both expected and authorised to give it should be prepared by study and experience for their solemn task. The Prayer Book urges that any whose conscience is troubled should " open his grief " either to the minister of his parish or " to some other discreet and learned minister of God's holy Word," who is by his discretion and learning competent for so great a responsibility.

Much of what has been said in the preceding paragraphs has application to the special case of auricular confession. But in this case the following principles are also to be observed :

(1) The confession is heard under the " seal " of absolute secrecy. This rule is necessary in order that freedom of confession may be secured. It is essential to the due discharge of the confessor's office that this rule should be

held to be so binding on the priest's conscience that he cannot consider himself liable to be released therefrom by the authority of the civil or other power. This, however, does not necessarily imply that he ought not in certain cases to refuse absolution except on condition of the disclosure by the penitent or with his consent of certain facts; the determination of the cases, if any, in which he should so act is one of the most delicate problems of moral theology, which it would be outside our province to discuss.

(2) The priest acts as a judge in certain necessary respects. He is bound to satisfy himself of the sincerity of the penitent, in particular by securing that there is no refusal to make any restitution that is on other grounds reasonable and desirable. He endorses (or in some cases mitigates) the judgment of the penitent upon his own conduct. In some cases he may have to estimate the extent to which the sin of the penitent has done injury to the fellowship. In pronouncing absolution he speaks for the whole fellowship, but with the authority derived from his office as priest, an office which carries with it the function of declaring the divine forgiveness and thus conveying the divine pardon.

(3) It is customary to impose a penance. This must be of such a character that it does not compel the penitent to make his offence public. Normally it is slight in character, and is not regarded as a penalty for the offence; it is prescribed and accepted in humble recognition and acceptance of the judgment of God, and as an admission by the penitent that his sin directly deserves punishment, even though by God's mercy that punishment is not exacted.

In those areas where a system of canonical discipline is in force—e.g., in parts of the mission field—the imposition of penance includes a judicial element, and the administration of the system is directly controlled by the Bishop.

3. Ordination

It is clear from history that the only "matter" which has always been used for conferring Holy Orders is the imposition of hands by a minister who is recognised as having the necessary authority to do so. The "form" is prayer of a character sufficient to express the intention of ordaining to the Ministry of the Church of Christ.*

The rite in the Anglican Ordinal presupposes that the candidate is inwardly moved by God and approved by the Church.

We are all agreed that the effect of Ordination is to set apart for life the person ordained as a minister of the Church, to convey the commission for the ministry and to convey grace for its exercise, and in the case of priests to confer commission to preach the Word and to administer the Sacraments. In the consecration of bishops authority for pastoral oversight is given.

4. Unction

Among "those five commonly called Sacraments" is Unction. Scriptural sanction was found for it in two passages—Mark vi. 13: "They cast out many devils, and anointed with oil many that were sick, and healed them"; and James v. 14, 15: "Is any among you sick? Let him call for the elders of the Church; and let them pray over him, anointing him with oil in the name of the Lord; and the prayer of faith shall save him that is sick, and the Lord shall raise him up; and if he have committed sins, it shall be forgiven him." Here the purpose is recovery from sickness rather than preparation for death. Later Unction came to be associated specially with immi-

* In some primitive Ordinals it is not always made clear in the form of service to what grade of the Ministry a man is being admitted. This is made clear in later forms, but actually there was never any doubt in the context of the whole ceremony.

nent death and thus acquired the name of Extreme Unction.   This was the current use in the Church of Rome
when the Thirty-Nine Articles were composed, and was,
presumably, in mind when reference was (apparently) made
to Unction as a "corrupt following of the Apostles."

According to the Roman Catholic view, Unction conveys forgiveness of sins.   But (though this opinion can
be traced to the words of St. James), it does not seem
to be necessary for this purpose, since in the developed
system of the Church those who are sufficiently conscious to receive Absolution and Holy Communion may
receive pardon thereby, while in the case of those who are
not conscious forgiveness of sins cannot be effected by
any external rite, except in so far as forgiveness may be
presumed to be desired, in which case Absolution may be
pronounced.

If and when Unction is used (as to which issue we make
no recommendation), it should be interpreted as an outward and visible rite, having a background both in the
New Testament and in Church tradition, which, expressing the Church's pastoral care for the sick and dying, is,
in the context of faith and of the Church's ministration,
a symbol of the grace of God for the strengthening of the
body and soul in their weakness.

We think that what has been said should be present to
the minds of those who have to decide whether or not
official provision should be made in the Church of England
for a rite of Unction; on this point the Commission is
divided, but does not think that the question falls within
the province of a body appointed to deal with doctrine.

5. *Marriage*

Marriage stands in a special position because, both as
a rite and as a state of life, it is not something peculiarly
Christian, but rather is an institution of the natural order
which is taken into and sanctified by the Christian Church.

The teaching of the New Testament, which clearly has

its basis in the teaching of our Lord Himself, implies that Marriage is in its own principle a lifelong and intimate union, and that anything short of this falls short of the purpose of God. Marriage so understood has the character which enables St. Paul to draw an analogy between it and the union between Christ and the Church.

The above statement expresses the essential principle of marriage, and may be fairly regarded as its theological basis. Further we desire to affirm that in the case of two Christian persons freely undertaking before God to enter on a lifelong marriage union, grace is afforded which, if reliance is fully placed upon it, will enable the persons concerned to fulfil the obligations involved and to rise to the opportunities offered in their married life in spite of all difficulties however grave.

The fuller consideration of the subject would involve questions which are not only doctrinal, but belong also to the fields of Ethics, of Moral Theology, and of Discipline; and the different aspects of the enquiry cannot be isolated from one another. We believe that many points might be clarified, to the great benefit of the Church, by a Commission specially appointed for the purpose, and selected so as to have competence in all the fields of enquiry that would be affected. We would urge that this task may be undertaken at an early date.

PART III

ESCHATOLOGY

ONE great subject remains as yet untouched. Here as before we are not making any attempt to write systematic theology. If this were our object, consideration of Eschatology could not have been avoided at an earlier stage; for its subject-matter is nothing less than the fulfilment of the purposes of God for the world which He has created and redeemed. It therefore has a vital bearing upon every department of Christian theology. But the scope of our enquiry here is more limited. We are concerned to note, and to relate to one another within the fabric of Christian truth as we understand it, certain prevalent tendencies of thought within the Church of England in relation to the ultimate destiny of man and the consummation of history.

(A) GENERAL CONSIDERATIONS

The interest of most modern people in the "Last Things" has an emphasis and perspective different from that disclosed in the New Testament. To-day the predominant concern tends to be with the personal destiny of individuals. People ask: What is the destiny of ourselves or (still more) of our friends? That concern is indeed present in the New Testament (*e.g.*, 1 Thess .iv. 13-18), but it is subordinate. The predominant concern is with the fulfilment of the purpose of God—so manifestly not yet fulfilled on the historical plane. The destiny of the individual is a subordinate part of the whole purpose of God. We are convinced that if we are to think rightly in these matters we must recover the perspective of the New Testament: we must begin with the world-purpose of God, and must see everything else in that context. The Gospel knows no private or merely individual salvation : the faithful departed shall not " without us " be " made perfect " ; and so neither shall we without them. The world-purpose of God is wrought out partly through history; but for its complete and full working out it requires not only a " new creation " of man, but a " new earth " and " new heavens."

Inasmuch as eschatological beliefs and doctrines are concerned, of necessity, with matters in respect of which " eye hath not seen, nor ear heard," these beliefs are inevitably expressed in symbolical language.* Often the different pictorial images employed will be inconsistent with one another. Their pictorial character having been once clearly grasped, there is no need to attempt to combine them into one picture. Moreover, the several pictures often represent tendencies of thought which are not, as they stand, compatible; we may seek to reconcile the elements of spiritual value found in these, but we must not expect to achieve this perfectly until we have that knowledge of the world to come which is only to be gained by entrance into it. Thus, there is important spiritual truth conveyed alike by the doctrine of the general " Last Judgment " and by the doctrine of the particular judgment of individuals at death; and while we may hope to make progress towards a reconciliation of these several truths, we cannot expect to have full knowledge of the relation between this life and the life to come while we still have direct knowledge only of the former.

From the point of view of a person looking before and after, neither a beginning nor an end of Time can be imagined, and yet the time-process can only be exhibited as significant in so far as it is imaginatively presented as a drama, with both beginning and end. But it appears vital to maintain that the time-process has a more than merely temporal significance, and that God achieves some-

* See p. 37.

thing through it. The world-outlook of Scripture, which
sees in the process of events in time the working out of a
divine purpose, appropriately sets at the beginning of
things a parable of Creation, and at their end a parable
of the End of the World.

The New Testament Scriptures, taken as a whole, are
dominated by the thought of the approaching " end "; by
the conviction that the new " Age " is " at hand "; that
its " powers " are already at work; and that human life,
here and now, stands in immediate relation to the Judgment, the Kingdom of God, Heaven and Hell, and the
Life of the World to Come. It is this conception of life as
being, so to speak, poised on the edge of judgment which
gives to the New Testament outlook its notes of finality,
absoluteness, and urgency. In the Pauline Epistles the
gift of the " Spirit " is already an " earnest " or first
instalment of the new order; in the Fourth Gospel the
phrase " eternal life " denotes similarly the present gift of
a new supernatural life which is to endure for ever.

In a literal sense, the *dénouement*, which in the New
Testament age was expected, did not take place, though
many scholars have urged that there is authority in the
New Testament, and notably in the Fourth Gospel, for the
view that there was a real Parousia of the glorified Lord
in the coming of the Spirit. Traditional orthodoxy has
tended nevertheless to take the scriptural imagery of the
Last Things and the hoped-for *Parousia* or " coming "
of Christ semi-literally, but to explain that the *time* of the
coming has been postponed. This explanation already
begins to be suggested within the New Testament period
(*cf.* 2 Pet. iii. 3 *sqq.*).

Inasmuch, however, as the moral urgency of the eschatological message (and, from one point of view, its real heart)
is to be found largely in the assertion of the *immediate*
relation of human life, here and now, to its consummation
in eternity, to the solemn realities of judgment, and to the
triumph of God, a truer perspective (it may be suggested)

is to be secured by taking the *imagery* in a symbolical sense, but by continuing to affirm, with the New Testament, that "the time is at hand." The "time" is, in this sense, *always* at hand; and from this point of view the spiritual value of the eschatological drama is best grasped when it is understood, not as a quasi-literal description of a future event, but as a parable of the continuous and permanent relation of the perpetually imminent eternal order to the process of events in time.

Moment by moment, the waves of time beat on the shores of eternity—it is not only the last wave in the series which washes those shores. Moment by moment, "the world hasteth to pass away." Moment by moment, we stand in the twilight of the dawn: "The night is far spent, the day is at hand" (Rom. xiii. 12). The supernatural is for ever pressing in upon the natural, the eternal upon the temporal. It is at all times true that the supreme and decisive verdict on human affairs is the verdict of God, before whom "all things lie naked and open." Despite the solid-seeming permanence of the natural order, the thought of which prompted the Old Testament author to write that "One generation goeth, and another generation cometh; but the earth abideth for ever," there is a deeper truth expressed by the words of St. John: "The world passeth away, and the lust thereof; but he that doeth the will of God abideth for ever."

But this account of the matter does not cover the ground. There is indeed a continuous process whereby, in accordance with the divine ordering of the universe, "things are what they are, and the consequences of them will be what they will be"; and in this ordered sequence the divine judgment may be in part discerned. But there is still more to be said: the divine judgment, which is thus always operative, is specially declared in certain events, such as, for example, the fall of Jerusalem, a doom upon which is pronounced in the Gospels.

Moreover, on any view, human history on this planet

must have an end; upon its course as then completed, as upon every separate episode, the judgment of God must be "made manifest" (Rev. xv. 4). It is the ultimate judgment of God upon human affairs, as thus conceived, which gives to human history as a whole its meaning as the sphere of the accomplishment of the divine purpose; and it is of this truth that the traditional imagery of the Last Judgment is the pictorial symbol.

As to the question whether, or in what sense, there will be a "Last Judgment," conceived as an *event*, supervening upon the conclusion of this world's history, the Commission is united in believing that it is impossible to pronounce; but we are agreed in the conviction that in the world to come the judgment of God on our earthly lives will be made manifest alike to our neighbours and to ourselves, and the meaning of God's "strange work" in human history will be disclosed.

The recognition that every moment is pregnant with eternal issues is in no way contrary to the conception of the Judgment as the culmination of history.

The drama of the Last Things, as set forth in the mediæval "Doom" pictures, rests on a tradition which makes use of a more or less literal conception of heaven and hell as specific "places," of which a picture was formed by drawing upon traditional material, more especially the imagery of the Book of Revelation, which is itself largely drawn from Jewish and other pre-Christian sources. The colours were no doubt heightened, the details embellished, in various ways; there was no completely fixed orthodoxy as to the details. Speaking broadly, there was a generally accepted consensus of ideas, though between Rome and the Reformers there was divergence concerning the doctrine of the Intermediate State. A quasi-literal interpretation of the imagery has in fact generally prevailed amongst Christians, and has been widespread, even in educated circles, almost down to the present day; though theologians, at least from the time of Clement and Origen onwards, have been aware that much of the language used was symbolical in character.

The various strands which have been combined together in this traditional scheme have in modern times been disentangled and traced out by Biblical criticism; and light has been thrown on them by psychological and historical enquiry. The point has been made, for example, that it is in times of stress that the apocalyptic outlook most flourishes. The perspectives of the traditional picture have, moreover, inevitably been affected by the substitution of a Copernican for a Ptolemaic cosmology, and by the vast vistas of time opened up by the researches of modern geology and astronomy.

As a result of all this the eschatology of the New Testament has been studied from new points of view; and the door has been opened to fresh methods of enquiry, both philosophical and scientific.

(B) THE FUTURE LIFE

1. *Resurrection.*

In all ages there has been philosophical argument with regard to the question of human immortality: in modern times there has been in addition to this a quest for what is described as scientific evidence of survival. In all such enquiry Christians, in so far as they are interested, must be concerned to distinguish between the purely scientific interest and the interests of religion. For example, although it is true that empirical evidence for the survival of physical death, if it be forthcoming, might for some people remove an obstacle to the acceptance of the Christian doctrine of eternal life,* yet such alleged evidence could never *establish* the Christian doctrine, and might even divert attention from it. For (*a*) the survival of death need not necessarily involve immortality—the

* *E.g.*, the idea that the mind cannot survive the dissolution of the brain.

mental and spiritual functions of human nature might conceivably survive the death of the physical organism and subsequently enter upon a process of dissolution; and (b) the Christian hope is not concerned with the mere prolongation of existence, without change of quality, but with fellowship with God.

So, again, we do not regard any one particular philosophical doctrine of immortality as being *de fide* for Christians. There are those who would regard immortality rather as a gift of God, bestowed in and through Christ, than as an inherent property or endowment of the human soul. As between the affirmation of the doctrine known as "*conditional immortality*," and the assertion of the *universal* immortality of mankind, the Commission as a whole does not feel itself called upon to make a pronouncement. There is a large number of Christians for whom it is sufficient in these matters to affirm that "the gift of God is eternal life through Jesus Christ our Lord."

For Christians the hope of immortality rests primarily upon faith in the love of God. To believe that the world is governed by a loving God, or is even truly rational at all, would, apart from this hope, be very difficult. A doctrine of immortality is a necessity for Theism and especially for Christian Theism.

Special difficulty has attached to the traditional doctrine of the Resurrection of the Body. No doubt the form in which it was originally accepted was largely due to the current Jewish beliefs, confirmed by the tradition of the Lord's appearances after the Resurrection, taken in conjunction with that of the Empty Tomb.* Thus in the Pauline doctrine Christ was the firstfruits, and the resurrection of the faithful, when it occurred, was expected to be after the pattern of His. But the fact of the disintegration of the bodies of departed Christians inevitably presents difficulties. Those modern theologians who accept the tradition of the Empty Tomb in the

* See p. 86.

case of our Lord, though they affirm the analogy, as for example does St. Paul in 1 Cor. xv., yet are not disposed to lay stress on the resemblance between the manner of Christ's Resurrection and ours, but rather to dwell on the difference between what was appropriate or even inevitable in the case of the divine and sinless Redeemer and what is possible in the case of sinners though redeemed.

Yet the doctrine of the Resurrection of the Body stands for an important group of truths:

(a) It excludes the notion that the future life is impoverished and ghostly. On the contrary, that life is as full as, and fuller than, the life here. We expect to be not " unclothed," but " clothed upon " (2 Cor. v. 4).

(b) It excludes the notion that our treatment and use of our bodies is spiritually irrelevant. The exclusion of this idea was of vital importance in the primitive Church, and is still important in many parts of the world. If it sometimes seems unimportant to ourselves, this is only because the truth emphasised by the doctrine is at present accepted among us. If the doctrine were abandoned, this truth might be jeopardised.

(c) It safeguards the conviction that we shall have the means of recognising each other in the future life.

(d) It expresses with serviceable brevity a truth which ought to be expressed, even though naïve interpretation of it may carry suggestions which ought to be discarded. While, in the judgment of the Commission, we ought to reject quite frankly the literalistic belief in a future resuscitation of the actual physical frame which is laid in the tomb, it is to be affirmed, none the less, that in the life of the world to come the soul or spirit will still have its appropriate organ of expression and activity, which is one with the body of earthly life in the sense that it bears the same relation to the same spiritual entity. What is important, when we are speaking of the identity of any person's " body," is not its physico-chemical constitution, but its relation to that person.

(e) There is a further point still. The doctrine of the Resurrection coheres with the conception of real continuity between the body of the earthly life and the resurrection body. What happens here upon earth is in some sense taken up into the life of Heaven, so that the character of earthly and bodily life is of eternal significance. The earthly life is something other, and something more, than a mere ladder up which we climb, but which we kick away when we have reached our goal. It has been pointed out already* that " for the Christian eternal life can only be fully attained through the sacrifice of the self in union with Christ's sacrifice," and that, in this connexion, " as means and conditions of such sacrifice, the natural facts of human decay and mortality take on a fresh significance, and death becomes not a mere gateway to be passed through, nor the mere casting away of a perishable body, but a loss which is turned into gain, a giving up of life which is made the means whereby that life is received back again, renewed, transfigured, and fulfilled." Thus the doctrine stands for the recovery, through the surrender which is death, of whatever has been truly and permanently valuable in life here.

But the question may be asked—and inevitably it is, in fact, asked—What is it exactly that happens when we die? There is the discarding of the physical frame; the soul, as we say, leaves the body. Are we to think of it as being *immediately* " clothed upon " with what St. Paul, in one passage, describes as its " habitation which is from Heaven "—that is to say, its new body of the resurrection? Or are we, in accordance with the literal and formal orthodoxy of the main Christian tradition, to think rather of a period of disembodied existence, an " intermediate state," as intervening between the death of the body and the day of " general resurrection " ? The problems of the relation of the temporal to the eternal order, and of the conditions of life here to the conditions of life hereafter,

* See p. 85.

are involved at this point. In the light of what has been said above, the notion of a period of disembodied existence presents difficulties, and it may be that some of the questions raised cannot be answered under the conditions of earthly life. We cannot expect a coherent scheme, but must be content to employ partially irreconcilable symbolisms, and to remain otherwise agnostic. The main tradition of the Church, as it came to be systematised in patristic and mediæval times, has postulated a period of disembodied existence as intervening between the death of the individual and the final consummation. Not only were the souls in purgatory regarded as disembodied, but those also who were classed as " saints " in the distinctive sense of that word, and who were regarded as being already " in Heaven " and as having already in some measure attained to the " beatific vision " of God, were nevertheless not thought of as having entered into the resurrection life, but as being destined still to " rise " upon the last great day. The expectation of a single great Day of General Resurrection, considered literally, and interpreted as a kind of Final Event in the temporal order, presents great difficulties. Nevertheless the traditional scheme at least calls attention to the truths (*a*) that the resurrection is to be regarded as being linked with the *fulfilled and completed* purpose of God, and with the idea of the " new heavens " and the " new earth," and (*b*) that the Christian salvation is a *social* salvation, and that the faithful departed shall not without us be made perfect.

2. *The Intermediate State.*

With regard to the idea of the Intermediate State there have been divergent views within Christendom. The more distinctively " Evangelical " tradition has been content to think simply of the faithful departed as being immediately " in joy and felicity." Any emphasis upon the ideas of growth, purification, or spiritual advance after death has been viewed with suspicion, and has indeed sometimes been held to imperil the reality and fulness of the Christian's assurance (linked, in the minds of Evangelicals, with the doctrine of Justification by Faith) of a present and joyful "salvation" through Christ.

On the other hand, there are those in the Church of England whose reaction from the cruder forms of the mediæval doctrine of Purgatory has not led them to reject the doctrine in all its forms. There are indeed crude forms of the doctrine and these ought to be rejected: thus, in the Middle Ages it was widely believed that Purgatory, like Hell, was a "place" in which souls were plunged into literal or quasi-literal fire, the difference being that whereas the fires of Hell were eternal, those of Purgatory were limited in duration, and the endurance of them was a temporal penalty which the sinner paid to the Divine Justice by way of "satisfaction" for the guilt of forgiven sins. We can to-day make terms neither with the legalistic conception of man's relation to his Maker here implied, nor with the theory of punishment according to which a specific amount of pain is inexorably "due," and must be rendered as satisfaction for a specific degree of guilt. But the crudity in these respects of some mediæval conceptions of Purgatory does not rule out the essential idea of a phase of progressive growth and, it may be, of needed purification of the soul after death. The chief defect of the traditional conception of Purgatory (apart from the points already criticised) has been its failure to recognise the manner in which not only pain or sorrow but also joy may minister to spiritual advance. It is true that (*e.g.*) in Newman's *Dream of Gerontius* the happiness of Gerontius' soul in Purgatory is emphasised, and it is represented as suffering only as the result of inability to bear the immediate vision of the "keen sanctity" of God's infinite and holy love. A similar thought is expressed by Dante in *Purgatorio* xxvi. 14, 15. The atmosphere of the traditional picture is none the less predominantly sombre, and a truer psychology would recognise, side by side with the deepening of penitence, a deepening joy in God's service and in the increasing knowledge of Him.

This thought of joy as characteristic of those who after death are awaiting the General Resurrection finds a natural expression in the use of the word "Paradise," which has often been used with precisely this significance.

In the Church of England to-day, both the view indicated above as having been characteristic of the "Evangelical" tradition, and also a doctrine of life hereafter which (whether or not the *word* Purgatory be used or the element of purification be emphasised) is at least conceived in terms of development and growth, are with varying degrees of emphasis, and in varying forms of statement, to be recognised as being current; and in the judgment of the Commission the Church of England deliberately leaves room for both views.

3. *The Communion of Saints.*

The New Testament doctrine of the Communion of Saints is not concerned with any communication between the living and the departed, but with the redemption of the human race. The faithful departed are in Christ; so also are we. The implications of this were not worked out by the Apostolic writers, partly, no doubt, because there were as yet few Christians who had died, partly because the Parousia was regarded as imminent. The primary concern of the New Testament in this connexion is to insist upon the reality of a fellowship in Christ in which living and departed share. Its concern is with the redeemed society, with incorporation into the Body of Christ, with the general assembly and Church of the first-born, whereof Jesus, by virtue of His perfect self-offering, is the Mediator.

Alike in the Eastern and the Western Church this thought has been prominent, both in the Liturgy and in popular religion. In particular the Eastern Church has kept it fully alive. The Communion of Saints is apprehended as a fellowship of mutual intercession. No distinction is drawn in this respect between saints and others; prayers are offered by the Church on earth even for the Mother of our Lord, and the prayers of friends lately departed in the faith of Christ are asked on behalf of those who seek this help. Thus for the Orthodox the approach to the Throne of Grace is made in a company at once august and friendly. Worship offered in that atmosphere can never seem to be cold or remote from the intimacies of human fellowship. But this fellowship is essentially a fellowship in prayer to God.

But such a conception may be perverted, and at the time of the Reformation the abuses arising from such perversion were very great. There has, however, been a real risk in the reformed Churches of a sense of remoteness in worship or else of a lowering of the thought of God to a level of familiarity. The latter is destructive of real worship; the former tends to correct itself by rash and groundless speculation. We are persuaded that the way of truth and safety is to remember that our fellowship with the departed is a fellowship in prayer and worship, as living and departed are united in yearning and aspiration towards the consummation of Christ's redeeming work. The only way to come closer to those who are departed in the faith of Christ is to draw near to God, and to draw near to Him is, *eo ipso*, to come closer to them.

It is impossible to declare that departed saints cannot hear our prayers, and we therefore must not condemn as impossible direct address to them as a private practice, provided this be to ask for their prayers whether for ourselves or for others; anything other than this seems to us both perilous and illegitimate. But also it is impossible to have well-grounded assurance that the saints hear us, so that direct address to them may well be thought inappropriate in the official worship of the Church. On the other hand, such formal expression within the liturgy of our fellowship with them in prayer as is contained, for example, in the Collect—" O God, the King of Saints "*—appended to the Scottish Liturgy represents a true balance of thought and is a legitimate enrichment of worship.

The vital point to be at all costs secured is that God alone is the object of our worship, and that our fellowship with the departed is in and through Him.

NOTE

PRAYER FOR THE DEPARTED

The Reformers mostly condemned any form of Prayer for the Departed. There had been widespread abuses, and when reference was made to Scripture no trace of the practice was found except in the Apocrypha, which the Reformers did not accept as canonical.† But the practice has never entirely died out in the Church of England; the position not only of Bishop Andrewes but of Dr. Johnson in relation to this matter is well known. It was declared by the two English Archbishops in the *Responsio* to the Papal Encyclical *Apostolicæ Curæ* that the words in the

---

* The Collect is this:

O God the King of Saints, we praise and magnify thy holy Name for all thy servants who have finished their course in thy faith and fear, for the Blessed Virgin Mary, for the holy Patriarchs, Prophets, Apostles, and Martyrs, and for all other thy righteous servants; and we beseech thee that, encouraged by their example, strengthened by their fellowship, and aided by their prayers, we may attain unto everlasting life; through the merits of thy Son Jesus Christ our Lord. Amen.

† Many modern scholars find such a reference in 2 Timothy i. 18.

Prayer of Oblation include the Church Expectant, when prayer is made that "we and all thy whole Church may obtain remission of our sins." Recently, and especially in times of great distress, such as those of war, the practice has increased, and the special Forms of Prayer issued by authority at such times have often contained petitions for the departed.

It is, of course, to be remembered that all Christian prayer aims at being prayer that God's will may be done; Prayer for the Departed is not, any more than any other prayer, an attempt to persuade or suggest to God some action that it was not already His will to take. If there is any such fellowship of living and departed as Christians have always believed, and if the thought of growth and of purification after death is not to be dogmatically excluded, there is no theological objection in principle to Prayer for the Departed. The question of the safeguards that may wisely be imposed in any given circumstances belongs to the realm not of theology but of pastoral expediency.

4. *Judgment, Hell, and Heaven.*

We have endeavoured to set out the Christian doctrine of Death and Resurrection as we understand it. The traditional scheme presents these as being followed by Judgment, a particular Judgment immediately after death, the general Judgment at the general Resurrection—the ultimate issue of Judgment being consignment to Hell or admission to Heaven.

Both on the ground of the varieties of interpretation accepted by the Church at large in all periods, and also on grounds of modern research (see above, p. 207), it is clear that this scheme can be accepted only as a symbolic outline of the course of spiritual destiny, not as a chronological account of future events.

The doctrine of Judgment pervades the whole of Scripture, alike in the Old Testament and in the New. We have already discussed the relations between the Divine

Judgment and human history in its totality. We are here concerned with the Judgment upon the individual. That man is ever subject to the Judgment of God is both the clear teaching of the Bible and a necessary part of any true Theism. There is great peril in the easy-going sentimentality of some modern Christianity, which supposes all who have departed this life to be forthwith " in joy and felicity "—a perversion of the Evangelical view mentioned above. Such a view is inconsistent with the solemn warnings of Scripture and especially the Gospels themselves, and converts the hope of immortality from a moral stimulus to a moral narcotic.

The Christian doctrine insists upon the reality of " abiding consequences " of every act of moral choice. When such a choice has been made, neither the world at large nor the person choosing can ever again be the same as if the choice had not been made or had been made differently.

According to the traditional scheme, the period of open choices closes with death, after which there remains only submission to the consequences of choices made during earthly life. This is, no doubt, consonant with the stern emphasis laid in the New Testament upon the decisiveness of choices made in the life on earth. On the other hand, it would not be easy to find in the New Testament a basis for definitely and rigorously excluding all hope of further opportunity; indeed, there are passages which taken by themselves are universalist in tendency, and there are some Christians who, partly because of these passages, accept the universalist position, and accordingly believe in further opportunities in the future life; moreover, one passage that seems to bear upon the matter (1 Peter iii. 19, 20) is at least patient of an interpretation which finds in the preaching of the Lord to the spirits in prison a hope that those who have not heard the Gospel before death may hear it after death and so receive the offer of salvation.

But it we extend this hope, as many feel bound to do, to a general expectation of further opportunities of grace for all, it will not be on account of specific declarations of Scripture, but rather as an inference from the Christian doctrine of God as a whole. That doctrine requires us to repudiate all conceptions of the Judgment which represent God as abandoning the appeal of Love and falling back on the exercise of omnipotent sovereignty to punish those who have failed to respond to the invitation of the Gospel. God is Love; and He cannot deny Himself.

But if any freedom of choice is attributed to the human will, this together with the universal facts of moral experience compels man to face the possibility that he may refuse for ever to respond to the call of the Divine love, and this possibility is prominent in the New Testament. Such a refusal must involve exclusion from the fellowship of that love. Some hold that the soul might continue for ever in that state of exclusion; others that at some point the soul which totally rejects the Divine Love must perish out of existence. Between these two we do not feel called to judge. Both may be held to be compatible with Scripture; both can be supported by ethical arguments. In either case, such a soul is "lost."

Whether in fact any soul will suffer final loss in either sense it is not possible for man to pronounce. But if we leave this open, as we must, that must not be allowed to obscure the reality of the final and irreversible " damnation " of evil. God's judgment upon sin is not provisional, nor is His repudiation of it reversible. For some the fundamental conviction is that the possibility of " loss " or " perdition " seems to be involved in the reality of human freedom; for others the fundamental conviction is that the Divine Love cannot suffer final defeat, and that such defeat seems to them to be involved in the perdition of any soul. There is here a real conflict of convictions and both sides of it must be fully recognised. There must be room in the Church both for those who believe that some will actually be lost, and also for those who hold that the Love of God will at last win penitence and answering love from every soul that it has created; while probably the majority feel strongly the force of the argument on both sides and are content to hold their minds in suspense.

As the essence of Hell is exclusion from the fellowship of God, so the essence of Heaven is that fellowship. It is not a selfish happiness offered in reward for selfsuppression at an earlier time; it is fellowship with God who is Love. Inasmuch as this is fellowship of the creature with the Creator, of the finite with the Infinite, its characteristic note is Adoration. This is infinite bliss to the soul which is purged of self-interest; to the self-centred soul the experience of that fellowship is not possible at all; but if it were possible, it would not be enjoyable. To put it crudely, if a selfish man could go to Heaven, he would be miserable there. Its joy is not only a joy won by Christ for the redeemed; it is the joy of actual union with God, and therefore for sinners the joy of actually being redeemed.

But for this reason Heaven is also a fellowship of finite spirits. It has been pointed out that though the life of Heaven is often described in musical terms, it is always as a chorus or an orchestra, never as a solo. It is the coming of the Kingdom of God, the new heavens and the new earth, the restoration of all things. It is the life in which all are united to one another, all enrich and are enriched by one another, in the adoring apprehension of the Divine Truth, the adoring contemplation of the Divine Beauty, and the adoring activity of co-operation with the Divine Goodness. As the finite creature thus enters into "fruition of the glorious Godhead" there can be no satiety or stagnation. This is a theme not for the definitions of Science, but for the glowing utterance of Poetry and Music: *Sanctus, Sanctus, Sanctus, Dominus Deus Sabaoth.*

> (*Signed*) WILLIAM EBOR: *Chairman.*
> F. R. BARRY.
> HENRY CHELMSFORD.
> J. M. CREED.
> JOHN DERBY.
> JOHN GLASGOW AND GALLOWAY.
> L. W. GRENSTED.
> WILFRED L. KNOX.
> W. R. MATTHEWS.
> WALTER H. MOBERLY.
> J. K. MOZLEY.
> OLIVER C. QUICK.
> C. F. RUSSELL.
> E. G. SELWYN.
> CHARLES J. SHEBBEARE.
> WILL SPENS.
> V. F. STORR.
> A. E. TAYLOR.
> L. S. THORNTON, C.R.
> CLEMENT C. J. WEBB.

APPENDICES

*(Contributed by individual members of the Commission
and published in accordance with its decision)*

I

ON THE PSYCHOLOGICAL ASPECTS OF SIN

The evolutionary inheritance of man involves not only kinship with the higher animals, but also close parallelism in the so-called "instincts." The exact nature and definition of these is a matter of dispute among psychologists, but whether they are explained as behaviour-patterns or as innate psycho-physical dispositions they indicate the typical ways in which individuals of any species feel and act with a view to the preservation and propagation both of themselves and of the race. The instincts of man have, of course, their own special range and organisation. In particular they come largely under the control of the conscious mind, and it is within this control that moral value becomes the criterion of right action. The "instincts," therefore, are not in themselves sinful. They are, in fact, the raw material of virtue as well as of vice. Nevertheless, they form a constant body of impulses capable of finding satisfaction in the pursuit of ends which are lower in value than the moral and spiritual ends proper to the developed human personality, and thus they supply the natural occasion of sin.

For our purpose what has been called the "social inheritance" is not less important than the instinctive. The environment, material, mental, and moral, into which each individual enters at birth, is the result, slowly built up, of the efforts, gains, and failures of countless generations. And the response of the individual to this environment is also affected by the past. Whatever be the truth as to the inheritance of acquired characteristics, it is only natural to suppose that the evolutionary process produces the same result in the moral field as elsewhere. The sinning of past generations must, in all reason, have strengthened the tendency to sin. Further, a wicked society gives survival value to characteristics which are morally bad, and this will produce a situation hardly distinguishable from the inheritance of an acquired sinful character.

This moral environment affects the child through personal relationship of all kinds, and most powerfully through the attraction or repulsion with which he is affected by those nearest to him. There is not only conscious imitation and adoption of ideals which appear to him desirable, but also unconscious reproduction of actions and habits based upon the direct and primitive influence of suggestion. This influence of environment continues during schooldays and throughout later life, though it then comes more under conscious control. Dispositions thus arise which are of fundamental significance for the formation of character. The behaviour of parents, and of others in close contact with a child's developing life, is now recognised to be of the most far-reaching importance in predisposing the child towards (or against) a corresponding attitude, and this importance sometimes attaches to acts apparently of the most trivial character. Thus the unwisdom and the moral imperfections of each generation form the natural basis of the unwisdom and the moral imperfection of the generation which follows, though the form which this failure takes will be constantly changing. It is obviously impossible to apportion the guilt for this corporate condition of sin, as between the individual and the race, just as it is impossible to discover in any given case the extent to which apparent moral defects may be due to inheritance in the more strictly physical or instinctive sense.

II

ON FINITUDE AND ORIGINAL SIN

A possible account of the universal tendency to evil may be sketched as follows : Man differs from the animals (if we conceive them rightly) partly by his capacity to choose in the light of general principles between various " goods " which he might pursue. In other words, he is not only aware that this is good or that is good, but he has a standard which he consciously applies in making such judgment. He has the " knowledge of good and evil " as principles. But his appreciation is limited by the speciality of his angle of vision. He sees the world, and judges it, from his own point of view   But the world is not really centred upon him; it is centred upon God. Only when seen as God sees it is it apprehended in true perspective and proportion.

There is no necessity preventing him from realising from the first his dependence on God, the like dependence of others, and, consequently, his own position as one among others. Therefore it was not necessary that he should be self-centred; and in that sense it must be held (on this view) that God is not responsible for his self-centredness. At the same time, such self-centredness was at least likely to develop, because of the ease with which each man exaggerates the importance of those goods and evils which he apprehends as directly affecting himself. Thus moral perspective is lost and moral perception is blurred. Such a development must be regarded as from the nature of the case so probable that it must be held to fall within the eternal purpose of God.

Some might be content to stop here, finding in the self-centredness of the finite the whole account of original sin as we meet with it in experience. Others, however, would not find this alone sufficient, but would combine with it the doctrine of " social inheritance." If it be true that human personalities are by their influence largely constitutive of one another, then it would follow that so soon as any one individual has adopted a self-centred view of life it becomes impossible for any human being influenced by him to avoid the tendency towards a corresponding distortion; and this must be expected to issue in actual sin unless there be such communion with God as delivers the soul from the self-centredness normally incidental to finitude. That this should be achieved in the midst of the mutual contamination of mankind is the marvel of the Incarnation.

It is to be noticed that on this view the process of evolution in a certain sense involves a real Fall. The best man, in so far as he is a sinner against the light, is, in that aspect of his character, lower than the beasts. The capacity for heaven is also the capacity for hell, as the capacity for sin is also the capacity for fellowship with God.

III

ON THE MEANING OF THE TERMS " BODY " AND " BLOOD " IN EUCHARISTIC THEOLOGY

This memorandum is concerned with the question, What meaning is to be assigned to the predicates in our Lord's words, " This is my Body " and " This is my Blood," as they are interpreted in the Eucharistic theology of the Church ?

There would perhaps be a considerable measure of agreement on the following points :

(a) In the New Testament a number of things are called Christ's Body: (1) the natural body in which He lived His earthly life and died upon the Cross; (2) the glorified body of His risen and ascended life; (3) His mystical body, the Church; (4) His Eucharistic body.

(b) That which is common to all of these is that each is in some sense an embodiment of our Lord—i.e., a means through which the life of the Incarnate is made accessible to man.

(c) The language of 1 Cor. x. 17 suggests some kind of interconnexion between the Eucharistic body and the mystical body. (" The bread which we break, is it not a communion of the body of Christ? For we, being many, are one bread, one body; for we all partake of the one bread.")

(d) On the other hand, the Eucharistic body is differentiated from the mystical body by the fact that in the Eucharist the Body and the Blood are so closely associated with one another.

In view of such considerations the questions inevitably arise: Has our Lord more than one body? And, whether or not we allow ourselves to speak of a plurality of bodies, how are the different entities which are called the Lord's Body to be related to one another? To these questions not all of those who would agree upon the propositions stated above would return the same answer. It is not enough to say simply that perhaps in all the four uses mentioned above, except the first, the term body is to be understood in a figurative or symbolical, rather than in a literal, sense. For, however true such a statement may be, the questions still remain: What is the reality which the figure is intended to express? and What is the relation of the one to the other? The Church has never been content to affirm that the partaking of Christ's body and blood in the Eucharist is just a metaphorical expression, or that the Church itself can only be said metaphorically to be the body of Christ, or that the glorified body of Christ in heaven is only metaphorically to be called a body. Indeed, the first and third of these propositions have been denied by the main tradition of orthodoxy. For language of this kind seems to suggest an element of unreality in that which to Christians is the most profound and fundamental truth. Some would urge, moreover, that if we are content to say that all terms such as " body," which primarily denote outward and material things, are in their spiritual application only figures of strictly immaterial realities, we are thereby led towards a falsely spiritual philosophy which misses the truth of the redemption of earthly and material things themselves through the Incarnation and Resurrection of the Son of God. We feel obliged therefore to particularise some further answers which may be given to the questions as to the meaning of the terms "body" and "blood" in their Eucharistic use, and as to the relation of the body and blood in the Eucharist to other entities which are called "the body of Christ."

(1) Some would maintain that the problem is essentially the same as that which concerns the relation of the body of the resurrection to our present body, a problem treated in the text of the report [see above p, 208]. Whatever be the principle of unity or continuity in a human body regarded simply as a physical object which somehow remains the same though changing in all its parts, it seems impossible to define the identity of *my* body at one time with *my* body at another time except by reference to the identity of its relation to myself whose body it is. It is the constancy of that relation which constitutes the identity of the body as mine. In the same way, in the relation to our Lord of His mortal body, His glorified body, His mystical body the Church, and His sacramental body in the Eucharist, there is an underlying identity which, in making each to be His body, makes it in that respect identical with the others. Each is the Lord's body, in so far as, in its own distinct sphere and for its own distinct purpose, it is the very organ of His activity and self-expression. And though, when we have in mind the distinctness of those spheres and purposes, we inevitably speak as though there were many bodies, yet the relation which constitutes each and all as His body is one and the same.

This thought, it may be urged, is of special help in conceiving what is meant when it is affirmed that the Lord's body in the Eucharist is the same as that which was born of the Blessed Virgin and was crucified. The words used by our Lord at the Last Supper designate Him to be a sacrificial victim. His sacrifice of Himself was completed through the breaking of the body and the shedding of the blood in the death of the Cross. This act and suffering were the perfect expression in His human nature of His love for men. And, in so far as the bread broken and the wine outpoured in memory of His Passion are effectual symbols by which He who is " the same yesterday, to-day, and for ever " now incorporates us as His members into His sacrifice, they enter into that very same relation to Christ Himself which made the crucified flesh also to be the effectual symbol of His unchanging love. This identical relation constitutes the enduring identity of what we speak of as Christ's body and blood.

Again, it is as the organ of His activity and self-expression that we affirm the Church to be Christ's body. But here a distinction has to be made. For though we speak of the Church as Christ's mystical body, we do not speak of it as His blood or His flesh. And there is theological reason for this distinction. For the body and blood constitute the outward vessel in which Christ's humanity was sacrificed upon the Cross and in which it is given spiritually to be our sacrificial food in the Eucharist. But the mystical body of which Christians are members comes into being as the *result* of Christ's redemptive sacrifice. Christians constitute this body, because they *have been redeemed* by Christ's blood.

(2) There are some who would follow the foregoing argument up to a certain point, but are quite unable to allow that Christ's sacramental body can be *identified* either with that which was crucified or with the society of faithful Christians. They would affirm all and each of these to be Christ's body, in so far as each is the organ of His activity and self-expression. But it seems to them unnatural and wrong to identify with one another for this reason such quite different entities, or to say that they

are in any sense one and the same body. Those who hold this view are content to affirm that there are several different things each of which in a different way may be called the Lord's body, because there is in all a certain underlying identity of relation to the one Christ. They would not wish to speak of several bodies of Christ, but rather of several things each of which in a certain aspect of its being is the body of Christ. It is not quite easy to determine how far the difference between this view and the former is really substantial and theological, or how far it concerns merely the proper and legitimate use of language.

(3) It is however to be observed that both the views so far described show an important divergence from the traditional use of terms in Eucharistic theology. According to them the body and blood of Christ are the *outward signs* in the sacrament of the Eucharist. On the other hand, according to the traditional language which has been universally used since mediæval times, both by those who have believed in the narrower doctrine of the Real Presence and by those who have not, the body and blood of Christ are the inward part or thing signified by the sacrament. They are the *res sacramenti* rather than the *sacramentum*. It is this traditional use of terms which has led believers in the Real Presence (in the narrower sense) to speak of Christ's body and blood as being present in the Eucharist *in or under the forms* (*species*) of bread and wine; and the whole logic of their doctrine has been complicated by the necessity of at once identifying the body and blood of Christ with the consecrated elements, and distinguishing the former, as things signified, from the latter, as signs. It is this traditional way of expressing the doctrine of the Real Presence which has largely determined the traditional expressions of opposition to that doctrine.

For a fuller discussion of the various doctrines of the presence reference may be made to documents in the body of the Report. It would seem that, if the traditional use of terms is strictly adhered to, "the body and blood" must be understood to mean the sacred humanity of Christ as distinct and separable from all material constituents;* in that case, the consecrated bread and wine, as sacramental signs, must be clearly distinguished from the body and blood, which are the spiritual reality signified, whether or not the thing signified is believed to be "in or under" the material sign itself. On the other hand, if that which is the organ of our Lord's activity and self-expression may properly be called His body, and if that which is the instrument and expression of His sacrificed life in its redemptive power may properly be called His body and blood, then there is a sense in which the consecrated bread and wine in the Eucharist may be directly identified with Christ's body and blood, in so far as these elements become that through which Christ in His sacred humanity both expresses Himself and actually gives Himself to faithful recipients. We may note in this connexion the words of a modern theologian: "By His 'body' our Lord meant and means that which makes Him accessible to us, and by His 'blood' that He was to be and is accessible to us as our sacrificial food, communicating to us His own life."

In conclusion it must be emphasised that the purpose of the foregoing statement is to explain certain views and points at issue, and to provide material for further study and thought. There is no intention to pronounce upon the relative merits, nor upon the legitimacy, of the views described. And we would add a reminder that the cautious language used above† concerning Traditional

---

* "The spiritual principle and life of Christ's manhood, inseparable from His whole living self" (Gore, *The Body of Christ*, p. 49). "Shall we say, then, that by His flesh we understand the spiritual principle or essence of His manhood, as distinguished from its material constituents?" (*ibid.*, p. 24).

† See p. 33.

Images and Phrases is peculiarly applicable to the subject-matter with which we have here been dealing.

IV

ON THE RELATION OF THE SACRAMENTS TO GRACE

Anglican theology, following the formularies of the Anglican Church, has in general consistently affirmed that the sacraments are "effectual signs"—that is to say, that they do not merely symbolise the reception of grace but are means by which grace is received. On the other hand, there has been in Anglican theology comparatively little exact discussion of the manner in which the sacraments are means of grace and can, therefore, be said to cause grace. In part this has been due to the extent to which the question has been confused by controversies and, in particular, by exaggerated fears, in some quarters, lest any allowance of a real sacramental causality should involve the admission of magical conceptions and, in other quarters, lest any rationalising of such causality should minimise its reality. In part, that reserve has been due also to the tendency common to Anglican and to Orthodox thought to distrust rationalising theology, regarding this as necessarily inadequate in the realm of grace. To whatever extent, however, this inadequacy is recognised, there remains a duty to use reason so far as it will carry us, and the controversies and fears to which reference has been made can only be resolved and allayed is so far as this is done. In consequence, it is desirable to state briefly but, so far as possible, exactly various possible views of sacramental causality, and this memorandum is an attempt to do so.

Four such views may be distinguished, and these are summarised below. It should be noted, and it is desirable to emphasise, that each, including that which will be first described and represents Anglican thought when furthest removed from Catholic tradition, regards the sacraments as real means of grace and as in a real sense causing grace.

(1) The sacraments may be regarded as symbols having their significance and effect simply as inculcating ideas and producing states of feeling which enable us to receive grace. By producing these effects the sacraments result in the reception of grace. This view of the sacraments is sometimes expressed by saying that they are " acted sermons," but it should be noted that when adequately analysed it is indifferent neither to the nature of the sacraments nor to their divine institution. It does not follow that other rites—or sermons which are not " acted "—would do as well. Symbolic rites may have a psychological efficacy which is real and may be peculiar to them; further, the symbolism of the sacramental rites is singularly appropriate to their purpose; and, lastly, but not of least importance, rites which were instituted by our Lord in His earthly ministry or through the guidance of the Apostles by the Holy Spirit, and which have been in constant use by Christians from the beginning, have on both these grounds a special value as serving to emphasise the ideas and to stir up the feelings which are proper to them. Nor need it be supposed that this view wholly associates the effect of the sacraments with the ideas and emotional state of the recipient at the moment of reception. The fact of reception of the sacraments and reflection on the meaning of this may well result in the reception of grace at a later stage even if the sacrament was received at the time without any adequate dispositions being aroused.

It is, of course, the case that on this view (as with that which will be described last) the sacraments do not cause directly the reception of grace but cause something which causes this reception. The traditional doctrine that the sacraments cause grace can, however, be interpreted, even in traditional Catholic theology, in accordance with the principle *causa causæ, causa causati*. From this point of view, it has to be admitted that the doctrine which has been described asserts that the sacraments are causes of grace, none the less so because the causation is " dispositive "— *i.e.*, because the sacraments have their effect by producing in the recipient a state or condition which directly causes the reception of grace.

From the point of view of consistency with Anglican formularies, it follows that this conception of the sacraments is not open to criticism on the ground that it fails to regard these as means of grace. It is open to more serious attack in another respect. If it is held that the sacraments are means of grace simply as producing or enhancing certain dispositions, it is difficult not to hold that these may be produced in the same degree otherwise. If so, however, it is difficult to maintain, as Anglican formularies require, that Baptism and the Eucharist are " generally necessary to salvation," since this phrase means that they are necessary in all but abnormal cases. On the other hand, it can be argued that, for a healthy emotional life in any field, external symbols are not only helpful but in practice necessary; and that, where this life is or should be of a corporate character, it is not only the case that this dependence on symbols is enhanced, but it becomes necessary that these symbols should have a corporate and, in some way, an authoritative character. It can fairly be argued also (as has already been suggested) that precisely this character is secured, in both respects, to a unique degree in the case of rites which have been practised by the Church everywhere and at all times, and which have their basis in our Lord's life and in the Scriptural accounts of His teaching.

(2) While all theologians, Catholic and Orthodox no less than Protestant, are, of course, agreed that faith and right dispositions are necessary to the reception of the grace of the sacraments, and are agreed also in recognising that, as symbols, the sacraments can and do play a large part in stimulating faith and in securing these dis-

positions, the great majority of Anglican theologians have felt bound both by Scriptural and more general considerations to endorse the traditional view that there is some further causal connection between the sacraments and grace.

In a sense the simplest, but also in a sense the most extreme, form in which such a connection is affirmed is found in the assertion that the actions and objects in the physical order, which constitute the sacraments, are not only signs but are instruments in the hands of God wherewith grace is directly caused by Him. Various objections are obvious: but some of these turn, in part at least, on misunderstanding. It can be argued that this view can imply no more than that God wills to give certain graces only when certain actions are performed, and that in consequence the sacraments are merely conditions *sine quibus non* and not really means or causes of grace. It can be replied that the objection fails to take seriously the theory in question. This regards the actions in the physical order as really causing grace, even if the manner in which they do so is a mystery. It can next be objected that such a conception has definitely passed over into the realm of magic. To this objection it can be replied that the manner of the causation of grace is admittedly a mystery, but that "magic" consists in an attempt by man to coerce his God or Gods and to secure benefits without moral effort. It can be argued that the doctrine in question is wholly free from suggesting anything of this character, since it is founded on the idea that it is God Himself who is freely using the sacraments as His instruments, and since it is fully recognised that spiritual dispositions (*i.e.*, penitence and faith) are necessary if grace is to result. A further objection is of another character. It is admitted on all sides that the sacraments are means of grace, even in cases where there are no proper dispositions at the time but where these arise subsequently: to take an extreme example, if a person seeks baptism in bad faith (*e.g.*, without belief or repentance and for some worldly motive), but subsequently comes to repentance and belief, it is not necessary that he should be re-baptised, but he secures the grace of baptism through the baptism which he has already received. It is not easy, although it may not be impossible, to account on the theory in question for the action of the sacraments which is thus involved.

These and perhaps other objections appear to have different weight to different minds. Some theologians, for example, feel that the accusation of relapsing into magical conceptions is only met by narrowing unduly the definition of magic; others may think that it remains difficult not to regard the gift of grace as merely conditioned by the signs, so that the latter are not really means of grace; yet others are primarily influenced by the last-mentioned objection and by the difficulty of accounting on this theory for the " revivification " of the sacraments in the circumstances which the objection contemplates.

(3) Whatever be the reasons, the theory in question has appeared unsatisfactory to many Catholic theologians as well as to almost all Protestant theologians. Among Roman Catholic theologians, at least until recently, its most serious competitor was the theory of " moral causation." This latter theory has been and remains so widely held and goes so far to meet many of the difficulties of the problem that it is important to understand its nature, and this can best be explained by an example. It is clear that King Edward III caused the release of the Burghers of Calais. If we suppose, for the sake of simplicity, that he released them with his own hands, he was the immediate and direct cause in their being set free. But he was led to release them by the plea of Queen Philippa. Her plea caused his decision to be what it was, and, in consequence, was a real although remoter cause of the Burghers' release. The Queen's plea affords an example of moral causation—*i.e.*, of the causation of an event when the direct agent is

moved to act by some other person who is able by request or entreaty to determine the action. It should also be noted that, in the case of the direct agent, either the agent or an instrument which he uses can be described as the cause of an event. Thus a man's death can be said to be caused either by poison or by the person who administered the poison—*i.e.*, we describe both "principal" and "instrument" as causes. In the case of moral causation the same distinction exists. We can speak of the Burghers being released either because of Queen Philippa's intervention or because of the actual means she employed, her actual spoken plea or, it might well have been in other circumstances, because of a letter which she sent. In, for example, the last-mentioned circumstances the letter would be the "instrumental cause" and the Queen the "principal cause," but each would be a "moral cause." In less unfamiliar language the letter would have been the means by which the Queen secured the King's clemency.

On the theory with which we are now concerned, the sacraments are not only or primarily "acted sermons"; they are rather "acted prayers." The Church impetrates for the recipients by the sacrament the particular graces which it implies. But this is not all. Since in the sacraments the Minister is doing something which our Lord commanded, the sacraments are, in a real sense, also the acts of Christ. If the sacraments are "acted prayers" the prayers are not only those of the Church, but those of Christ through the Church. In view of such impetration by Christ, and in virtue of His Sonship and Passion, grace will certainly result to the measure of the recipients' capacity to receive grace—*i.e.*, in accordance with their faith and general dispositions.

The principal difficulty in regard to the above conception of the sacraments turns on the particularity which it assigns to our Lord's impetration of grace. It is urged that our Lord prayed (and prays) that grace should be given to all who should believe on His name; that the administration of the sacraments may serve to express this more general intercession and may emphasise its applicability to the individual; but that it does not and cannot add to it and, as a consequence, that the sacraments are not a *necessary* element in the impetration of grace by Christ and cannot properly be said to be the means whereby He impetrates grace. If we accept the view on which this objection is founded (namely, that our Lord impetrates grace generally on all who may come to believe in Him), then it is difficult to deny that the theory falls to the ground and we are driven back at first sight on the first of the above views—namely, that the sacraments are means of grace only as " acted sermons "—as enhancing our capacity to receive grace. At the least the conclusion is inevitable that any doctrine of the sacraments which goes beyond this necessarily involves a definite rejection of the view that our Lord's impetration of grace upon believers is so unconditioned as to make their reception of grace depend further only upon their faith and good dispositions.

The rejection of this view (and the assignment in consequence of more than a psychological causality to the sacraments) rests in general on its being regarded as unduly individualistic, and as mistakenly supposing the salvation of each soul to involve in principle only God and that soul. It is held that this conception of salvation was the outcome of an excessive individualism which after the end of the Middle Ages increasingly permeated and characterised both secular and theological thought; that this view was read into the Scriptures, but that the New Testament as a whole, so far from supporting it, emphasises very strongly the corporate character of salvation. It is argued that, just because man is a " social being," he can only find salvation in and through a redeemed community, and that, as a consequence, while salvation can and must be thought of as freely offered to all, it must normally be so offered in the first instance as to con-

vey membership of such a community, and its further
development must normally be dependent on participation
in a corporate religious life.

It is possible on this ground to revert to the theory of
" moral causation," and to regard the sacraments as impetrating grace, this impetration as being morally
(*moraliter*) the act of our Lord, and the particularity of
His impetration of grace, and the adoption of visible rites
for this, as being accounted for and, indeed, necessitated
by the above consideration. But there are substantial objections to this solution. It remains difficult not to feel
that even allowing for the above considerations there
is involved an undue narrowing of our Lord's impetration of grace. In the second place, not only is there difficulty in thinking of our Lord as impetrating grace otherwise than on all believers in the measure of their capacity
to receive it, but there is difficulty in not thinking of God
the Father as giving grace to all in this measure. It remains difficult, in consequence, to think of the sacraments
as means of grace unless it can be said that they render
man more capable of receiving grace.

(4) It does not follow, however, that any increased
capacity which the sacraments convey is necessarily due
only to their psychological effect. It is possible, and it is
maintained on the theory which we have now to consider,
that the reception of grace as a result of the sacraments
depends on these being the means by which a new status
is conferred, and on the fact that this status determines
and brings about the reception of grace. The view in
question is traditionally described in the phrase that the
sacraments confer directly a " title exigent of grace "; but
this phrase is open to objection as unnecessarily forensic.

Baptism affords the simplest illustration of the view,
although a corresponding line of argument can be
developed in other cases. It is agreed on all sides that
it is only as being " accepted by Christ " that man can
seek and obtain grace. The above considerations are

held to justify the conclusions that such acceptance should involve admission into the Christian community and that, for this reason, it is afforded in an overt and recognisable act. This act is properly regarded as morally the act of Christ Himself, since it is performed on His behalf by those who are authorised so to act on His behalf. While it is possible, in consequence, to think of the act as impetrating grace from the Father, yet it is widely felt that this way of regarding the matter is less satisfactory than one which goes further and regards our Lord's ministerial action in the sacraments as the act also of God the Father through His Son. On this view God the Father gives grace to (and God the Son impetrates grace for) all men in the measure of their capacity to receive. But a certain status—namely, acceptance by Christ—is an inherently necessary condition and the determining cause of Christian grace, and this status is in fact conferred (and must normally be sought and obtained) in and through Baptism.

It will be observed that the dependence of this view on the fact that the life of grace involves a corporate life, and is conditioned by this, links this view with what was said earlier about the special importance and necessity of symbols where a corporate life is involved. It is linked also with the conception that the sacraments are not only signs but instruments, since, although they are regarded as signs, they are regarded as signs which do not only signify something but effect something which does not depend on the degrees of apprehension of the recipient.

The obvious objection to this view is that what is thus regarded as conferred by the sacraments is not grace directly, but a status which enables us to receive grace, whereas many would claim a certainty that in the sacraments they receive grace itself. It can, however, be replied that it is not disputed that, given proper dispositions in receiving the sacraments, grace results simultaneously with reception. It is maintained that what the sacraments convey is status and that this causes grace to result given right dispositions; but, if these last exist, there is no temporal separation, although there is a logical separation, between the sacraments and the actual reception of grace. It should be noted, however, that temporal separation will result if the proper dispositions are absent when the sacraments are received, but that the status will be received and remain to cause grace to result when proper dispositions arise. The further objection that the sacraments cause only the reception of status, and not the reception of grace, can be met by the principle *causa causæ, causa causati*, to which reference has already been made. It should be emphasised, however, that while preserving the real instrumentality of the sacraments in bringing about the reception of grace, through conferring a status which determines this, the view in question emphasises the importance of faith and of appropriation of grace by faith.

––––––––

It is desirable in this connexion to refer to the controversy which is associated with the statement that the sacraments convey grace *ex opere operato*. The issues have been stated so clearly by Billot as to justify the following somewhat lengthy quotation:

"In sacramentis, inquit S. Thomas in IV., D. I, q. I, a. 5, est duo considerare, scilicet ipsum sacramentum, et usus sacramenti. Ipsum sacramentum dicitur a quibusdam *opus operatum*; usus autem sacramenti est ipsa operatio, quæ a quibusdam opus operans dicitur." Ex quo quidem testimonio apparent non ita antiquas esse hujusmodi locutiones, quæ ineunte tantum sæculo XIII. inceperunt esse in usu, et postmodum a theologis communiter receptæ, tandem in Concilio Tridentino fuerunt consecratæ.* Est autem opus operans, seu melius operantis, ipsa actio

* "Si quis dixerit per ipsa novæ Legis sacramenta, ex opere operato non conferri gratiam, sed solam fidem divinæ promissionis ad gratiam consequendam sufficere, A. S."—Sess. 7, Can. 8.

hominis prout e potentia ejus egrediens. Opus vero operatum (sensu passivo) est opus exterius factum, puta sacramentale signum rite positum secundum legem suæ institutionis, et a Deo ordinatum in instrumentum productionis gratiæ. Bene enim id quod ex divina institutione vim habet instrumentalem opponitur ei quod ab homine operante consequeretur valorem et efficaciam.

Cum ergo dicuntur sacramenta conferre gratiam ex opere operato, sensus est quod causant illam, non in quantum subsunt virtuti hominum ministrantium neque etiam in quantum nata sunt excitare in suscipiente fidem per quam ipse homo sese ad justificationem disponeret, sed pure et simpliciter secundum quod sunt instrumenta Dei sanctificatoris, ita ut nihil aliud sub Deo considerandum sit velut causa inductionis gratiæ, præter sacramentum valide positum juxta institutionem Christi.

*   *   *   *   *

Rursus cum dicitur nihil aliud considerari in linea *causæ inductionis gratiæ*, manifestum est non ideo negari necessitatem dispositionum quæ sint ab homine operante, sumendo nunc dispositiones, non pro eo quod appellat et exigit formam, scilicet gratiam, sed pro eo quod, removendo prohibens, reddit animam susceptibilem effectus sacramenti. Causa enim quæ inducit hujusmodi dispositiones, nequaquam dici potest causa inductionis *ipsius formæ*, sicut qui emollit ceram non est causa figuræ quæ formatur ab artifice, sed tantum est causa cur materia illa sit capax recipiendi actionem agentis; quippe nullum activum inducere potest suum effectum in passivo quod non debito modo ei subjicitur, et sic etiam in sacramentis. (*De Ecclesiæ Sacramentis*, 6th Edition, Rome, 1924, pp. 67-69.)

For convenience a translation of the above passage is appended :

" In Sacraments," says St. Thomas, " two things may be considered—the Sacrament itself and its use.

The Sacrament itself is by some called *opus operatum*, 'the act done': the use of the Sacrament is the doing of the act, which some call *opus operans*, 'the act doing'." This passage shows that the kind of phraseology here mentioned, which came into use only at the beginning of the thirteenth century, and afterwards, having been adopted by theologians generally, was eventually consecrated by the Council of Trent, is in fact of no very great antiquity. The *opus operans* or "act doing" or, as it may be better expressed, the *opus operantis* or "act of the person doing," is the action of a human agent considered as proceeding from his own ability to perform it. But the *opus operatum* or "act done" is the action outwardly performed—that is to say, a symbolic action belonging to a sacrament, performed in accordance with the law of its institution and ordained by God to be an instrument by which the presence of grace is brought about. For that which by God's appointment is capable of acting in this way as an instrument may properly be contrasted with that which should derive its value and efficacy from a human agent.

When, therefore, sacraments are said to confer grace *ex opere operato*, the meaning is that they are causes of grace not in so far as they are determined by the ability of the human beings who administer them nor, again, in so far as they are apt in their own nature to excite in a human recipient a faith by which he might put himself into a condition to be justified; but purely and simply in so far as they are instruments employed by God in sanctifying the recipients, so that there is nothing (under God) to be taken into account as the cause of grace being imparted except the sacrament validly performed according to the institution of Christ.

*   *   *   *   *

Again, when it is said that nothing is taken into account in reckoning the cause of the imparting of grace, it is plain that we do not deny the necessity of dispositions due to the human agent, if such dispositions be regarded not as evoking and bringing into existence the "form," that which it is the essential nature of the sacrament to impart—namely, grace

—but only as removing an obstacle and merely rendering the soul capable of being acted upon by the sacrament. For the cause which effects such dispositions can by no means be called the cause which brings about the presence in the soul of the "form" itself, which we call "grace," any more than the man who softens the wax is the cause of the shape imparted to it by an artist; he is only the cause of the wax being capable of being moulded by the other: for no activity can produce its effect on anything which is not fitted to be acted upon thereby; and this rule holds in the case of sacraments as well as elsewhere.

It is obvious that if the sacraments are regarded as causing grace by conveying a status which causes grace, the significant fact is the act performed, rather than "the action of a human agent considered as proceeding from his own ability to perform it." What matters is not any personal ability of the minister, but the fact that he has a delegated authority to confer a certain status. Further, whether we think of the sacrament as instituted by our Lord directly in His earthly ministry or mediately through the Apostolic Church, the delegated authority is not authority to confer the status in any manner the minister pleases, but to confer the status by a prescribed rite which will serve as direct evidence that the status has been conferred. The primary importance of the due performance of the action turns not on any magical quality attaching to particular actions in themselves, but on the desirability of its being manifest to all concerned that the status in question is being conferred and on the fact that, with a view to securing this, the delegated authority has the above character.